Confidence
in
Mutual Aid

A biography of the Methodist Local Preachers
Mutual Aid Association, 1849 – 1999

Fear held them mute: alone, untaught to fear,
Tydides spoke – 'The man you seek is here.
Through you black camps to bend my dangerous way,
Some god commands, and I obey.
But let some other chosen warrior join
To raise my hopes, and second my design.
By mutual confidence and mutual aid
Great deeds are done, and great discoveries made;
The wise new prudence from the wise acquire,
And one brave hero fans another's fire.'

[from *The Night Adventure of Diomed and Ulysses* –
Book X of Homer's *Iliad*, translated by Alexander Pope
(1688 - 1744)]

CONFIDENCE IN MUTUAL AID

ACKNOWLEDGEMENTS

My thanks go first to my General Committee colleagues of 1990 who assigned to me the task of writing this record. 1999 seemed a long time ahead then, but the past eight years have shown the wisdom of the decision to put the matter in hand at an early date. During most of the research and writing period the project has been splendidly supported by a group which has included Leonard Green, Clifford Hare, Lois Morton, Danny O'Donnell, Brian Scorer, Albert Syson and, in the later stages, Ian Day and Ken Bowden. I say 'thank you' to them for all their encouragement and active involvement. Honorary Officers, past and present, past-Presidents and other senior members of the Association have assisted out of their own extensive experience of its work. I am grateful also to those District and Branch Officers and members of LPMAA who have worked in their own localities, provided hospitality and transport, and made arrangements for access to libraries, Record Offices and other useful sources.

Particularly important have been the John Rylands University of Manchester Library, the Wesley Historical Society Library (at Westminster College, Oxford), Queens College, Birmingham, Wesley College and John Wesley's New Room, Bristol. All these have been valuable complements to the Association's own records at Head Office, Rickmansworth. I want to thank the General Secretaries, Derek Bolton and Godfrey Talford, and Head Office staff who have willingly helped in both the administrative and research aspects of the project. The managers, staff and residents of LPMAA Homes have brought their experience and reminiscences to bear upon the official records.

Against that background, I accept responsibility for any shortcomings, errors and omissions. Many authors have gratefully quoted Dr Samuel Johnson, who, when challenged over a mistake in his famous dictionary, replied, 'Ignorance, Madam, pure ignorance.' Defects there will be, but where records have been lost, members have died or information has not been shared, I say, with Dr Johnson, 'Ignorance, pure ignorance.'

There are two further groups of people whose help I gladly acknowledge. First, some Methodist District Archivists have supplied details of archives and locations in their Districts, sometimes with regret that they have not been asked to arrange secure storage for LPMAA records. Secondly, a number of officers and members of the Wesley Historical Society and its Branches, and others interested in Methodist history, have suggested useful sources and provided information themselves. This includes the Chairmen of some Methodist Districts; all whom I have met in connection with the project have shown great interest.

The advice and guidance of the Chief Executive of the Methodist Publishing House, Brian Thornton, and staff of the Publishing House, have been greatly appreciated. The Association is deeply grateful to Rev Brian Beck for his gracious Foreword. Finally, I refer to the Connexional history of local preaching, also published by the Methodist Publishing House under the title *Workaday Preachers*. It was a special pleasure to contribute the chapter on 'Self-help Among the Local Preachers'. Involvement in that project gave access to information and advice from its editor, Geoffrey Milburn, and some of the Methodist historians who wrote other chapters. I hope this book will appeal to them as much as to all members of LPMAA, for whom especially it has been written.

Alan Parker
Stockton-on-Tees, September 1998

List of Illustrations

* Photograph by Derek Byfleet. Used by permission

FOREWORD

The office of local preacher has profound theological significance. It bears witness to what preaching truly is. Preaching is more than the expounding of the Scriptures. That limited task can be quite adequately done on the basis of a good modern translation and some reliable commentaries. True preaching goes further, and engages with the contemporary world, so that the general truth given in the incarnation of the Son of God and attested in the Bible becomes the particular truth for here and now, for this person, this situation, this moment.

For that to happen, preachers must be part of the contemporary world, carrying in their own experience the meeting-point between God's word and everyday life. All preachers do this to some extent. Local preachers, because of their secular calling, whether in employment, in the home or experiencing involuntary unemployment, are particularly well-placed for it. They know about the hard places where God's illuminating word is needed, they can test for themselves whether it rings true, and they can bear witness to it when it does.

There is, of course, a complementary ministry of those who are set apart by ordination, detached to some extent (but never altogether) from the everyday world. Both ministries are needed. History shows, however, how hard it has sometimes been for ordained and unordained to recognise their need of each other. Sometimes local preachers have been thought of as an unfortunate necessity, a second-best needed to fill the gap left by a shortage of ministers. Such condescending attitudes miss the theological point.

In the pages that follow the story is told of Methodist lay preachers banding together for mutual support. It is a story of struggle and conflict, of mutual suspicion and misunderstanding between Mutual Aid and official Methodism, and of the gradual emergence of new attitudes and new relationships. Given the social and religious context of the nineteenth century it is difficult to see how the story could have been other than it was. Then as now Methodism was better at providing for the needs of the ordained than of its lay people. Mutual aid by the preachers to support the very poor among them was as much an expression of the gospel as preaching itself.

Times have greatly changed. The Local Preachers Mutual Aid Association, though still distinct, is now officially related to the Conference, and it is a privilege, as a sign of that new relationship, to be invited to write this Foreword to Alan Parker's fascinating account. I commend it to all those who would seek a better understanding of an important but often ignored aspect of our Methodist history.

Brian E. Beck

PREFACE

A *Goodly Fellowship*, by Harold Buss and Richard Burnett, was published in 1949 as a Centenary History of LPMAA. It presented the story of the Association's first hundred years very much through the personalities of those who formed it and who guided its development during that time. The book is long out of print, but the eagerness with which copies are still sought, begged, borrowed, and sometimes even stolen (i.e. not returned!) is not the least of the tributes that are paid to it. The publication of *More Precious Than Rubies*, written by Alfred Gilliver to mark the 40th Anniversary of Mutual Aid Homes in 1989, stimulated interest in the idea of a reprint of the 1949 volume, perhaps with the MAH Ruby Anniversary booklet incorporated. The Officers of the Association favoured a different approach. At that time action was being taken to bring MLPMAA and the Connexion closer together by the end of the century, so a new history should be written for the Association's 150th Anniversary. This was endorsed by General Committee in June 1990, and the project was put in hand.

The Foreword to the report of the important COPEC Conference of 1924 (see chapter 30) included certain observations about its author. Substituting 'MLPMAA' for COPEC, part of that Foreword is reproduced here:

> If a movement such as MLPMAA is to be widely understood, it needs an interpreter who must be in full sympathy with it, must have wide sympathy with others, must have some creative imagination, and a measure of detachment. Otherwise he will never be able to understand the movement, nor convey his understanding to others, he will have neither the vision nor the sense of perspective for a true and living presentation.

Others must decide whether my sympathies, imagination, detachment, have been adequate for this task, and whether my understanding, vision, perspective have been appropriate to the purpose. There is one factor, however, which seems to be of particular importance, and that is whether the vision and perspective should be from within or from outside the organisation. LPMAA, like many individual Christians and the Church itself, has been criticised for being too inward looking and insufficiently mindful of the wider church and society of which it is part. The available records do not support that view. There have always been those who have taken a narrow, even insular view of the Association and its work, but they have rarely prevailed. In formal pronouncements, and through the work of its members, the Association has shown itself well aware of its place in Methodism and of the fact that, like all Christian organisations it has functioned in the context of a constantly changing society. Considerable encouragement can be derived from that as we look back to the past and forward to the future.

It is unfortunate in one way that the 150th Anniversary of MLPMAA falls at the end of the 20th century. Lectures, books and published articles are inevitably being written with a 'Janus' perspective, looking back over the century (even the millennium) and looking towards the century and millennium soon to begin. This book can hardly avoid doing the same thing. History cannot be written in advance, but neither can the story of the origin, growth and development of a great Christian organisation be brought to a full stop. Further chapters will need to be written in the future, and it is interesting to contemplate what they might contain.

- That the work of preaching the Gospel of Christ in the context of Christian worship will continue is not open to doubt. Neither is there doubt that both the forms and styles of worship and preaching will continue to change and develop.

- We have an unshakeable conviction that it is right and necessary for lay Local Preachers to continue their unique contribution to that work, though again ways and means will continue to evolve and adapt to change.

- Most of all the Good News of Life in Christ will – in the future as in the past – have to be demonstrated in deeds as well as declared in words. If the messengers are not seen to be concerned about the needy amongst their own number, the message they proclaim is undermined.

Caring for all in need, Christian and non-Christian alike, is part of our response to the Gospel we preach. In this also, needs and ways of meeting them are still changing, but the care and support of fellow-preachers continues to be a distinctive privilege of the calling. This includes those who have stepped aside from the work. The themes of continuity and change flow through this book – they will surely do so in the years to come.

In his Observations in *The Local Preachers Magazine* of May 1982, the Senior Honorary Secretary, Alfred Gilliver, reported that the desire had been expressed for more information about the Association's history. After alluding to *A Goodly Fellowship*, he continued:

> The last 33 years have been as eventful as any that have gone before and there may well be need now for an up-to-date history to be written. It would not be an easy task, but it would be worth undertaking in order to help sustain the work of the Association into an uncertain future. History is recorded not only in books but in the lives of pioneers and in the buildings associated with them.

Having quoted Henry Ford's famous comment – 'History is bunk' – Alfred Gilliver concluded:

> History . . . provides the understanding and the incentive for the enthusiasm needed in the present and the future.

He may not have anticipated, at the time of writing those *Observations*, that before the end of the decade he would have written the history of Mutual Aid Homes from 1949 to 1989. Neither could it have been foreseen that work would then be put in hand for a new substantive history of LPMAA to mark its 150th Anniversary. His statement, noted above, that it would not be an easy task but that it would be worth undertaking, has proved on both points to be prophetic. It has not been easy, but it has been thoroughly worth doing. A contributor in a much more recent issue of *The Local Preachers Magazine* commented that history helps us to understand how we got where we are, which for him makes it so worthwhile. I trust that the opinions of both writers will be shared by all who read this book.

Alan Parker

Section One

BEFORE LPMAA

The story of a movement or an organisation cannot properly begin at a point in time. The word 'movement' suggests life, growth, development, change, and the word 'organisation' derives from the same root as 'organic' and 'organism', again denoting something which is alive and which breathes. If LPMAA has a starting-point it might be the conversation between Pearson and Marsden on 21st May 1849, or perhaps the first of Pearson's letters to *The Wesleyan Times* in June of that year, or possibly the preliminary meeting on 24th July in Birmingham, but if any one of these was chosen, it would still be necessary to ask why it happened at that time, in that place, in that way.

The chapters of this opening section seek therefore to explore the background, the climate, the atmosphere of the times, so that the origin and growth of the Mutual Aid Association can be seen as a natural development, part of a process whose direction and outcome were very much influenced by the diverse elements which contributed to it. This is not a comprehensive social history of the second quarter of the 19th century, but gives a framework within which the evolution of LPMAA can be understood.

Chapter 1   Who Were the Local Preachers?

Chapter 2   Public Policy for Relief of the Poor

Chapter 3   The Friendly Society Movement in the 19th Century

Chapter 4   Wesleyan Methodism in the 1830s and 1840s

Chapter 5   Mutual Aid amongst Local Preachers before 1849

Chapter 6   Mid-19th Century Society

1

Who Were the Local Preachers?

Men of Mutual Confidence • *Mr Wesley's Preachers*
The Tolpuddle Martyrs • *Men of Mutual Aid*

MEN OF MUTUAL CONFIDENCE

The context of the lines from Homer's *Iliad*, quoted on the title page of this book, is very different from the context of Mutual Aid amongst Methodist local preachers in 19th and 20th century Britain. In the *Iliad* they refer to the confidence and comradeship between soldiers on a battlefield. On first thought this is quite unlike the beneficence amongst Christian preachers which is the distinguishing mark of the Mutual Aid Association. Further reflection does, however, suggest some meaningful similarities. The vocabulary, metaphors and images of warfare appear in a number of places in the New Testament. Some of the language used by early Christians to express their faith and experience was explicitly borrowed from the military sphere. Hymn-writers have also found rich inspiration from the same source ('Like a mighty army . . .' and 'Put on the gospel armour . . .' are just two examples).

The battle in which Christians have been engaged for over 2,000 years is simply the battle against everything which is alien to the Kingdom of God – selfishness, sin, ignorance, poverty, oppression, violence, neglect, and so on. The weapons for this battle are described in New Testament letters in interesting ways, eg: '. . . put on the armour of light' and 'Let Christ himself be your armour' (Romans 13:12, 14), '. . . the weapons of righteousness in right-hand and left' (the gladiatorial image, 2 Corinthians 6:7). The metaphor is extended to the whole suit of armour in Ephesians 6.

The same writer is, however, careful to urge not only attack on evil, with defence against its threat, but also the positive qualities of Christian discipleship, eg: 'Let love of the Christian community show itself in mutual affection' and '. . . contribute to the needs of God's people' (Romans 12:10, 13). Other writers affirm the same principle: 'Whoever loves God must love his fellow-Christians' (1 John 4:21), 'Never cease to love your fellow-Christians' (Hebrews 13:1). It was mutual confidence and mutual aid in this latter sense that motivated and inspired great deeds and discoveries amongst some Methodist local preachers in the mid-19th century. That is why they attempted to deal with the poverty and neglect experienced by others of their company.

Mr Wesley's Preachers

There are two questions that must be asked and answered before the story of their endeavours can be told. First, who were these Methodist local preachers? Secondly, why were they faced with a problem of poverty? It is not known precisely how many local preachers there were in the Wesleyan Methodist Church in the middle decades of 19th century. Informed conjecture suggests there might have been over 12,000 as the 1850s began. (Wesleyan Methodism did not start to record their numbers until 1883, the total in that year being 14,183.) What is reasonably certain is that they came from widely-varying social and economic backgrounds, and differed greatly in education and employment. The first purpose of this chapter is to explain briefly how the office of Local Preacher originated, and the place of local preachers in the Wesleyan Church in the early years of the 19th century. [These matters are dealt with in greater detail in the collection of essays, *Workaday Preachers*, published in 1995 as a Connexional history of local preaching, to mark two hundred years since the first Conference minute on the subject.]

Before that time, i.e. throughout the Wesleys' evangelistic ministry and beyond it, the position of lay local preachers was anomalous. The maintenance and development of Methodist work would not have been possible without them, yet their role was neither fully accepted nor properly regularised. Indeed the minute referred to does not deal unambiguously with these matters. Wesley himself had been equivocal about non-itinerant lay workers, allowing and encouraging them to lead meetings of members of his Societies in prayer, to read scripture and exhort the gatherings, but – perhaps being fully absorbed with his own travels and the management of his travelling colleagues – he did not formalise their position.

One result was considerable diversity of conduct and practice on the part of many of these local leaders. Some of them caused considerable concern to those itinerant preachers whom Wesley had appointed as 'assistants' to supervise the work in different areas (circuits). He added to the responsibilities of his 'assistants' the supervision of those who were allowed to preach in their own localities. Thus it was partly for reasons of discipline that the office of Local Preacher was identified. Only those to whom the Superintendent ('assistant') accorded recognition were authorised to preach, and any who failed to meet standards acceptable to the Superintendent were disciplined by him, if necessary to the point of exclusion.

When the all-ministerial Conference, the repository of Wesley's authority after his death, addressed the question of ordering and organising the work of local preachers in 1796, it was inevitable that there would be both undertones and overtones of discipline and control. The Minute affirmed the customary practice that those styled 'local preacher' should be subordinated to the authority of Superintendents, and also the importance of attending to the rules laid down by Conference, that 'all things may be done decently and in order'. The direction in which the Connexion would move in 19th century was becoming explicit – it would develop as a denominational church, not primarily as an evangelistic movement.

It is not surprising, therefore, to find diverse perceptions of the local preachers' role, and of those who fulfilled it, in various articles and pamphlets published in the early decades of the 19th century. The quarterly meeting of local preachers had been formally recognised by the Conference, including its place in the process of approving new preachers. Superintendents were still left to exercise their own judgement as to whether or not they should be added to the Plan, or appointed to preach. The situation was made more difficult by the political background of religion and the restraints still imposed upon Nonconformity and Dissent at the beginning of 19th century by legislation from previous years [see John Munsey Turner in *Workaday Preachers*, chapter 2].

THE TOLPUDDLE MARTYRS

Some of the best-known lay Methodists of the 1830s are the Dorset farm-workers, commonly called the 'Tolpuddle Martyrs' who were sentenced at Dorchester Assizes in March 1834 to seven years transportation. The man generally regarded as their leader, 37 year old George Loveless, was a local preacher, as was his brother James. They had learnt to read by studying the Bible and to speak in public through their calling as local preachers. In this they can be seen as representative of many preachers who were active in seeking improved living conditions for themselves and their fellow-workers during the decades prior to 1850. They and four colleagues were brought to trial for allegedly administering an unlawful oath at a meeting of the Friendly Society of Agricultural Labourers in December of the previous year. Admission to membership of such a society at that time involved giving a pledge of loyalty taken on oath, necessary for the protection of its funds and the safety of its members. This practice had continued from the days before 1824, when the combination of workers for the pursuit of their interests was illegal.

The Society's meeting of December 1833 had been infiltrated by an informer, whose report to the magistrates resulted in the arrest warrant being issued, the trial held and the sentence passed. George Loveless was offered his freedom if he would reveal the identity of the members of the Society, but as a man of faith and conviction he refused to do this. The weaknesses in the legal proceedings are described in Garth Lean's pamphlet *The Tolpuddle Martyrs* [published by Luton Industrial College and the Industrial Pioneer]. Loveless and his friends, although shocked by the severity of the sentence, accepted it without bitterness and encouraged each other to maintain their faith. In a letter to his wife just before his departure from England George wrote:

> I shall never forget the promise made at the altar . . . Be satisfied my dear Betsy . . . it will work together for good and we shall yet rejoice together. He who is Lord of the winds and the waves will be my support in life and death.

It is not surprising that a trade union historian (quoted by Garth Lean) said that the labourers learned self-respect, self-government, self-reliance and organisation in the chapels, and as preachers to speak, read, write and lead. Loveless was far from being an isolated example. Many less famous local preachers, restrained by the church which appointed them, found opportunity to use their abilities in movements for political and social reform, e.g. trade unions and Chartism. Identification with such bodies was sometimes regarded in Wesleyan Methodism as ground for expulsion from membership, and attempts to achieve reform in the Wesleyan church itself led in some cases to the same result (see chapter 4).

MEN OF MUTUAL AID

The treatment of the Tolpuddle Martyrs aroused nationwide sympathy for them. After political pressure and public petitions they were brought back to England, though only one of them remained here for the rest of his life. Their story does, however, illustrate some important points.

First, whilst substantial numbers of local preachers in the 1830s and 1840s were professional men, merchants, shopkeepers or craftsmen, a significant proportion were unskilled labourers. The balance between the groups differed in various parts of the country. [The occupations of local preachers are dealt with by Clive Field in chapter 11 of *Workaday Preachers*.]

Secondly, it was the latter group who were most exposed to poverty, and therefore most in need of support from some kind of collective association.

Thirdly, Methodist local preachers in that group were likely to be motivated by their faith to take action to deal with the consequences of poverty. Because of their work as preachers they were able to play a leading part in organising it. Put simply, they felt they ought, and they knew they could.

The chapters of this Section examine briefly the state of public relief for the poor, the place of Friendly Societies in compensating for its deficiencies, the situation in Wesleyan Methodism, and some efforts by local preachers to develop Friendly Societies before LPMAA was formed.

2

Public Policy for Relief of the Poor

*Christian Concern for the Poor • Evolution of the Poor Law
The Poor Law Amendment Act, 1834*

CHRISTIAN CONCERN FOR THE POOR

> You have the poor among you always.
>> Matthew 26:11; Mark 14:7; John 12:8;
>> Deuteronomy 15:11 (REB)

Poverty and wealth have always commanded Christian attention. With the Old Testament behind them, the New Testament writings, especially the Gospels, make many references to wealth, how it is obtained and used, and to the attitudes of Christian believers towards its unequal distribution. Christ's own statement that the poor are always with us, suggests that disparities of material wealth were recognised and accepted by people of his earthly lifetime, and that his aim was to promote particular attitudes towards the creation and use of wealth.

The early Christian community continued to discharge obligations, inherited from its Jewish forebears, to care for its poorer members – orphans, widows, elderly and sick folk – together with those whose need stemmed from other causes. As early as 200 AD Clement of Alexandria, a wealthy Christian, wrote in a book called *Who Is The Rich Man Who Is Saved?* that wealthy Christians should sit lightly to their wealth, adopt a simple lifestyle and give alms to poor people.

You cannot give money to God, so he sends the poor as his representatives and you must give to them. Redemptive alms-giving, according to Clement, is a cement that holds the church together. It benefits the poor who receive what they need, and saves the wealthy from the snare of trusting in riches. The idea of poor people as 'stand-ins' for God was given some emphasis in a

9

17th century work called *The Whole Duty of Man*, published only a generation before the birth of John Wesley.

The present book is an account of how one particular group of Christians in mid-19th century England was moved to make careful provision for the needy in its midst, and how the organisation that was founded for this purpose has grown, developed and changed as it progressed towards its 150th Anniversary year. The Wesleyan Methodist Local Preachers Mutual Aid Association is the title by which it was known at its inception in 1849. Before examining the circumstances of its birth, it is helpful to consider the nature and extent of both public and private provision for the poor in this country in the early 19th century.

Some Methodists, local preachers amongst them, were closely identified with movements for social change at that time. There were also powerful forces for change at work within the structures of Wesleyan Methodism itself. These are also relevant to the history of LPMAA, for it is not to be seen in isolation, either from society or from the church. The work of local preachers is carried out with the commission of the church and in the social context of the times. To understand LPMAA some attempt must be made to understand both the ecclesiastical and the social history surrounding it.

The early decades of the 19th century were a period of rapid and far-reaching change. The population of England and Wales, which had been increasing gradually during the 18th century, began to increase much more rapidly. The first population census (1801) recorded almost 9 million people; by 1851 this had doubled. Population in our country has never expanded so rapidly in any comparable period of time, but it was not only the increase in the number of people that was important. Most of the increase was concentrated in relatively few areas where water transport and water power facilitated the development of factory industry. As steam power superseded water power, areas on or near coalfields became more important and saw the growth of many small settlements into substantial towns. Expanding trade also led to the development of new ports as well as to growth in existing ones. This had considerable implications for parliamentary representation and for municipal government. As an increasing proportion of the population lived in towns rather than rural parishes, it was also significant for social issues such as law and order and the relief of the poor. All these matters received Parliamentary attention during the decade of the 1830s.

The view of early, medieval and Puritan Christendom that private and personal charity is the duty of better-off and property-owning people, and that poor people have an important role in reminding wealthier folk of this duty, gradually declined. The view that individual beneficence is inadequate and unreliable, and that collective charity is the only satisfactory way of ensuring a place in society for the less fortunate gained ground. The question then became – how can this best be achieved? For over 200 years, poor people had been dealt with under the terms of the Elizabethan Poor Law (1597 and 1601) and its many subsequent modifications. Changes in the economic and social context of life in early 19th century England resulted in the 'old' Poor Law arrangements becoming unsuited to the needs of a rapidly-industrialising nation. The formation of voluntary associations for mutual assistance was given some impetus by an Act for the Relief and Encouragement of Friendly Societies in 1793. The development of the Friendly Society movement in the 19th century is considered in more detail in chapter 3. It is relevant to note here that the laws which restrained the combination of working people for the pursuit of their interests were not relaxed until 1824. Friendly and similar societies and clubs were somewhat inhibited by the risk and fear of being confused with illegal combinations.

EVOLUTION OF THE POOR LAW

In 1832, (the year the first Reform Bill became law) a Royal Commission was appointed:

> to make diligent and full inquiry into the practical operation of the laws for the Relief of the Poor in England and Wales, and into the manner in which those laws are administered, and to report its opinion whether any and what alterations, amendments, or improvements may be beneficially made in the said laws, or in the manner of administering them, and how the same may be best carried into effect.

The Commission's inquiry was constrained by the difficulties of securing comprehensive, consistent and comparable information.

It was the largest investigation of its kind, and the first to be attempted in the context of an industrialising society. It did not, however, have the benefit of detailed information about population structure and movements, employment and wages, industrial development, and so on, which would be part of the raw material of any similar investigation in the late 20th century. The commission worked speedily and by August 1834 the 'Poor Law Amendment Act' was on the Statute Book. A brief summary of Poor Relief before the 1830s will assist understanding of the intentions of the Act and its effects.

Poor Law practice in 18th and early 19th centuries was based on principles derived from Tudor legislation. A distinction was made between able-bodied people and the impotent, the latter having a moral claim for support which was made into a legal claim upon their own parish. The able-bodied were also supported by their own parish, where landholders were required to pay rates in order to provide work for them. A distinction was recognised, however feebly, between wilfully idle beggars and those without work through bad harvests, decline in trade, severe weather or other temporary causes. It was clearly expected that each community should be responsible for its own poor. The church had two roles. The first was collection and distribution of alms by the churchwardens. Secondly, the clergy were required to preach sermons, exhort people at confessions, and urge charity immediately after the reading of the Gospel each Sunday. Bishops were empowered to send uncharitable persons to Quarter Sessions, where Justices could ultimately impose gaol sentences on any who refused to pay.

Thus the role of the Christian church in stimulating individual generosity was complemented by state action from the end of Elizabeth's reign. The administration of poor relief through a parish-based system was embodied in the Acts of 1597 and 1601. The Justices appointed Overseers for each parish with complete authority to collect and distribute relief. This power was exercised in such widely-differing ways that the process was often described as corrupt, profligate, arbitrary and lax. It was inevitable that unpaid and annually-appointed officers would interpret their duties variably. No amount of money was prescribed for relief; a farmer serving as overseer might find his crops vandalised if he was not generous in giving relief, a shopkeeper would be tempted to give relief too generously to any of his customers who applied, whilst employers quickly realised that by restricting wages they could throw some costs on to the parish. If it became known that relief was more readily available in a neighbouring parish, people seeking it would try to move there.

Legislation of the late 17th century sought to deal with the latter abuse by strengthening the powers of Justices of the Peace, and establishing a role for a Vestry meeting of rate-payers to whom Overseers were to be responsible. Such a system, with three different focal points of authority, was open to other abuses, especially as many Magistrates, being country gentlemen, did not understand labourers' lifestyles and tended to apply over-generous criteria. Eighteenth century legislation sought to deal with these problems, whilst still retaining the parish basis of the system, but was not wholly effective. Acts of 1723 and 1782 authorised parishes (or groups of parishes) to maintain workhouses for the accommodation of their poor, but then provided that these should be for the aged and infirm, the able-bodied poor being found work outside the poorhouse.

The parish principle was now being seen as a serious impediment to economic development, as it inhibited the movement of labour to areas where it was needed, and there was massive increase in the cost of poor relief. This led to scales for assessing relief, known as the Speenhamland System after the parish in Berkshire where it was first introduced. This had the effect of extending the application of relief in lieu of wages or to compensate for inadequate wages. After the Napoleonic Wars, Parliament enacted further changes to Poor Law administration, including the election of Vestry members, the appointment of full-time paid Assistant Overseers, and limitation of magistrates' powers to order relief. The last attempt to adapt the old Poor Law to the rapidly-changing situation was the Labour Rate of 1832 under which employers were required to employ a certain number of labourers or pay the equivalent wages to the parish. Like other measures, it proved difficult to enforce, and imposed heavy costs for little return.

Poor Law Amendment Act, 1834

It was recognised that adaptation was not effective and that major revision was necessary. The Royal Commission was set up in 1832. Whatever the weaknesses of the Commission's Report, the abuses and malpractice which it revealed certainly existed. The fundamental principle underlying its recommendations was 'less eligibility'; parish relief, whether in or out of a workhouse, should not make paupers better off than those who were in work. The report contains statements such as

> The diet of the workhouse almost always exceeds the diet of the cottage. . . Paupers within the workhouse enjoyed a diet profuse compared with that of independent labourers of the same district.

Examples were found in farming and fishing of labourers who refused employment and preferred parish relief because it was sufficient to live on, the work was lighter and the hours fewer than in a normal job. The Commission took evidence from many people, including the barrister appointed under a law of 1829 to advise Friendly Societies about their rules (see chapter 3). He was particularly asked about the benefits paid by Societies to members unable to work and he replied that the average allowance was about one-third of what a member could earn. For example, if wages in a particular area averaged £1-4s a week, then the benefit would be about 8s, as it was generally believed that more would encourage members to stay in the Society rather than take work. The 'less eligibility' principle was applied rigorously by the friendly societies, and benefit was not allowed to anyone in employment. The Commission was influenced by this in framing its recommendations, but its report was most significant in the arrangements it proposed for implementing those recommendations. It set a pattern for most of the public service reforms of 19th century, that is, a centrally-appointed body to ensure uniformity of practice and locally-elected bodies to administer the service in each community, financed by locally-determined and collected rates.

The Poor Law Amendment Act did not embody all the recommendations. A new Poor Law Commission was introduced, the notable Edwin Chadwick being appointed its secretary. The Act did not include the 'less eligibility' test, nor was outdoor relief declared illegal. The Poor Law Commissioners, with the Royal

Commission Report for guidance, were left to determine these things. The Act did require the election of parish Boards of Guardians, and by July 1837 over 90% of all parishes had been provided with them. By 1846 almost all unions had their own workhouse, and in 1847 the Poor Law Commission was replaced by a Poor Law Board whose President was a minister of the Government. There was still variability of practice, some unions applying the law more strictly than others. The harsher aspects of the new Poor Law were critically exposed by Charles Dickens, and also in writings such as the famous poem 'Christmas Day in the Workhouse' by George Sims. Two verses from the middle and end of the poem make the point:

> I came to the parish, craving bread for a starving
> wife –
> Bread for the woman who'd loved me through fifty
> years of life;
> And what do you think they told me, mocking my
> awful grief,
> That the 'house' was open to us, but they wouldn't
> give 'out-relief'.
>
> Yes, there in a land of plenty, lay a loving woman
> dead,
> Cruelly starved and murdered for a loaf of the
> parish bread;
> At yonder gate, last Christmas, I craved for a human
> life,
> You who would feed us paupers, what of my
> murdered wife?

Nevertheless, in the longer term the reforms did help to check the demoralising pauperisation of the growing numbers of working people. A final point may be noted: the 1834 Report concluded by urging the benefits of religious and moral education in improving the condition of poor people. Perhaps the Report and the Poor Law Amendment Act did something to encourage the educational work of Christians, and in due course the promotion of public education by the state.

James Uriah Walker, proprietor of *The Halifax Guardian* and a Wesleyan local preacher, was a member of the small gathering in Birmingham on 24th July 1849 which planned the inaugural meeting for the formation of the Association later that year. There he told of his experience as a Poor Law Guardian some years earlier. He sat as a member of the Board when a fellow-preacher came in to ask for relief. Another Guardian, a Church of England man, said, 'This ought not to be. This Methodist preacher ought not to have to come to this Board for relief.' Incidents of this kind stirred some local preachers to the actions that eventually brought LPMAA into being. The many allusions in early writings, in speeches at meetings, and at the inaugural Aggregate, to parish relief, the workhouse and to paupers' funerals, indicate the mixture of disgust and distress that local preachers felt at the thought of fellow-labourers in the Gospel having to depend on parish support. In the face of misunderstanding, misrepresentation and mistrust, they moved when the time was ripe to try to eliminate this stigma from the church through which they served the cause of Christ.

3

The Friendly Society Movement in the 19th Century

*Friendly Societies in the Early 1800s • Developments in the 1830s
A Change of Emphasis*

FRIENDLY SOCIETIES IN THE EARLY 1800S

In the previous chapter it was noted that the established practices of Friendly Societies, so far as they could be ascertained in the 1830s, were influential in shaping some of the recommendations of the Royal Commission on the Poor Law. They were influential because they indicated the general attitude and expectations of many working men towards the provision they might make for their own and their families' needs when they were unable to work. Friendly Societies were not new then, though they had been known by a variety of descriptive titles. In essence, a society or club was a voluntary association of working men who agreed together (on certain terms) to make financial provision for any member who, through illness or injury, might be unable for the time being to continue in work. The Friendly Society movement was thus the first systematic and organised attempt at collective self-help amongst working-class folk, combining a desire for sturdy independence with concern for fellow men. It is appropriate, therefore, to consider its growth and development in the decades leading up to 1849, for it is part of the tradition out of which Mutual Aid amongst Local Preachers emerged.

There was no obligation under the Friendly Societies Act of 1793 for rules to be registered with the magistrates in Quarter Sessions. It is impossible therefore to give accurate figures for the numbers of Friendly Societies and their members at the beginning of the 19th century. Estimates of the time seem to point to about 8,000 societies with 700,000 members. The number of Societies exceeded 10,000 by 1815, with membership of nearly 1 million, approximately 10% of the population. Most Societies were small and local, with average membership about 100.

As a consequence of early industrial development, Lancashire was foremost in the establishment and growth of Friendly Societies. It was in that county that the co-operative movement originated, and some of the earliest known local preacher Friendly Societies began in that area (see chapter 5). Most Societies had members from many occupations. Where the majority of members were of the same occupation, a Society sometimes assumed the character of a trade union, but could evade the restrictions of the Combination Acts (not relaxed until 1824) by being officially a Friendly Society. Registration gave a measure of protection for a Society's funds, for example, power to sue dishonest officers, and priority in claiming any funds in possession of a bankrupt or deceased officer. Other Societies did not have these benefits. Societies were known to collapse because sickness benefits and death grants were offered at higher levels than contributions could support. Younger men often preferred to form a new Society of their contemporaries, rather than join an existing Society of older men whose claims would be greater. Competition between Societies sometimes took the form of spending greater sums from funds on liquor at meetings. Rules might require members to spend a minimum amount on drink at each meeting, the landlord in return providing a room for meetings and keeping the Society's box.

DEVELOPMENTS IN THE 1830S

Legislation in the early 19th century was aimed at strengthening the position of Friendly Societies in order to reduce the burden on the poor rate, and to help develop self-reliance amongst working men. Acts of 1817 and 1819 gave the right to deposit funds in savings banks and to invest in the National Debt. In 1829 registration procedure was amended, Societies wishing to register being required to have their rules certified by the barrister who performed the same function for savings banks. This was the origin of what later became the office of Registrar of Friendly Societies. As well as providing for certain insurance needs of members, Societies also met the social and convivial needs – a regular (monthly) evening, an annual feast, and support from fellow-members at a funeral. It is probable that in many cases the social dimension was more important than the insurance aspect in keeping Societies in existence. They were often anxious to stress their soundness, reliability and trustworthiness, so that words like 'Ancient' and 'Loyal' appeared in their titles.

It was normal for members to be actively involved in the management of a Society's affairs, by serving in turn as officers or stewards. The box containing the Society's funds was usually secured by three locks, the keys being held by different officers as a precaution against theft. The difficulty that many Societies experienced in finding a member able to read and write well enough to keep the records, especially the accounts, was noted until the last quarter of the 19th century, by which time popular education was almost universal. Benefit levels varied widely both between Societies and between different parts of the country. Sick pay probably averaged about one-third of normal wages; funeral grants varied much more widely, perhaps from £2 minimum up to £10 in larger, wealthier Societies. The underlying difficulty in relating subscriptions to benefit levels was the lack of actuarially-sound tables. Many existed, but they were frequently misleading or unreliable, especially when the rates of sickness differed between occupations and between localities.

Friendly Society rule-books give some insight into the concerns and expectations of those who joined them. Complex systems of fines were included to deal with matters such as disorderly behaviour, failure to pay subscriptions, refusal to serve in office, absence from (or even lateness for) meetings, embezzlement or misuse of funds, fraudulently obtaining benefit by feigning sickness, or claiming benefit when in work. One Society (The Town Porters Friendly Society, Edinburgh) printed on the title page of its 1833 rule-book a statement of its objects in the form of a rhyme:

> To aid each other in distress;
> to make the wants of old-age less;
> or should a Member die,
> His new-made Widow to assist,
> to lay his body in the dust;
> These are the objects, surely just,
> of our Society.

Many Friendly Societies set rigorous standards in the application of their rules. This is well illustrated by the case of a member in the printing industry who was 'on the box'(receiving benefit), whilst still working at his trade. The Society concerned required lists of its members and the benefits they were receiving to be printed, and sent the 'copy' to a local firm. The man who was given the material to set up in type realised that one of the allegedly sick members was actually employed in the same workshop. He reported the situation to the Society's officers, and as a result the offending member was expelled, forfeited his contributions and lost his job.

A CHANGE OF EMPHASIS

Some reference has been made to early legislation affecting Friendly Societies. In many respects the Act of 1829 marked the turning point in the attitude of the State towards the Friendly Societies movement. Up to that time the perceived purpose was to encourage independence and self-help in the labouring classes, thereby helping to control the rapidly escalating costs of publicly-provided poor relief. A framework of regulation helped Societies to survive and expand in reasonable security. After that time, the emphasis changed. The year 1834 saw an Act of Parliament relating to Friendly Societies, as well as the Poor Law Amendment Act. Together they created a new context for the development of self-help through Friendly Societies. The paternalism of earlier decades was replaced by a more centralised system of registration and legal support. This left Societies and their members almost complete autonomy in the matter of contributions and benefits. The range of purposes recognised by the law was extended to include 'any purpose which is not illegal'.

In 1846 the title 'Registrar' was given to the barrister who certified Friendly Societies' rules; the first holder of the office, John Tidd Pratt, held it until his death in 1870. Societies wishing to have the advantages of registration had to submit their rules to the Registrar. These then became legally binding. Periodical returns of sickness and death amongst members were also required. Many Societies preferred not to register, fearing Government interference in their affairs. The strict administration of poor relief by the Boards of Guardians after 1834 had the effect of stimulating self-help amongst working-men and encouraging the growth of Friendly Societies.

Less than 40 years after the changes of 1834, when a Royal Commission on Friendly Societies was sitting in the early 1870s, there were over 32,000 Societies, with more than 4 million members and invested funds exceeding £11 million. It is not surprising that, when Methodist local preachers determined to find ways of assisting their brethren in need, they adopted the widespread and rapidly growing method of forming Friendly Societies in order to do it.

4

Wesleyan Methodism in the 1830s and 1840s

An Unsettled Church • Disturbances Before 1849
1849 and Some Consequences

AN UNSETTLED CHURCH

The Methodist Local Preachers Mutual Aid Association is, first of all, an association of Methodist Local Preachers. It would not, indeed it could not, exist unless the Methodist Church recognised that some lay people are called by God to the work of preaching his Word in the context of corporate worship, and commissioned them to do that work. If there were no local preachers there would be no need for an association to support them in the pursuit of their call and commission. Local preachers have always served under the discipline required of them by the church within which they hold their allegiance to Christ, and which has recognised their call. If that was all there was to be said, this chapter and some other parts of this book could not have been written. However, in the history of the Christian Church, including Methodism and its institutions, things are rarely as simple as they seem, and the origin of LPMAA cannot be properly understood without some reference to the Methodist context of the times. There were occasions when the discipline of the church was imposed unreasonably or in a heavy-handed way, just as there were local preachers and other lay people who tried to reject the discipline or who behaved in an unconstitutional manner.

In his *Historic Sketches of Free Methodism* of 1885 (originally published as a series of articles in *The Sheffield Independent* ten years earlier) Joseph Kirsop made some strong assertions:

> All the secessions from Methodism have taken place
> on grounds of church government or discipline.
> . . . The secessions that have taken place in England
> have all been through disciplinary action, or on

account of the governmental constitution of the Wesleyan body. Pastoral supremacy is at the root of the disruptions of Methodism.

The word 'secessions' may not be appropriate in every case, for in some of these disruptions many members were deprived of their membership, i.e. they were expelled, and others left merely to avoid expulsion. Then, as throughout the history of Methodism, loss of membership meant also that a local preacher ceased to be recognised, which presented a difficulty for Local Preacher Friendly Societies, as will be noted in subsequent chapters.

DISTURBANCES BEFORE 1849

The second quarter of the 19th century was a period of substantial secessions and expulsions, coinciding with political agitation in Britain and revolution in some parts of Europe. Movements for greater participation by the citizenry in political affairs were matched by movements for a positive role of the membership in the decision-making processes of Wesleyan Methodism. The end result was the separation of a number of groups retaining many of the characteristics of Methodism but rejecting the authority of an all-ministerial Wesleyan-style Conference, and the pastoral supremacy of ordained ministers within the circuits.

It was in context of an upheaval over the installation of an organ in Brunswick Chapel, Leeds, in 1827 that Rev. Dr Jabez Bunting, a powerful and influential figure in Wesleyan Methodism at the time, made one of his most famous statements:

Methodism knows nothing of democracy; Methodism hates democracy as it hates sin.

This would not have seemed so extreme then as it does in the late 20th century, though in his book on *The United Methodist Free Churches* (originally the Wesley Historical Society Conference lecture of 1957) Dr Oliver Beckerlegge recalls that the Vice-President of Conference 1955 warned against importing political vocabulary such as 'democracy' into the church. He points out, however, that many political and trade union leaders learned much from Methodism that they applied in public life, including the principle of participation in the political process. It was this, in the life of the church, that the reformers sought, even at the expense of their own membership in it. In her book *Stages in the Development and Control of Wesleyan Lay Leadership* Dr Margaret Batty examines the Leeds organ case in detail. She concludes that it was the breaking of its own rules by the Connexion which led to the secession of a thousand members, including a significant number of local preachers, in Leeds. The formation of the Protestant Methodist Connexion, which followed, soon found support in Barnsley, Sheffield, Keighley, in Lancashire and in London.

A few years later (1834) Wesleyan Methodism was shaken again, this time by a dispute over the establishment of a theological institution for the training of travelling preachers. Again the disruption centred as much on the way the matter was handled as upon objection to the institution and its purpose. True, there were those who had reservations about the idea, fearing, as many have done in subsequent generations, that education might displace inspiration in preaching. When the committee appointed by Conference in 1833 to plan the scheme went so far as to nominate Dr Bunting as President of the Institution and then submitted its proposals for approval by the next Conference, the opposition cohered, led by Dr Samuel Warren. Joseph Kirsop (*Historic Sketches*), refers to a letter from Rev. James Everett to Dr Warren in December 1834, which suggests that part of the ground for opposition was the fear that such an institution would foster ideas of ministerial supremacy.

Warren's attack on the scheme resulted in his suspension from his Circuit. During the Autumn of 1834, lay members (including local preachers) were expelled from Circuits in Lancashire, Yorkshire, the Midlands and London, and in November a meeting in Manchester formed the 'Grand Central Association'. By 1836, that Association had been joined by the Leeds Protestant Methodists and had adopted the name 'Wesleyan Association'. Dr Warren was elected President of its first Annual Assembly (not, let it be noted, Conference!) and Matthew Johnson, leader of the Protestant Methodists, its Secretary. During the next three years a small group of seceders from Derby (the Arminian Methodists), some from North Wales, and others from various places overseas came in. The word 'Methodist' was then added, and it became the 'Wesleyan Methodist Association'(WMA). This was the principal body of reformers until the last and greatest upheaval, which followed the events of 1849, described later in this chapter.

Other things happened before 1849 which were part of the background to the formation of LPMAA. Amongst these was the refusal by Conference in 1839 to allocate any part of the Centenary Thanksgiving Fund for the support of local preachers and their work. It will be seen in chapter 5 that, in response to poverty amongst local preachers in some parts of the country, local preacher Friendly Societies had been formed during the 1830s. Their continuation, and the establishment of further such Societies, would certainly have been restrained had Conference decided in 1839 to set up a Necessitous Local Preachers' Fund. However, it did not do so until 1882, in spite of an offer from a prominent layman, James Wild (later to be first treasurer of LPMAA), of £100 to initiate such a fund.

Official Methodism has always recognised that it cannot live without local preachers, but has sometimes found difficulty in living with them. In deploying the money actually received at that date, the Conference made allocations to a number of uses related to the training and support of ministers, including retired ('worn-out') ministers and widows. Nothing was set aside, however, to meet needs amongst the unpaid lay ministry, although need had been identified and some action taken by local preachers to try and deal with it themselves. The Conference decision meant that pressure for the expansion of their work increased.

Meanwhile, movements for change in the political and constitutional sphere (following the first Reform Act, 1832) had captured the interest and enthusiasm of many people including some lay Methodists, local preachers amongst them. The principal movement for Parliamentary reform in the late 1830s and early 1840s was Chartism. The People's Charter pressed six points to give further participation in the democratic process:

   (i)   Universal adult male suffrage
   (ii) Removal of property qualification for M.P.s
   (iii) Payment of M.P.s
   (iv) Equal constituencies
   (v)   Secret ballot
   (vi) Annual Parliaments

All except the last were eventually achieved, though universal adult male suffrage did not come about until 1918, the year that the first women were enfranchised. In the 1830s and 1840s, however, some of these demands would have seemed revolutionary. In her essay on Lord Shaftesbury, in *Christian Social Reformers of 19th Century*, Constance Smith, a former Deputy Chief Inspector of Factories, writes of 1840 as a year

> ... when the promise and menace of Chartism lit the horizon for half the nation and brooded darkly over the minds of the other half ...

It is not surprising that a church which had already experienced schism over its unwillingness to allow lay members a full place in its affairs should view Chartism with alarm. In some parts of the country Wesleyans were expelled if they were suspected of espousing the Chartist cause. For example, the ministers of the Bath District at their District Synod Meeting in May 1839 (as reported in *The Bath Post*) resolved that

> ... any member of the Methodist Connexion who should join himself with the Chartists should be removed from membership.

It appears that reform activity outside the church was thought to indicate the likelihood of reform activity within it; Wesleyan authority was taking no risks. An article in the *Methodist Times* (29 June 1899) includes a further example of the feelings that membership of 'other organisations' aroused in Wesleyan Methodism in the years before LPMAA was formed. The preacher at Fillongley on 11 June 1899 wrote about his visit to the first occupants of the Fillongley Local Preachers Retirement Cottages (see chapters 13 and 14). He referred to one who recalled objections to his being placed on the plan, nearly sixty years earlier,

> because of his connection with the Order of Oddfellows, there being strong feeling in these days against what were considered secret societies; but to remove the obstacle to his becoming a local preacher he gave up the club.

1849 AND SOME CONSEQUENCES

In this climate of opinion collective action by local preachers for any purpose would have been viewed with suspicion. This may well have discouraged the expansion of local preacher Friendly Societies, notwithstanding the Conference decision of 1839 and the extent of perceived need. However, the biggest turmoil in

Wesleyan Methodism – which had significant effects for LPMAA at its inception and in its early years – was yet to come. It followed the sequence of anonymous circulars, sent to all Wesleyan ministers through the newly-introduced 'Penny Post', which became known as 'The Fly Sheets'. There were five of them altogether, published in the years 1846-49. The first dealt with 'Location, Centralisation and Secularisation' of Connexional authority; the second attacked 'the Presidency, the Platform, and Connexional Committees'. The later Fly-Sheets repeated and reinforced the arguments, keeping the controversy about the dominance of Connexional leaders, especially Dr Jabez Bunting, very much alive. Dr Bunting had been a central figure in the Warrenite dispute over the Theological Institution in 1834, and had held most major Connexional offices. He had been President of Conference four times. Published correspondence shows how influential he continued to be, many people writing to him for advice and guidance over problems in the Circuits.

It was decided to hunt out the authors of the Fly-Sheets by requiring all ministers to sign a statement to the effect that they were not connected with them. By the Conference of 1849 over 30 ministers had still refused to do so. Some of them were orally examined in Conference, being required to answer the question 'Are you the writer or author of the Fly Sheets?' No accusation was made nor evidence presented; the underlying issue was loyalty to the Connexional hierarchy and concentration of authority in a handful of senior ministers. One minister in particular, Rev. James Everett, who had travelled forty-two years, objected to this manner of conducting proceedings. His most-quoted statements were:

> I demand the name of my accuser, the charge against
> me in writing, and an opportunity to defend myself
> in a constitutional way . . . If I am the most
> suspected, there must be most evidence against me;
> produce it.

There was no response to this; a charge could not be made because there was no evidence. Two other ministers, Samuel Dunn and William Griffiths, also refused to answer, and all three were expelled. Over subsequent years there has been a widely-held belief that Everett was *an* author, if not *the* author, of the Fly Sheets, though this has never been proved. All that the Conference of 1849 could do was to pass a resolution referring to 'the strong and generally-prevalent suspicion', and made that the ground of his expulsion.

As chapter 7 explains, all this occurred at the time when initial steps were being taken to convene the great assembly of local preachers that formed LPMAA two months later. They were parallel events but were not at that stage directly related. There was widespread opposition amongst both ministers and lay members of Wesleyan Methodism to the action of the Conference. This meant that any unofficial activity (especially amongst laymen) was regarded with disapproval and was likely to face difficulty, if not active resistance. The reaction spilled over into the public domain, the Conference proceedings incurring the displeasure of *The Times*:

> The rule of all our courts . . . assumes every man innocent until he is proved guilty. These gentlemen are punished on mere suspicion, and for refusing to incriminate themselves. We take these proceedings on the statement of the Conference, and we pronounce them at once a gross outrage on our old English principles of fair play.

The three expelled ministers travelled extensively, addressing large crowds in many parts of the country; there was a war of words between the Wesleyan establishment newspaper, *The Watchman*, and the more liberal *Wesleyan Times*. Many who supported reform had no desire to leave Wesleyanism, hoping that Conference would accede to some clearly-worded requests for giving lay people a fuller role in the ordering of the church's affairs. This did not happen, and the expulsion or secession of members in the early 1850s totalled 100,000. Zealous Superintendents, influenced by Dr Bunting's principle of the supremacy of pastoral authority, expelled anyone thought to be in sympathy with the reformers. Long-serving members, class-leaders, local preachers were put out of membership, for reducing their giving to the church, preaching to reform congregations, or simply attending unauthorised meetings. In his chapter 'Years of Tension and Conflict', in *Workaday Preachers*, John Munsey Turner summarises the situation in a sentence:

> There was angry abuse on both sides, with rival magazines and newspapers, and mass expulsion of 'rebels', including many local preachers.

Sometimes whole Societies seceded, retaining possession and use of their chapels; others formed new congregations and built new chapels. Almost certainly some expelled members were lost to the church entirely, whilst some joined other branches of Methodism. Others drifted back when it became clear that reconciliation was impossible.

By the middle of the 1850s the reformist cause had begun to lose some support. There had never been a desire to fragment the church. Those who left often did so reluctantly, regretting that conditions in Wesleyan Methodism made unity impossible. The Wesleyan Association's first assembly (1836) expressed its desire for a union of all branches of the Methodist family. In 1851 the Reformers of the post-1849 schism sent an address, to which the WMA Assembly responded warmly, again looking forward to union of all Methodists. In 1853 and 1854, the 1836 resolution was reaffirmed, with a decision to negotiate with any branch of Methodism prepared to do the same. The Reform delegates of the latter year made a similar decision, and communicated with the Wesleyan Methodist Association and other denominations.

The Methodist New Connexion seems to have been determined to retain its own constitution, but the Reformers and the WMA formed a joint negotiating body early in 1855, which agreed a draft basis of union later that year. After some modifications of detail, the scheme was implemented at an amalgamated Assembly in July 1857 at Baillie Street WMA Chapel in Rochdale. James Everett, from whose expulsion by the Wesleyan Conference the Reformers had stemmed, was elected President. Approximately 20,000 Reformers combined with a similar number of WMA members to form the United Methodist Free Churches. As many again did *not* join the UMFC, and established the Wesleyan Reform Union in 1859.

1857 thus marks the first major stage in the process of Methodist Union. In spite of the loss of members, ministers and local preachers that followed the events of 1849, the Wesleyan Church remained the strongest of the diverse branches of Methodism right through to the Union of 1932. It did not survive unchanged, however, and almost certainly stayed strong because changes *did* take place. Many of these resulted from the 1849 upheaval. The most significant of these was the admission of laymen to the Conference in 1878 (women came later), though there was a long period of debate about the respective roles and responsibilities of the ministerial and representative sessions of the Conference. Before that date there remained a degree of doubt and uncertainty about the propriety of independent lay action, which clearly affected the recognition and growth of the Local Preachers Mutual Aid Association.

The disturbed state of Wesleyanism in the 1840s did, however, provide a climate in which some were prepared to take initiatives, even if cautiously, to try and deal with matters which they believed required action. The previous decade had seen some disruptions in the Wesleyan body, as well as scattered endeavours to support needy local preachers by the formation of Friendly Societies. It is to this that we now turn. Much bigger things happened before the end of the decade, but they owed a great deal to what had been done earlier. Public provision, self-help and ecclesiastical politics were major factors influencing these developments.

5

Mutual Aid amongst Local Preachers before 1849

The Earliest Societies • Rochdale
Bristol • The Momentum Builds

THE EARLIEST SOCIETIES

It was in that context, and against that background of public provision for poor people and self-help amongst the growing number of workers, that the first Methodist Local Preacher Friendly Societies were formed. Caring for fellow-Christians was clearly required by the faith that Methodist preachers proclaimed, though other influences contributed to the development, both in Wesleyan Methodism and in the political and social sphere. There were several initiatives by groups of local preachers in widely scattered parts of the country during the 1830s and 1840s.

The earliest Wesleyan Local Preachers' Friendly Society so far traced held its 4th Annual Meeting, according to a report in *Stephens' Methodist Magazine* (Vol.1, No.4, September 1834), in the Schoolroom of Rochdale Wesleyan Methodist Church, on 5th August 1834. It must therefore be presumed to have been formed in 1830. The report mentions a membership of 300, stating that over 100 were present at the meeting, representing 21 different Circuits in North West England. The Society had £250 in its funds. Its President that year was a Manchester preacher, Thomas Taylor. Perhaps anticipating a tradition which has been followed by LPMAA in later years, that the District Chairman or President entertains the meeting in his own circuit, the Society arranged to hold its next meeting in Manchester.

The preceding chapter gave some account of the main disturbances that afflicted the Wesleyan church in the 1820s, 1830s and 1840s, pointing out that local preachers were sometimes in the forefront of these upheavals. They were often affected by them, either by expulsion for unauthorised activity or by secession (sometimes with ministers and lay leaders), to register their discontent at the way the Wesleyan body was conducting its affairs. It appears that some local preachers had been excluded from the Plan in Ashton and Oldham, over their involvement with Rev. Joseph Rayner Stephens (brother of the founder of the magazine mentioned above). He had been forced to resign from the Wesleyan ministry for publicly supporting disestablishment of the Church of England, and a number of local preachers had identified themselves with him. This posed a problem for the Society, membership being open only to recognised Wesleyan local preachers. Other Societies were faced with the same difficulty over eligibility for membership when preachers were expelled by Wesleyan authorities, including LPMAA itself very soon after its formation.

Self–help amongst local preachers was not confined to Wesleyans, though only a little detail is available. On Whit Monday 1826 a small group of local preachers of the Nottingham New Connexion Circuit held a conference in one of their chapels. This became an annual event, and in 1876 a booklet was published for the Jubilee Conference, giving an account of its origin and progress. It included information about a Local Preachers Relief Fund which had originated soon after the first conference. The objects of the fund were to give financial assistance 'towards the interment of a deceased brother' and 'to assist in providing suitable clothing for preachers actively engaged on the plan'. Subscriptions were sixpence per quarter, and at a later date the Quarterly Meeting requested the Societies in the Circuit to contribute one penny per member annually to the Relief Fund.

It appears that in 1857 the fund was in deficit by £3-14s-2d, but by 1875 the balance in hand was £41-17s-9d. By that time a total in excess of £400 had been distributed in allowances and funeral grants. In 1926, a centenary booklet *Heralds of the Cross* was published, which included some account of the winding up of the fund, in 1897. In that year the Methodist New Connexion paid £1,500 to LPMAA to secure eligibility for its local preachers to join (see chapter 12). The Nottingham Circuit Relief Fund paid £50 in entrance fees for its own local preachers, and gave the rest of its funds towards the Connexion's £1,500.

ROCHDALE

Another Local Preachers Friendly Society dating from this period was established at a meeting held in Rochdale on 27th May 1836. Its minute book has been preserved in an unusual way, as described by Jean Reid, a General Committee member for many years:

> The book was found at Petrie and McNaught's factory, Crawford Street, Rochdale, about 1970, 134 years after the Society's origin. When it came to light in an office safe it was handed to a member of the staff who was a Methodist. Seeing that it had to do with local preachers' self-help, he passed it on to me, knowing my connection with LPMAA.

John Petrie was a prosperous engineer, and a leader at Baillie Sreet, Rochdale, the earliest Wesleyan Association chapel. It seems possible that the Local Preachers' Friendly Society may have been given facilities at the factory for some of its meetings, and that the minute book had been left there when it was full (1866). The inaugural meeting, attended by 14 members, including officers and committee, adopted comprehensive rules. Rule 1 specified that:

> This Society shall be for the benefit only of the Wesleyan Local Preachers in the Rochdale Circuit.

However, the disruptions over the founding of a theological institution (the movement led by Dr Warren) were affecting Rochdale, and many lay people, including local preachers, separated from the Conference body to become part of the Wesleyan Association. The rule was therefore deleted and all subsequent rules renumbered. A comparable situation faced the Wesleyan Methodist LPMAA immediately after its establishment in 1849. It adopted an interpretation of its own rules, but with the same purpose as the earlier Rochdale Society, which was to retain local preachers in membership even though they had left or been expelled from Wesleyan Methodism.

For some years the Rochdale Friendly Society held most of its normal quarterly meetings in the home of one of its members, J. Pollitt, in Mill Street. The annual meetings were held at the Temperance Hotel, quite often on Good Friday. In October 1845 it was decided to apply to the Trustees of Baillie Street Chapel for permission to hold the meetings there, and from 1846 the meetings usually took place in No. 7 Vestry (how many Vestries did the Chapel have?). The minutes are generally very brief, recording the date and place of the meetings, names of members present and of the stewards appointed for the succeeding quarter.

From time to time particular items of business arose: in November 1836 the Treasurer, John Milne, was awarded 5 shillings 'for composing and writing the Rules'. In May 1837 it was agreed that the Secretary, Charles Renshaw, who served in this capacity throughout the whole period of the Minute Book (i.e. 1836-66), should receive 5 shillings annually for his services. The Annual Meeting of 1839 authorised the printing of 250 copies of the Rules, indicating a modest confidence in the likely recruitment of members. Membership figures were not regularly reported, but attendance at ordinary meetings was usually between 8 and 12, rising sometimes as high as 20 for annual meetings. At the Annual Meeting in April 1865 the Committee was instructed to prepare a revision of the Rule Book, to incorporate all amendments made over the years, ready for reprinting, which had not been done since 1850.

This early Local Preachers Friendly Society had to grapple with the same kinds of problem that confronted other similar Societies of the period, including LPMAA itself after 1849. They fall into two related categories – members *and* money. There were, of course, regular resolutions on the admission of new members, and the suspension or expulsion of members in arrears with their subscriptions or who defaulted in other ways. The Society also had to address the matter of local preachers who left or were expelled from Wesleyanism and ceased to be recognised as Local Preachers. In April 1844 a resolution of the Annual Meeting decreed that they should not be allowed to hold office or vote in the management of the Society. This was rescinded a year later and replaced by a ban on holding office only if such a person joined a religious body that did not accept the doctrine of Atonement. Provision was made for members who went to live more than three miles from Rochdale to continue in membership, to receive benefit in sickness, and to be visited by the Stewards. If the committee agreed 'the propriety of visiting such members', a travelling allowance of 6d per mile (after the first three miles) was approved. At the same Annual Meeting (April 1849) it was resolved that those appointed to collect the Honorary Members subscriptions should be paid at the rate of 5 per cent of the amounts so collected.

Occasionally consideration had to be given to members who, in the vernacular of the time, were 'on the club'. One had been found going about his business whilst receiving benefit. At the meeting in January 1856 he refunded the money and was pardoned for his offence. A special meeting called in May 1842 decided that a member was not eligible for the sick pay he was receiving. Before any disciplinary action was taken he 'took himself off the club' and nothing further was done. At the Annual Meeting in April 1865 the request of another member who wished to continue preaching whilst 'on the club' was granted.

The financial soundness of the Rochdale Society caused concern after only a few years. In April 1846 a select committee was appointed 'to devise means to adjust the income and expenditure of this Society'. Its recommendations were adopted at a meeting in January 1847. Two years later the contributions for funerals were discontinued, and far-reaching changes made to the scales of subscriptions and benefits. By 1855 it was deemed desirable to mount a recruitment drive amongst preachers of the Wesleyan Methodist Association, the New Connexion and the Primitive Methodists in Rochdale, as well as the Wesleyans. This could link with the decision in March 1861 to decline the invitation of Thomas Cuthbertson, President of Wesleyan Methodist LPMAA, to amalgamate with the national association. Finance was prominent again in 1864, the Annual Meeting of that year resolving to approach 'a few of the wealthy friends' for Honorary Subscriptions. One of the last minutes in the Book records that on the advice of several Honorary Members it was decided not to proceed with a request to the Quarterly Meetings of the various Circuits for collections for the Society.

BRISTOL

A third pre-1849 Local Preachers' Friendly Society operated in Bristol for some eighteen months before the inauguration of the Wesleyan Methodist Local Preachers Mutual Aid Association. None of its records seem to have survived, but *The Wesleyan Times* of 30th January 1849 carried a full report of one of its meetings, and the August 1857 issue of *The Local Preachers Magazine* contained an article by one of its founders describing its origins. This is of special interest as it makes some reference to Francis Pearson (see chapter 7), who was invited by the editor to comment on the article.

The writer, J. D. Woolcock, referred to some conversations he had with a fellow-preacher, Henry Curnock, as they were travelling to preaching appointments. Woolcock was out of work through illness at the time, and described his predicament to his colleague – loss of wages and doctor's bill together cost him £11-0-0d, and because of weakness he was unable to return to his former employment. Curnock's response was:

> Something might be done among ourselves to assist
> such cases as yours. Let us see if we can form a little
> company among ourselves for Mutual Aid.

A meeting of local preachers from both the Bristol circuits (North and South) was called and drew up rules. The first quarterly subscriptions of 15 pence (1s-3d) were paid in July 1848, no benefits being payable for twelve months. John Russom, who later played a part in establishing LPMAA, was elected President.

On 22nd January 1849, the Bristol Local Preachers Mutual Aid Association held a public meeting to make itself and its purpose better known. *The Wesleyan Times* report gives a detailed account of proceedings, but Woolcock's 1857 article provides some interesting background to the event. It appears that the Superintendent

> . . . unwisely surmised we were concocting
> something against Methodism.

He refused use of a room at King Street Chapel, informing the officers that they

> . . . had no right to meet together as local preachers,
> unless the Superintendent were at the head, and the
> meeting were called by his authority.

At the next quarterly meeting of preachers he questioned their loyalty to Methodism. Being denied use of Methodist premises, the Association hired the Broadmead Rooms in Bristol for its public meeting, which was preceded by tea. John Russom, as President, naturally took the chair at the evening meeting; Woolcock notes an attendance of 'several hundreds of kind friends'.

It was at this point that Francis Pearson became involved with the Bristol Society, but there is some difference of recollection between Woolcock and Pearson about the precise timing. The latter, we know, engaged in correspondence through *The Wesleyan Times*, during June 1849, about the possibility of a large gathering of local preachers to inaugurate a national Friendly Society for Wesleyan Local Preachers. As a commercial traveller he went to many parts of the country, and in the course of a visit to Bristol he was invited to meet with some members of the Bristol Mutual Aid Association. Woolcock says that, when the work of the Society was explained to him, the visitor responded:

> It is a pity such a praiseworthy object should be confined to such narrow limits

and that when he went home he wrote the first of his letters to *The Wesleyan Times*. Pearson's comments put events in a different order. He affirms that after he had initiated the correspondence of June 1849 in *The Wesleyan Times* he received over 150 letters from gentlemen in various parts of the country, including Messrs Samuel Tuckey and Henry Curnock in Bristol. He arranged to call on Tuckey when next in Bristol which he did, and was entertained to tea along with a number of Bristol preachers. He reports discussions about

> . . . forming a Society for the purpose of affording pecuniary help to sick and necessitous local preachers. The subject was taken up with the warmth and fervour of men imbued with the benevolent spirit of Christ.

He goes on to state that Mr Russom (President of the Bristol Association) was appointed to meet in Birmingham with friends who had already agreed to confer there on 24th July 1849. The members indicated their intention to dissolve the Bristol Society if the new one matured. They were obviously pleased to be identified at an early stage with what proved to be a major initiative. Woolcock rather overstated his own position by saying:

> I am proud in being one of two individuals who first suggested and raised this noble, this brotherly, this Christian association.

He did, however, express cogently the spirit of Local Preachers' Mutual Aid.

> If the paid labourer in the vineyard is to be cared for when worn out, the labourer who works without pay ought to have some sympathy

though he distorted the order of events again when he wrote:

> I am glad the Lord put it into Bro. Pearson's heart to
> make the principles of the little band at Bristol so
> extensively known.

In addition to the benefit which he personally received from
Mutual Aid, he referred to more aged brethren who, but for the
Association, would have been in the workhouse.

The existence and vigour of the Bristol Society without
doubt encouraged Pearson and his colleagues in their efforts to
organise mutual aid on a connexion-wide basis (chapters 7 and 8).
The Wesleyan Times report of the public meeting in the Broadmead
Rooms on 22nd January1849 gives a very good impression of its
liveliness and impact. One of the Bristol ministers, Rev. John
McLean, vindicated the Society and its object against the position
taken by the Superintendent, by attending and taking part in the
meeting. The President (John Russom), in his opening address,
diplomatically recognised this ministerial support. He placed great
emphasis on the purposes for which the Bristol Local Preachers
Mutual Aid Association was formed – promoting brotherly love,
relieving the distressed, ministering to the wants and necessities of
the afflicted, and smoothing the pillow of death. Including within
those purposes the widows and orphans as well as local preachers
themselves, he went on to say:

> We have not forgotten the worthy men whom God
> has placed over us, we have not forgotten the church
> to which in principle we belong, and to which we
> are all so largely indebted. We meet as Wesleyan
> local preachers, and as a body of men we give the
> right hand of fellowship to our ministers. We
> deprecate the idea that we are desirous, by holding
> this meeting, and having a member of our own class
> in the chair, to supersede the authority of those 'over
> us in the Lord'. We do not meet to legislate on
> Methodism, or to interfere with the duties of any of
> its officers; no, we meet as men to promote each
> other's welfare, and we contend we have an
> undisputable right to do so.

He was followed by several other speakers who supported
the work of local preachers and of mutual aid in various ways. One

remarked that he had been pressing the subject of this association or something like it for 15 years. Another considered the local preachers, in unison with the regular ministers, as an army to go and battle with error in all its varied forms. Rev. John McLean, who had led the meeting in prayer, said how pleased he was with the wise and able speech of the President. He seemed to understand his position, and had steered clear of danger on delicate points. On the preaching of the Gospel, Mr Mclean said it was of little moment whether it was done by *you* or *us*, the world will be Christianised and civilised by the preaching of Christ's Gospel.

THE MOMENTUM BUILDS

These discretions and courtesies illustrate well the tensions of the time. Ministers took different views of laymen and their actions; some laymen, especially some local preachers, were anxious to establish a constructive partnership with the full-time paid ministry, whilst others would defer entirely to them, and yet others would try to ignore them. Action was strongly desired to build up the fellowship amongst local preachers and to support each other in time of need, but where ministers (especially Superintendents) regarded such action as irregular, to press forward might affect the cause adversely. However, momentum gradually increased as information about the work and achievements of these small localised Societies spread, aided by the Penny Post after 1840 and the facilitation of travel by the growing railway network.

The existence of other Societies is referred to incidentally in LPMAA records, but no original sources or contemporary reports are known. There was a Society, for example, in Cambridge, and John Smith of the Cambridge Branch of LPMAA (himself now in his 90s) recalled hearing senior members speak about it when he was a young preacher On Trial. It did not become part of LPMAA until 1921 (see chapter 16). It seems that by the end of the 1840s both the necessary and the sufficient conditions were in place for the idea of a Connexion-wide Local Preachers' Friendly Society to be an idea whose time had come. There was:

- awareness of both the nature and the extent of need
- consciousness that public provision was insufficient fully to meet the need

- realisation that some preachers were unable to provide for themselves or their families
- recognition that Wesleyanism was unwilling to accept or to deal with the situation
- above all a Gospel imperative for those who preached to care for each other when in need

After a brief look at the world in which this idea was born, we shall turn to the man generally recognised as the founder of LPMAA and to its formation and early struggle to survive.

6

Mid-19th Century Society

How Things Were • The Great Exhibition of 1851
Literature, Politics and Art

How Things Were

> The past is a foreign country – they do things
> differently there.

The opening of L. P. Hartley's novel *The Go-Between* might be
compared with some of the statements at the beginning of Charles
Dickens' *A Tale of Two Cities*:

> It was the best of times, it was the worst of times, it
> was the age of wisdom, it was the age of foolishness,
> it was the epoch of belief, it was the epoch of
> incredulity . . . it was the spring of hope, it was the
> winter of despair, we had everything before us, we
> had nothing before us . . .

Written in the late 1850s, they refer to 1775, but could equally well
apply to mid-19th century England. For some it was a time of great
optimism, for others there seemed no future to work for, at least in
this world. It is appropriate to pause between the pre-LPMAA
years and the period from 1850 onwards to look briefly at some of
the events and movements of that time. In the literary, artistic,
political, economic, social and religious spheres things were
happening that influenced the values, attitudes, standards and
organisation of society significantly. They help to give the 'feel' of
life as the second half of the century began.

The Great Exhibition of 1851

At the same time as initial discussions concerning the
formation of LPMAA were taking place, Queen Victoria's consort,
Prince Albert, convened a committee of the Society for the
Encouragement of Arts, Manufactures and Commerce (of which he

was President) to plan a major exhibition celebrating peace, prosperity and progress. Speaking at the Mansion House a few months before the Exhibition opened, he made a statement which reflected the confidence that some Victorians had in the future:

> The Exhibition of 1851 is to give us a true test and a living picture of the point of development at which the whole of mankind has arrived in this great task, and a new starting-point from which all nations will be able to direct their further exertions.

The Great Exhibition of 1851 is often taken to mark the climax of Britain's international standing. It attracted six million visitors, including many foreigners, to Joseph Paxton's Crystal Palace in Hyde Park. The use of glass for this massively enlarged version of the Lily House at Chatsworth (where Paxton was Head Gardener to the Duke of Devonshire) was encouraged by the recent removal of a heavy tax on it. *The Times* reported the opening of the Crystal Palace by the Queen (1st May 1851) in famous phrases:

> . . . a sight the like of which has never happened before, and which can never be repeated. . . . an effect so grand and yet so natural, that it hardly seemed to be the work of human artificers.

The Queen herself wrote, in a letter to her uncle (the King of Belgium):

> I wish you could have witnessed the 1st May 1851, the greatest day in our history, the most beautiful and imposing and touching spectacle ever seen . . . Many cried, and all felt touched and impressed with devotional feelings.

Half of the space was occupied by Britain and the Empire, France and Germany being the principal exhibitors in the other half. An American reaping machine attracted much attention, as did the Jacquard loom, things indicating what was to come later in the century. The display of Sheffield edge-tools particularly impressed foreign visitors. The Exhibition was open for 141 days, though closed on Sundays, of course. The average daily attendance exceeded 40,000, and the profit (over £186,000) was used to acquire the site for the Victoria and Albert Museum. The railway companies operated excursion trains, and the recently-built Euston Station, opened in the year that LPMAA was formed, gave easy access to central London for visitors from the Midlands and the North-West. This may have had something to do with a smaller than expected attendance at the Aggregate Meeting of 1851, which assembled in Sheffield a few days before the Great Exhibition closed. The Crystal Palace was dismantled and reconstructed in South London; the Queen presided over the re-opening in 1854, the year the Crimean War began.

1851 was also a year for the decennial Census of Population, which in that year included a census of the religious life of the country. This provided some illuminating information about the churchgoing habits of the nation, as well as the fact that the population of England and Wales, at 18 million, had doubled since 1801. It appeared, for example, that of the 7.25 million people at worship on census day, almost 3.5 million were in nonconformist congregations.

LITERATURE, POLITICS AND ART

The middle years of 19th century were an important period for literature, too. The Brontë sisters, under the assumed names of Acton, Ellis and Currer Bell (partly to hide their female identity) produced five of their seven novels in the late 1840s. Emily and Anne died within six months of each other. The latter's *The Tenant of Wildfell Hall*, which appeared in 1848, the year before her death, was the story of a woman who flouted convention and behaved illegally by leaving her drunken husband, a subject well ahead of its time. Charlotte lived until 1855, having enjoyed the friendship of Elizabeth Gaskell, who subsequently published a biography of Charlotte.

Mrs Gaskell herself was a notable contributor to the literary output of this period. Her *North and South* was serialised in Charles Dickens' weekly magazine *Household Words* during the autumn of 1854. The magazine had already passed 200 issues when it carried his own *Hard Times* in serial form earlier the same year. Both novels portray something of the hardships of life in northern industrial towns in mid-19th century. Mrs Gaskell, the wife of a Unitarian minister in Manchester, had the advantage of living in an industrial community and being able to write with greater authority about life in that kind of setting. A few sentences from *North and South* give some idea of the ways people of the time thought about themselves and their society:

I'll tell you it's their [the masters'] part – to beat us down to swell their fortunes; and it's ours to stand up and fight hard – for justice and fair play. We help to make their profits, and we ought to help spend 'em!

(Nicholas Higgins, chapter 17 – What is a Strike?)

The Americans are getting their yarns so into the general market, that our only chance is producing them at a lower rate. I wish the old combination laws were in force.

(John Thornton, chapter 18 – Likes and Dislikes)

These matters also commanded the attention of political writers. In 1844 Friedrich Engels wrote *The Condition of the Working Classes in England,* based on his experience in the Lancashire cotton industry, and in 1848 Karl Marx produced the Communist Manifesto. Some important Christian political insights were formulated around this time by the small group that became known as 'Christian Socialists'. The leading members of this movement were the theologian F. D. Maurice, the writer Charles Kingsley, and a lawyer, J. M. Ludlow. The latter had witnessed some of the revolutionary events in Paris at the beginning of 1848. The term 'Christian Socialism', first used in 1850, arose from Maurice's earlier book *The Kingdom of Christ* to denote his understanding of the relationship between Christianity and society. The group's concern was for the redemption of the structures and institutions of society but – in common with many others of their time – they had an inadequate grasp of the economic fundamentals to turn that concern into policy. The Christian Socialists' importance lies in their conviction that Christianity is about social organisation as well as about individual human beings. [The word 'socialism' was not in general use as a political term at this date.] The group lasted until about 1853 when F. D. Maurice turned his attention to working-class education.

In other spheres, also, the years around 1850 were important. Art was unsettled by the work of the Pre-Raphaelite Brotherhood, formed in 1848. This was a small band of young men who sought to recapture the naturalism of art from the period before Raphael (15th century). Its founders were Dante Gabriel Rossetti, Holman Hunt, and John Everett Millais. The first pictures signed with the secret initials PRB were exhibited in 1849, but the Brotherhood was short-lived; when Millais was elected an Associate of the Royal Academy the other members and their followers went their own ways. The influence of the Pre-Raphaelites was, however, considerable and lasting, in part because of the support given by the critic John Ruskin against the condemnation of their work by (amongst others) Charles Dickens. They used real people as models and painted from actual landscapes in their pursuit of honesty and simplicity. Ruskin's advice to reject nothing, select nothing, scorn nothing, underpinned their down-to-earth realism and the poignant comment on social issues in some of their work.

Many more features of life in mid-19th century England might be mentioned in this brief survey, but two must not be omitted. One is the publication in 1848 of the first two volumes of Macaulay's *History of England*. This was an attempt to present English history in the light of mid-Victorian progress and prosperity. Macaulay himself asserted that the history of England since 1688 is 'the history of physical, moral and intellectual improvement', and he convinced many people of the validity of this view. Finally 1850, the year in which Tennyson was appointed Poet Laureate, saw the publication of his *In Memoriam*, a cycle of lyrics in memory of his deceased friend Arthur Hallam. In this he captured the mood of much mid-19th century religious thought; parts of it have been incorporated into various Christian hymnals (for example, 'Strong Son of God, immortal Love'; 'Ring out, wild bells'.) In it Tennyson also gave the language some powerful and still-quoted phrases, such as 'Nature, red in tooth and claw' and ''Tis better to have loved and lost than never to have loved at all'.

These, then, are some – perhaps some of the most important – currents of thought, writing and activity that were influencing the direction of development and change as the Mutual Aid Association was formed and took shape. They help in understanding how its founders felt about their life in the society of that time.

Section Two

THE ORIGIN AND EARLY YEARS OF LPMAA

It is not easy to enter into the thoughts, feelings and experiences of previous generations. Where records exist it is quite possible to learn what happened, but it is much harder to interpret events and to share the motivation and responses of those who were involved in them. There is an irresistible tendency to assess past events by the attitudes and values of our own time. In this section an attempt is made to capture something of what the founders, early leaders and members of LPMAA thought and felt about what they were doing. The chief sources for this are the Association's own records, *The Local Preachers Magazine*, official Wesleyan documents, Wesleyan and secular newspapers, and personal papers of the period. Conjecture and comment are part of this process, and are intended to illuminate rather than to impose a particular view of events or of the behaviour of people caught up in them. It must be remembered that, like people in all ages, folk of the middle and later years of the 19th century were responding to the circumstances of their time, as well as to their own ambitions, aspirations and visions, just as we do today.

7

Francis Pearson, the Initiator of Wesleyan Methodist LPMAA

Events in Focus • Francis Pearson
Expulsion from Wesleyan Methodism

EVENTS IN FOCUS

The first part of this book set the tensions and turmoil in Wesleyan Methodism of the late 1840s in their social and political context. It was against that background that decisive action was taken to establish a single national Friendly Society for Wesleyan Methodist local preachers. The poverty and distress that afflicted some of them would, unless action was taken, doubtless afflict many more. The motivation was quite clear: the Christian gospel requires its advocates to care for the poor and needy. Those who took the lead in this matter were determined that the proclamation of the gospel should not be hindered by the lack of its practical application amongst their colleagues in the work.

They were, of course, concerned about the relief of poverty in wider society, and many were associated with other initiatives, both public and private, directed towards that end. This particular enterprise was specifically to ensure that those to whom they were bound by faith and calling were sustained in their pursuit of that calling. For that reason mutual help and encouragement in the preaching work was seen as an entirely proper objective of the Association from the beginning. However, the immediate thrust of its organisation and activities was towards meeting those basic needs without which no work of any kind was possible. What *was* excluded was involvement *as a body* with the ecclesiastical controversy of the time.

Many leaders and ordinary members of the newly-formed Mutual Aid Association were identified with the reform movement. A number either left or were expelled from the Wesleyan church because of it. There is little doubt that some members of the Wesleyan hierarchy suspected the Association of being a reformist organisation and dealt with any local preacher known to be a member accordingly. All these things were ventilated at the inaugural Aggregate Meeting of WMLPMAA in October 1849, as will be seen in chapter 8. First, however, it is appropriate to look at the man who is generally regarded as the initiator of LPMAA.

FRANCIS PEARSON

The Association's records and articles in its magazine in the 19th century, give some account of the action he took during the summer of 1849 which led to the formation of a national Friendly Society for Wesleyan local preachers. A fuller picture of the man, his family, friends and experiences, can be constructed by drawing on other sources, including official Wesleyan documents and secular records.

Fern Cottage, Stoney Way, Matlock Green

Following a conversation in the Spring of 1849, Pearson wrote to the leading Methodist newspapers of the time commending the idea of an assembly of local preachers. This conversation involved a fellow-preacher by the name of Marsden, later identified as Joseph H. Marsden. His house, near the bottom of a steep footpath called Stoney Way (Matlock Green), still stands and is known today as Fern Cottage. Francis Pearson visited the Marsdens on 21st May 1849; a letter from Joseph Marsden's son William, to the editor of *The Local Preachers Magazine* in August 1889, gives some details of the visit. Joseph's wife and son were both present, as well as a William Blanksby who later became a local preacher and then emigrated to Australia.

William Marsden, 18 at the time, recalls the relevant part of his father's conversation with Francis Pearson, indicating that the latter's reaction to the suggestion of a society for the relief of needy local preachers was:

> That would be a splendid thing, but I don't think it practicable.

Marsden senior urged the idea more forcefully, and Pearson then said:

> Do you think the Editor of the Wesleyan Times would insert a letter proposing such a thing?

Marsden said that he had no doubt about it, as *The Wesleyan Times* had suggested something of the sort in a leading article earlier in the year (see reference to the Bristol Society in chapter 5). The two men prepared a letter which went, over Francis Pearson's name, to *The Watchman* and *The Wesleyan Times*, though only the latter published it. The ensuing correspondence is reviewed in the next chapter. The 18 year old William Marsden became a reformer in later life, served as President of Wesleyan Reform Union in 1881, 1888 and 1903, and was its General Secretary for a number of years from 1890.

Another family of Marsdens is important in the Francis Pearson story. The 1841 census return shows a William Marsden, farmer and coal-merchant, of Oaker Side, near Wensley, and it was the youngest daughter of this family, Elizabeth (after her mother), whom Pearson married at Darley on 31st May 1845. She was born on 29th March 1824, and upon marriage went with her husband to live in Manchester, where their first child was born the following year, and named Francis after his father. The boy was baptised at Matlock Methodist Church on 6th July 1846. Pearson's name does not appear in Cromford Circuit Plans or other local preacher records up to this time. He is first mentioned in the minutes of the Circuit Local Preachers' Meeting of September 1846, when his transfer to the Cromford Circuit is recorded. The Local Preachers' Meeting minutes of the Manchester South Circuit give September 1844 as the date when he was placed 'On Trial'. At the meeting of 24th January 1845 arrangements were made for his trial sermon.

His occupation as a commercial traveller seems to have made him reasonably prosperous, although a tendency was noted in him to worry about this and be anxious about the future. He was known as a generous man, always ready to forward the interests of other people. Both these characteristics appear to have underpinned his determination to do something about the poverty that he knew existed amongst some local preachers. As a commercial traveller he was unavoidably away from home a great deal. They moved to Matlock in the summer of 1846 so that his wife could be nearer her relatives during his absences It is interesting to consider what might have been the case if Elizabeth Pearson had not been unsettled when her husband was away on business. They would probably not have moved to Matlock, and the idea of a 'great gathering of preachers to establish a mutual aid association' might have been conceived by someone else, somewhere else. Indeed, because it resulted from conversation between Pearson and Marsden, it might not have been conceived at all.

EXPULSION FROM WESLEYAN METHODISM

Wesleyan Methodism in the village of Wensley began in the 1820s, as a meeting in a cottage called 'Green Stile', still in use as a dwelling. It was then the home of yet another William Marsden, cordwainer, who is listed in the directories of the 1840s trading as a boot and shoe repairer with a Joseph Marsden, probably his son. This William Marsden, of Wensley, appears in the list of local preachers on the Cromford Circuit plans of the time. The Wensley society became well established, and by 1829 a chapel had been built, both William Marsdens (the farmer and the boot maker) being trustees. The membership increased to over 40 by the 1840s. It is not surprising, therefore, that Francis and Elizabeth made this their regular place of worship, and as an accredited preacher he fulfilled frequent appointments there.

Green Stile Cottage

Wensley Chapel

When the reform agitations spread through the Wesleyan Connexion in the late 1840s, the Cromford Circuit was affected. Suspecting that Francis Pearson was involved, the Superintendent stated at the September Local Preachers' Meeting 1850 that he would bring objections against Pearson 'at another tribunal', almost certainly a Leaders' Meeting. [Some Superintendents at this time, out of zeal for the authority of the pastoral office, loyalty to the Wesleyan establishment, or both, dealt autocratically with any lay-leaders and local preachers whom they saw as a threat to the stability of the system.]

It was while this matter was pending that Elizabeth wrote a typically encouraging letter to her husband, in which she said:

> My Dear Frank,
> I hear charges will be brought against you at the next Leaders' Meeting. My dear husband, I can only recommend you to keep your own conscience clear in the sight of God, and then you need not be afraid what any man or number of men can do to you. May the Lord direct you in all these proceedings! Do all with a single eye to his glory.

The end of the matter was that Pearson was expelled from membership, and thus lost his status as a Wesleyan local preacher. Whether this was the sole reason for their removal to Birmingham early in 1851 is not known – that it was a factor in the case can hardly be doubted. In Birmingham they became members of a reforming congregation, and were still active there when Elizabeth (who was an honorary member of the Association) died on 14 April 1858, aged 34, leaving five children. Her body was interred in the Key Hill cemetery in Birmingham.* Francis Pearson continued in business at various addresses in the city, as a wool merchant, then as a tailor and draper, serving the Association as a member of General Committee until the mid-1860s.

We can only speculate about the effects of all this on him.

(i) Did he realise that the Association might be seen, as it clearly was by some Wesleyan authorities, to be an organisation for promoting reform on a wave of anti-clericalism, a rebellion against the power-structures of the church? The correspondence summarised in chapter 8 suggests that he did.

(ii) Did he consider what the effects of that might be on the success of the venture? Even a different name could have disarmed the critics, for in the 1840s the word 'Association' still carried connotations of opposition, and 'mutual aid' of fighting for rights.

(iii) Was he aware that his involvement with the movement might cost him his membership in Wesleyan Methodism, and did this influence him initially in refusing nomination for the Presidency of the Association? (He declined nomination on three subsequent occasions – 1850, 1855, 1858).

We may never know. What we do know, however, is that LPMAA prospered slowly, that it had to face resistance in several forms, and that it existed for over 30 years before even a quarter of eligible local preachers had joined.

[In the same burial ground the mortal remains of three distinguished Presidents of LPMAA were later laid to rest:

  (i) *Edwin Benson, President 1877, died 17 February 1886. Like Francis Pearson he had been expelled from Wesleyanism (1851) on the grounds of involvement in the reform movement. He later served twice as President of the Wesleyan Reform Union (1865 and 1885).*
 (ii) *David Barr, founder of Fillongley Retirement Cottages (see chapter 12) and President 1906, died 9th March 1910.*
(iii) *Brigadier-General Sir John Barnsley, President in Jubilee Year, 1899, died 19th January 1926.*

  Also in Key Hill cemetery is the Melson family tomb, where the body of Dr John Barritt Melson was buried after his death on 30th May 1899. He was one of the Association's original six trustees and was noted especially for his powerful and lengthy preaching at the first two Aggregate Meetings.]

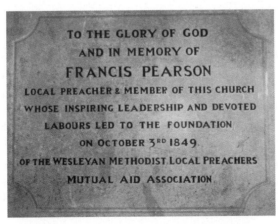

TO THE GLORY OF GOD
AND IN MEMORY OF
FRANCIS PEARSON
LOCAL PREACHER & MEMBER OF THIS CHURCH
WHOSE INSPIRING LEADERSHIP AND DEVOTED
LABOURS LED TO THE FOUNDATION
ON OCTOBER 3RD 1849
OF THE WESLEYAN METHODIST LOCAL PREACHERS
MUTUAL AID ASSOCIATION

Memorial tablet to Francis Pearson in Wensley Chapel
(unveiled in 1950 after the centenary of LPMAA)

8

The Wesleyan Times Correspondence

The First Letter and Its Results • Francis Writes Again . . .
. . . and Again • He 'Signs Off'

THE FIRST LETTER AND ITS RESULTS

Francis Pearson's 'letter to *The Wesleyan Times*' is known about and often mentioned amongst members of LPMAA. There was, in fact, extended correspondence over several weeks in that paper's columns, including no fewer than *four* letters from Pearson himself. The following extracts show how the idea of a large gathering of local preachers, to constitute a national friendly society, evolved during the summer of 1849. On 5th June *The Wesleyan Times* carried Pearson's first letter, headed:

> To the Local Preachers in Connexion with the Wesleyan Methodist Societies.
>
> Honoured Brethren – Whatever may be said, or written, in Fly Sheets or other Papers – whatever may be the doings of the regular ministry in their impeachments and accusations of each other – whatever clamourings there may be for office or imaginary honours, or elevated positions, or extended influence or snug sinecure, it is our noble, disinterested, Christ-loving task . . . My object in addressing you is to suggest the propriety of us, as local preachers, assembling together . . . for the purpose of exchanging friendly salutations and greeting each other with fraternal regards . . .
>
> Our meeting together . . . would strengthen our faith . . . and consolidate us into one great brotherhood. It would nerve us for fresh toils and enterprise . . . and whilst no harm could result from it, incalculable good might be the necessary consequence. Can any reason be assigned why we should not for once meet each other in the flesh? Our object is not political,

> neither is it to express an opinion on the events of
> the day, nor yet to interfere with those exciting
> topics which now distract the minds of men. If it be
> *supposed* we have political objects . . . ? Should it be
> insinuated that we might interfere with matters
> ecclesiastical . . . ? But we aim at a nobler object, the
> unity and harmony of a Christian brotherhood.

He concluded by inviting response from circuits, with suggestions
of time and place for meeting. The Editor of *The Wesleyan Times*
supported the idea, recommending Birmingham later in June. The
cautious wording of the letter, and the absence of any reference to
the formation of a Friendly Society, suggests that Pearson was
conscious of the dangers of provoking avoidable opposition, at
least until he felt assured of positive interest from a substantial
number of his fellow-preachers.

In the issue of 12th June 1849 five letters from widely-
scattered circuits were printed from (in the Editor's own words) 'a
host of others'. One of them raised questions about Francis Pearson
himself:

> Mr Pearson's name, and attachment to the interests
> of the Connexion, are not known . . . His name does
> not appear in any list of subscribers to any of the
> funds of the body . . . seems to indicate a want of
> deep interest in the prosperity of the Church! The
> special question seems to be the Wesleyan character
> of the originator. Is he a person on whose
> suggestion the local preachers can be recommended
> to act?

The other letters approved in general of Pearson's proposals; one
floated the idea of a Local Preachers' Magazine, and of a society to
promote the welfare of the aged and infirm preachers. Another
dealt in detail with the objects of the gathering and practicalities
such as hospitality and travelling expenses. The editorial comment
urged that nothing be contemplated which was not strictly social
and devotional.

FRANCIS WRITES AGAIN . . .

Pearson's second letter appeared in *The Wesleyan Times* of 19th June 1849. In it he proposed:

> . . . the great specific object of the formation of a society, composed of local preachers only, for the purpose of affording pecuniary relief to the sick and necessitous amongst us. This is not a deep-laid scheme to undermine or revolutionise our much loved Methodism. There is no design to organise into a great central confederation the scattered power existing among you for any such purpose. We as a body, are decidedly opposed to schism, faction, and party.

Again, his anxiety to allay fears of disguised improper purposes can be discerned. He then returned to the main theme:

> The establishment of such a society would wipe away a stigma that has long been attached to us, whilst its necessity has been for many years acknowledged, and its want deeply deplored. . . . I think it is utterly impracticable without a large meeting. How necessary it is that the wisdom and prudence of the entire body should be brought to bear upon this institution, so that it may be established upon a broad, firm, and durable basis.

In arguing against the formation of circuit clubs, he pointed out that 'many of our circuits are very small and very poor'. The closing paragraph gives an interesting insight into Pearson's personality:

> I shall be happy to receive your advice and assistance, for without you I can do nothing; when this is accomplished, I will retire from public notice, and by God's grace try to continue worthy of a name and a place amongst you. In the meantime until other and abler men come forward, I will do my best to promote a society that will be an honour to Methodism and to the land in which we live.

Below this letter there appeared a short note from six Matlock preachers, including Joseph Marsden (in whose house the conversation of 21st May took place) and Joseph Hogkinson who, with Francis Pearson, attended the planning meeting in Birmingham in July. In this they affirmed Pearson's exemplary character, devotion to Wesleyan Methodism, and his liberality in contributing to Methodist funds.

... AND AGAIN

In the next issue (26th June 1849) *The Wesleyan Times* printed Pearson's third letter. He emphasised again the need for a connexion-wide Friendly Society for local preachers, and his conviction that a large meeting would be the most likely means to achieve that object. He assessed the potential support for the idea from a number of sources, including the ministers, stewards and leaders, members of congregations, the world, and the preachers themselves. He estimated their number at around 13,000, and thence calculated – on certain assumptions –that annual income of around £3,000 was achievable, sufficient to assist more than a hundred 'poor brethren' with 10s per week for a full year. The penultimate paragraph reads:

> It remains with you to carry out the design. One man, or a small number of men, are . . . utterly inadequate for a task so great and important; nothing less than the combined wisdom and piety of the whole . . . can form such a society upon a basis that shall be firm, durable and abiding.

Correspondence continued into July with two letters, published in the *The Wesleyan Times* of 3 and 17 of that month, from a writer using the intials LP CL WMS, which could stand for Local Preacher Class Leader Wesleyan Methodist Society. This writer first answered the criticism of the correspondent who questioned Francis Pearson's status, and his giving to Wesleyan funds:

> The pecuniary contributions of an individual are not to be an index of his mental or moral qualifications for any work in which he may engage . . . Of the ability to give or of aught else respecting Mr Pearson, I know nothing; but it is quite plain he is a member of our society and a local preacher, etc.

The letter goes on to deal with an objection to Pearson's youth, raised in a letter to the Wesleyan 'establishment' newspaper, *The Watchman*, saying:

If it be well for local preachers to meet together, it matters little whether they are summoned by young Brother Pearson, or by the oldest man in the Connexion.

Turning to what the projected assembly might achieve, this writer commends the publication of a regular magazine for preachers and the formation of an annuitant society:

> . . . so that the locals [preachers] may have a superannuation fund to look to in the sear of life. Many of our Brethren are poor, and the Church should not let them fall on the parish for relief.

Yet again there is concern that no suspicion of hidden plotting against the Connexional authorities should be aroused. The concluding paragraphs rebut this forcefully:

> It may be said, 'There is danger, lest, making these things the ostensible reason of your meeting, you should have some ulterior designs'. What can they be? Are we not to be trusted? What, or who, is to prevent our 'hatching treason' now, if we wish? Shall we, who do it not when we are covered from discovery by secrecy, do it openly? Shall any dare to charge us as designing to oppose ourselves to the constituted authorities? If there are, 'they do us foul libel'.

The reasonableness of these observations is underlined by the statement in an adjacent column, in a report of a District Meeting (Synod):

> We live in times when men are made offenders on the most frivolous pretexts imaginable.

In a subsequent letter LPCLWMS considered 'Where and When Shall the Local Preachers' Meeting Be Held?' He favoured London, not later than the first week in September, and said that he was writing with Brother Pearson's authority. A brief letter followed this, from a writer in Brandon, co. Durham, lamenting that:

> . . . servants of Christ who have laboured with unwearied zeal for 20, 30, 40 years should become

chargeable to the parish, or be inmates of some union workhouse.

He 'Signs Off'

By this time the case was made, Pearson felt assured of adequate support, and a planning meeting was arranged for the following week in Birmingham. He invited those attending it to call on him at a Birmingham hotel the previous evening. After a full day's deliberations, *The Wesleyan Times* was able to report that preparations were in hand for an Aggregate Meeting of Local Preachers in London early in October. The proceedings of the Wesleyan Conference dominated the late July/early August editions of the paper, but it found space on 6th August for Pearson's fourth and very brief letter. In this he thanked *The Wesleyan Times* for its co-operation, saying he was grateful that he was now free from responsibility.

9

The Inaugural Aggregate (Day 1)

This chapter and the following one give a fairly full summary of the detailed report of the two days' proceedings. This conveys some impresssion of

- *the atmosphere in which LPMAA was inaugurated*
- *the concerns which the representatives had*
- *the ways in which they expressed those concerns*
- *the economic and ecclesiastical pressures when the Association was formed.*

Wednesday 3rd and Thursday 4th October 1849
Freemasons' Hall • Great Queen Street • Lincoln's Inn Fields

Wm. Harris Elected Chairman • The Chairman's Address
Pearson Names the Association • The Object of the Association
The 'Twelve Months' Rule • Two Long Sermons

3RD OCTOBER (MORNING)

WM. HARRIS ELECTED CHAIRMAN

The assembly began with the Charles Wesley hymn 'Behold, how good a thing it is to dwell in peace' (a hymn retained in the 1904 hymn book, though not in later collections). The scripture reading was from Ephesians 4, still a frequent choice at LPMAA gatherings, and which has been the basis for at least one Presidential address. William Harris, of London South Circuit, was elected 'by acclamation' as Chairman of the meeting. He had represented London, together with Isaac English, at the planning meeting in Birmingham in July, and had been an active member of the pro-tem Committee in London which was responsible for arranging the October meeting.

Harris had probably been anticipating the appointment as Chairman; his opening address certainly had the flavour of a 'keynote' speech. In it he set out clearly the fundamental importance of their common calling as preachers and the duty laid upon them by the gospel they preached to care for the poor amongst them. He then outlined the background to their assembling together, and the widespread support amongst preachers and others for the object of the assembly. He appealed to the members of the gathering, who numbered over 500, to avoid contentious matters in their debates. The meeting was taking place within three months of the expulsion of three ministers from Wesleyan Methodism by the Conference of 1849. In the wake of that event sides were being taken by ministers and lay members throughout the church. Assemblies of lay people, especially of local preachers, were viewed by some in Wesleyanism with suspicion. This may be part of the reason why the meeting was not held on Methodist premises.

THE CHAIRMAN'S ADDRESS

Being only 36 years of age Harris was amongst the younger members of the inaugural Aggregate. His election as first President at the end of the meeting makes him the youngest but one to serve in the office. He prefaced his address with an apology for his youth '. . . I should have been better pleased if an elder had been chosen . . .' but went on quickly to refer to the honour he felt in having a name and a place amongst the local preachers. He stressed the strength and support which all gain, in the pursuit of their calling, from the knowledge that there are many sharing in it. Part of the purpose of their coming together was to encourage each other in the preaching work. Referring then to verse 28 of the opening scripture reading ('. . . working that which is good, that we may have whereof to give to him that needeth'), he developed the argument for their main purpose, to make practical provision for achieving the objective embodied in the text. He dismissed the sentimental approach of indiscriminate charity, as well as the attitude that 'suspects every poor man to be a criminal'. He urged those who were involved as Overseers and Guardians in the administration of poor relief to discharge their duties in the fear of God.

> The best means of providing for the poor of the land is one of the questions of the day. . . . Notwithstanding the Act of Elizabeth, it has ever been the opinion of the Church . . . that it was the peculiar duty of the Church to care for the poor.

With a brief mention of the practice of making an appeal for the poor at the Lord's Supper, Harris went on to affirm that whatever the enactments of the Legislature, it is the duty of the Church to make provision for the needy.

> Whatever others may do . . . it is our duty . . . to be careful that nobody belonging to our section of the Church shall need.

He reinforced the point by quoting an experience of James Walker (proprietor of *The Halifax Guardian*), a fellow-preacher, who, whilst serving as a guardian of the poor, had been faced with a brother local preacher seeking relief. He was persuaded by this that action must be taken to prevent recurrence of such things, and the meeting wholeheartedly agreed.

In summarising the events that had resulted in their gathering together, the Chairman paid tribute to the initiative of Francis Pearson, in writing to Methodist newspapers on the matter. This was greeted with prolonged cheering, and he promised that the meeting would hear Pearson speak later. The press correspondence had resulted in the preliminary consultation in Birmingham, which drew up resolutions on the formation of a Friendly Society to be put to Aggregate for adoption or amendment during these two days. After the Birmingham consultation the task of organising the present assembly was entrusted to the London representatives. The company now gathered was truly representative of the realm, preachers from all four countries being present. [A list of all those named in the report as taking part in the debate is given in an Appendix to chapter 10.]

He then mentioned the names of a number of gentlemen who had sent or promised donations, as evidence of the widespread support for what was being undertaken. He was immediately interrupted by further spontaneous promises of donations from the floor. The attention of the meeting was then directed towards the resolutions, but before calling Francis Pearson to propose the first one, the Chairman exhorted members to confine their speeches to the purposes of the gathering. 'There are,' he said, 'topics which I would not have you refer to.' As will appear, this exhortation was not entirely heeded. There was an interesting interpolation, before Pearson began his speech, from a Staffordshire representative who enquired whether the provisional committee had considered the possibility of legacies to the new society. It seems that an important source of funding for LPMAA in modern times was in mind even before the Association was formally established.

PEARSON NAMES THE ASSOCIATION

So the moment for which everyone was waiting arrived; Francis Pearson was greeted with an ovation of several minutes, and seems to have been overcome by the enthusiastic reception. He began by disclaiming the honour of originating the idea of forming a local preachers Friendly Society. 'It appears to have existed in your hearts for years,' he said, adding that he had heard fellow-preachers say, 'I have thought about this for twenty years.' As we have seen, small local societies of this kind had been in existence for almost that length of time.

Pearson followed the Chairman's example in stressing their duty of Christian charity to the needy amongst them, and related an experience in his own Circuit of a preacher whose funeral he had conducted. This man's premature death had come about through starvation, though help had been given in time to save his family. His duty now was to propose, as the **first resolution**, the formation of a Friendly Society, to be called 'The Wesleyan Methodist Local Preachers Mutual Aid Association'. He therefore concluded his remarks by emphasising the benefits to their work as preachers which would result from their being united in this way. This would be as lasting as Methodism itself. 'May all our doings be owned of God.'

The seconder (Mann, of Hinde Street) spoke at length. He was convinced that the fellowship in which they would share in the new society would be as great a blessing as the relief they would bring to those local preachers who were dependent on the parish. Some were dying and being buried as paupers. He urged that these things which had been shall not be again. Local preachers of the Wesleyan Connexion must have their comfort in sickness, old age, and death. The Chairman then asked for brevity in the speeches, whereupon Samuel Johnson (Isle of Man) supported the resolution by telling of a preacher in the island who had been 60 years in the work and was now in great poverty.

The assembly addressed itself with vigour to the intentions and wording of the rules it was adopting. On this very first proposal a question was asked (B. Hardy, of Swaffham) about the meaning attached to the words 'mutual aid'. Were they to be taken in a pecuniary sense only, or to include spiritual aid? The Chairman commented that it would need a very long time to discuss the full extent of mutual aid, and said the meeting should be content to set up an organisation to give relief in sickness, distressed old age and death. Hardy nevertheless moved an amendment to include the words 'mutual, pecuniary, and spiritual aid.' Keed, of Lynn, seconded. The amendment was not supported; 'Mutual Aid' was already understood to be an inclusive phrase. [see also chapter 29.]

THE OBJECT OF THE ASSOCIATION

Isaac English (Deptford) moved the **second resolution**:

> The Association shall consist of accredited Local Preachers in Great Britain, and its object be to provide relief in sickness, old age and at death.

In his brief speech, he expressed the view that the Association would commend itself to others in the Connexion because it was the local preachers helping each other, and not depending on other people. Samuel Blake (Exeter), in seconding, regretted that some people – not understanding the intentions – regarded what they were doing with disfavour. Read (Reid) of Birmingham East, proposed that 'Ireland' should be added to the resolution. Taylor (High Wycombe) and Unwin (Sheffield) supported this proposal. The Chairman, in response to a question, said Ireland had a separate Conference, and delegates from that country had not been invited. Upon assurance that a future meeting might deal with the matter, the amendment was withdrawn. The Chairman assured a questioner from the Isle of Man that, as connexionally it was in Great Britain, it was included in the Society.

The resolution was not going to have an easy passage, however. Many representatives had points to make regarding the scope of the Association, both in its membership and its beneficent objectives. First, the inclusion of unemployment as a ground for assistance and the making of allowances to widows of deceased preachers were urged. Next, the extension of membership to include other than accredited preachers (for example, exhorters) was suggested. The Chairman recognised the worthy motives of those who put these points, and observed that assistance at death would give some relief to families, but said that membership could not easily be defined in a broader way. Another speaker moved the addition of 'cases of extreme distress' to the resolution, for which he secured a ready seconder, but the amendment was opposed by the Cambridge representative. He referred to the society which had existed there since 1846, and said they had found it impossible to contemplate aid to such a broad category within the resources they could procure. The amendment was withdrawn. One of the Bristol representatives said the experience in the society recently formed there was completely different; they sought to relieve need arising from unemployment, and to help bereaved families, and hoped the new society would be able to do the same.

The Chairman was then challenged about his earlier remark concerning the Conference. The York representative said that while the York preachers were loyal to Methodism, they would have nothing to do with the new society if in any way it was under Conference control. The report of the meeting does not cover the ensuing discussion in detail, being content to state that there was discussion of the matter. The Chairman was able to satisfy those who spoke that the tenor of his remarks did not imply any role for Conference in the present business. In further debate speakers mentioned other local societies with which preachers were connected, and expressed the hope that the new body would do something more. This view did not find favour, and the meeting was reminded that if funds permitted in the future they could make fresh rules on the subject. They dare not say, 'Be warmed, be clothed' until they had means to provide relief. The last business of the first morning was to approve the second resolution almost unanimously.

Aggregate meeting lunches have frequently overrun the time allocated for them, thus delaying the start of the afternoon session, a tradition which seems to have originated in 1849. The company did not reconvene after dinner until a quarter to three!

3RD OCTOBER (AFTERNOON)

THE 'TWELVE MONTHS' RULE

The afternoon's business was again concentrated on just two **resolutions**, numbers **three** and four. The first of these was moved by Parker (4th London), to the effect that no funds should be distributed until the Association had been in existence for twelve months. He recalled the famous story of Thomas Maxfield, and how John Wesley's mother prevailed on her son to recognise Maxfield as truly called of God to preach, the possible origin of the office of local preacher. His seconder was Brumwell of Gravesend. In the course of debate on this motion, the need to begin distribution of benefits immediately was argued. The longest speech, in parts having the character of a sermon, was made by James Wild, of Fulham (Hinde St. Circuit), later to become Treasurer.

Wild referred to his more than forty years on the Plan and mentioned his connection with the late Dr Adam Clarke, three times President of Conference (Wild had been his executor). He then lamented that from more than £200,000 raised to mark the centenary of the beginnings of Methodism, the Wesleyan Conference had not seen fit to allot any amount to help local preachers in need. He had offered to give £100 to commence a fund for that purpose, but to no avail. So the local preachers must do it for themselves. He affirmed his loyalty to the Methodist system, and encouraged all present to work hard to win support for preachers and their work. The Report records 'great applause' at the end of Wild's speech. He was, and continued to be until his death in 1866 (aged 83), a popular figure in the Association, serving as President in 1854.

Later speakers also argued for earlier payment of benefits. One of them proposed a formal amendment to that effect. Ellison (Liverpool) pointed out that the Friendly Societies Act of 1846 governed enrolment with the Registrar of Friendly Societies. A table of anticipated income and its proposed distribution, passed by an actuary, had to be presented to prove that its affairs were properly manageable. There was further opposition, on grounds of financial stability and prudence, to distribution before twelve months. The amendment was lost and the original resolution adopted.

The **fourth resolution**, moved by Edward Cope (Birmingham), required that members had to subscribe for twelve months before being entitled to any relief. The proposer explicitly admired the word 'entitled' – members would receive as a right, they would not come as beggars. Integrity was also safeguarded because that entitlement only came when members had done something. Grosjean (Hinde St.) seconded this motion. Again an attempt was made to amend so that relief could be claimed after three or six months, but this was not passed, the original resolution being carried almost unanimously. The afternoon session closed at 5 o'clock, when tea was taken before the evening sermon in Great Queen Street chapel.

Two Long Sermons

During tea a tale was told, according to the record, of a 'mile-long sermon', a suitable preface to Dr Melson's hour and three-quarters address. A certain preacher, engaging in open-air work, was moved on by a constable, so he announced a text and began walking, preaching as he went. A crowd followed, and after half a mile the preacher turned round and walked back, still preaching, until he reached where he had begun. The tea meeting dissolved into prayer for blessing on the evening's gathering.

Dr John Barritt Melson was a well-known preacher in mid-19th century Methodism. The full text of his sermon to the 1849 Aggregate survives. His father, Rev. Robert Melson, is believed to have been the first Wesleyan minister to become an Honorary Member of LPMAA. J. B. Melson was a doctor of medicine of Cambridge University, Fellow of Cambridge Philosophical Society, and served 62 years as Justice of the Peace in Birmingham. He was in great demand as speaker on a wide range of subjects, as well as for preaching appointments. For example, within the space of eight days in March 1849, *The Wesleyan Times* reported two meetings at which he gave the major speech, one on Popery, to a gathering of 2,000 (the lecture lasted three hours), and another on 'The Christian Churches and Their Poor.' As late as 1883, at the age of 72, he is recorded as preaching at a chapel anniversary in Lancashire for a fee of £4! He died in 1898, aged 87, his mortal remains being interred in the family tomb at Key Hill Cemetery in Birmingham. [See Footnote to chapter 7].

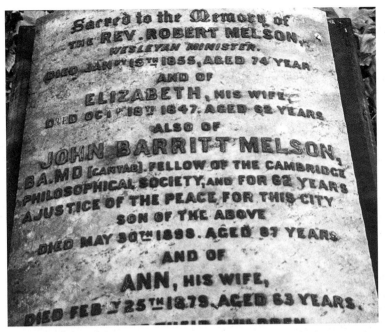

The Melson family tomb in Key Hill Cemetery, Birmingham

The sermon of 3rd October 1849 was so well-received that, before the main business next morning, a resolution of thanks to Dr Melson was proposed and carried by acclamation, with the request that he allow the sermon to be printed. The Chairman intimated that the Doctor had come to preach at his own expense, and that copies of the sermon would be sold for the benefit of the Association's funds. There is an amusing note at the conclusion of the Report of the Aggregate business. Having stated that the sermon would be available in print at 1s per copy, the note continues:

> It is requested that all who intend taking copies will signify the same, and the number required, to the Secretary; as the subscription list made out at the Meeting was taken from Freemasons' Hall, on the Friday morning, by some unknown person.

10

The Inaugural Aggregate (Day 2)

General Committee • Trustees and Officers
Subscriptions and Benefits • The Basis of Membership (again)
The First President • Election of Officers
Trustees and General Committee

4TH OCTOBER (MORNING)

At the start of the second day's business William Harris expressed the conviction of all present that God will accomplish his ends if we employ means that he approves and use the talents he has given us. 'Charity is spurious,' he said, 'which is not founded on the employment of means.'

GENERAL COMMITTEE, TRUSTEES AND OFFICERS

The **fifth resolution** provided for the election, by an annual aggregate meeting, of officers and a central committee of 30 members to conduct the Association's business. It was proposed by Summersides (Belper), who made it plain that members of committee would be elected by, but not necessarily chosen from, the members of Aggregate, and that they should be representative of the whole country. Here is a reflection of the concern, generated by the Fly Sheets of the previous few years, that the Connexion was London-oriented and London-dominated. The WMLPMAA would have none of that. The seconding speech was made by Edward Cresswell (7th London). He was able to draw on his experience as secretary to the pro tem committee which had been responsible for arranging the Aggregate meeting. He had been made aware of preachers buried in paupers' graves, and of one preacher serving on a Circuit plan who was an inmate of a parish union workhouse. He appealed for the uniting of means and energies – '. . . our hearts and purses should go together . . .' – to rescue suffering brethren from want and distress.

Again, however, controversy lurked in apparently innocent wording. An amendment was moved (by Tuckey of Bristol) to the effect that the committee members should be elected by the Districts, not by the Aggregate. He was warm in his appreciation of the spirit in which they were meeting and of the openness and honesty with which everything was being done. Nonetheless he upheld very strongly the view that those who lived in the provinces knew their men best, and would send those most suited to serve. Any list laid before them by the pro tem London Committee would resemble the work of the Connexional Nomination Committee, of which much had been heard elsewhere. Pearson (Tadcaster – not Francis) seconded. Those in his part of Yorkshire were suspicious about London; he believed that the preachers in each Circuit should form a committee, and that there should be an aggregate meeting in each District to choose the committee members.

The Chairman explained that members from many parts of the country (he cited particularly the West of England and the NE) had been involved in preparing and revising the resolutions now being considered. They had spent most of the day before yesterday on it. They were quite prepared to have what they had done thoroughly sifted. Smithson (York) questioned the connotation of the word 'central' in the resolution. Customary usage relates everything central exclusively to London; he could only support the resolution if it clearly embodied a statement to the contrary. The problem was solved by a suggestion from Flatman (Downham) that in all the resolutions the word 'general' should replace the word 'central'. Thus the General Committee got its name and has retained it ever since.

The **sixth resolution**, concerning the appointment of Trustees (six or more) was moved by Pearson (Tadcaster). He was most complimentary about the London Committee, which drew cheers from the assembly. Hanson (6th London) seconded, and the resolution was carried unanimously. Similarly, the **seventh resolution**, requiring that all officers of the Association shall be accredited local preachers, proposed by Smithson (York), seconded by Eggmore (Norwich), was adopted without dissent.

SUBSCRIPTIONS

The **eighth** and **ninth resolutions** were taken as one, proposed by Flatman (of Downham –to which the report adds 'in Norfolk'!). This prescribed subscription levels – 10s entrance fee, and 3s per quarter. One poor preacher in Flatman's Circuit had said, 'If an individual would not try to help himself, he was not worthy of being helped.' The contributions should not prevent any local preacher from joining, and would enable all who were in need to come upon the funds in time of sickness. Tagg (Leyton) seconded, and paid tribute to the admirable way in which the Chairman had performed his duties. He rejoiced in the rich fellowship of their gathering, which he trusted would be the first of a series continuing as long as Methodism endures. They were not making laws like those of the Medes and Persians; if the rules were found not to work well, they could be changed. When no needy Local Preacher remained, they could talk of enlarging the basis of the Association.

Inevitably, very diverse views were expressed on the subject of subscriptions. The first speaker (Palmer, of Belper) moved that the entrance fee should be 5s and the quarterly payment 2s. Both he and his seconder (Crockford of Rochester) believed that any higher level would preclude many preachers from joining. Pearson (Tadcaster) said that 3s per quarter was less than had been expected. In his circuit they had decided that those who could afford to do so would pay for those who were unable to pay. The Chairman intimated that he had received numerous letters from the country in which the writers undertook to guarantee payments for all the preachers in their circuits. Francis Pearson observed that 3s per quarter was not quite 3d per week. Far more than this was raised by other clubs, and much more was spent uselessly. He agreed that there were many who would pay for anyone genuinely unable to pay for himself.

Summersides (Belper) pointed out that the first full year contribution would be 22s. There should be a contributions fund to let the poorest come in free. They were a society for justice as well as mercy; the contributions must be adequate to meet obligations, but they should assist the weak to pay it. Lovely (London) said it was the members from the country who had succeeded in having the entrance fee raised to 10s from the committee's original proposal of 5s. Ways and means would be found to meet it. If the subscription was reduced from 3s to 2s they would be unable to meet need. Reid (Read) of Birmingham, believed that without 3d per week they would never achieve their purpose. Cheetham (Leeds 1st) took the same view. The amendment was lost, and the resolution carried by a large majority.

BENEFITS

The **tenth resolution** (now ninth) fixed sick relief at a minimum of 8s per week, and was proposed by Gunter (Ely), seconded by Pybus (Bakewell). Nichols (Queen St) raised the problem of guaranteeing that 8s, or any fixed amount, could always be met. They had no idea of the funds they would need. The Society should simply give what it could afford, and no amount should be stated in the rules. Jephson (Huddersfield 1st) moved an amendment that relief be not less than 10s per week. His colleague (from Huddersfield 2nd), Pogson, seconded. The latter referred to a sick club in his home town which collected half-a-crown per quarter (2s 6d) and gave relief at 7s per week. It now had £127 in hand. His opinion was that the travelling preachers in Conference would propose an annual collection for the society in every chapel. The Chairman advised most strongly against the idea of a connexional collection. They must let it be known they had no intention of burdening the Connexion. They would say with Paul, 'We are chargeable to no man.' He added that all information available indicated that no more than 8s could safely be afforded at first.

Luckham (Bath) and Lovely (London) both illustrated their comments with statistics, drawn from different sources. The former said that extraneous help would enable the society to make greater allowances, but they must rely upon themselves. The latter reminded everyone that they had not formed an annuitant society, but one designed to meet need arising from sickness. Pearson (Tadcaster) remarked that there would be fewer such cases in proportion to numbers because of the temperate and active lives of local preachers! The Chairman's final observation was that the more they gave for sickness, the less they would be able to afford on death. The amendment was lost. An addition to the resolution was moved by Parker, of Southwark, to empower the Committee, as soon as funds permitted, to deal with the cases of extreme distress which might arise from unemployment or prolonged illness in a member's family. Isaac English (Deptford) expressed strong objection to giving such power to a committee, and was supported by Shaw (Halifax), Nichols (Queen St), and Sharman (Sheffield). The Chairman explained to a questioner that the word 'distress' had not been included in any resolution because it could raise hopes that it may not be possible to fulfil. The addition was lost, and the original resolution carried by a large majority.

THE BASIS OF MEMBERSHIP (AGAIN)

The eleventh resolution (now tenth), proposed by Towne (Melton Mowbray), dealt with the continuance in membership of any member ceasing to be a local preacher. Shaw (Halifax) seconded. Heritage (Leamington) queried the phrase 'for any cause whatever' in the resolution. The Chairman cautiously avoided reference to the expulsions that had taken and were taking place from Wesleyan Methodism, but gave as an example the case of a local preacher becoming a travelling preacher; the matter was left open. Topham (Derby) said that his co-delegate had been expelled for something with which he had no connection, and this perturbed members of the Derby Friendly Society, as much as members of the the new Association. He ventured to say that local preachers did not know where they were in respect to the constitution of Wesleyan Methodism. As he proceeded to refer to an instance of the agitations in Wesleyanism, the Chairman asked him to confine his remarks to what bears directly upon the interests of Local Preachers. Topham said that local preachers were allowed by Conference to think, but if they went beyond that they might be in a perilous position. On the issue of continuing membership in the Association, he suggested there should be a right of appeal to the Annual Meeting.

Atkinson (Barnard Castle) said that the opinion in his Circuit was that while there were many causes why a preacher might lose his standing, he should never lose his right to relief from the Society unless a majority of the preachers in his own Circuit concurred. He moved to amend accordingly and was seconded by Pearson (Tadcaster). His chief concern was the anxiety of some of his fellow-preachers that they might step over a certain boundary and be put off! The debate continued to be controversial; one speaker's statement that no man can be excluded from the Local Preaching Plan without the consent of the majority was greeted with shouts of 'Yes, he can.' This led to a protest against discussing connexional rules in that meeting. Further grounds for preachers being removed from the plan were mentioned; it was questioned whether such causes should require expulsion from the Association, and whether investigations might be better conducted by members in the same or a neighbouring circuit. Other contributors to the debate asked about re-admission after any possible exclusion. Towne (Melton Mowbray), saying that the discussion had thrown light on a difficult issue, urged unanimity on it and asked for the amendment, with the right of appeal to the Aggregate meeting, to be put. It was carried and thus became substantive resolution 10. Following the previous day's experience, the meeting adjourned for only half-an-hour for dinner!

4TH OCTOBER (AFTERNOON)

The afternoon session dealt speedily with all remaining resolutions. These made provision for:

- the removal of members from the Society in certain circumstances and the financial consequences thereof
- the establishment of a category of Honorary Membership (annual contribution of one guinea or more, about an average week's wage at that time), though not without some debate on the position of local preachers who chose to pay this higher rate subscription
- the appointment of a paid secretary
- the handling of money by the Secretary and Treasurer
- the responsibilities of the Trustees in respect of the investments
- the drafting of rules to implement the resolutions of the Inaugural Aggregate Meeting, and the power of future Aggregate Meetings to amend them

THE FIRST PRESIDENT

The meeting then moved to the election of the Association's first president, clearly anticipating the unanimous appointment of Francis Pearson. It was moved by Flatman (Downham) and the record states that before any seconder could speak there was 'continued general acclamation'. During this Pearson approached the Chairman and said 'I cannot.' Briefly but emphatically he declined the honour, assuring the brethren that he would give his best efforts to advance the Association. Thereupon John Harrison (editor of *The Wesleyan Times*) proposed that William Harris be elected; he had performed most ably in the chair for these two days. This was immediately seconded, but there was a dissentient voice. Nichols (London, Queen Street), one of the most frequent contributors to the debates, urged caution. Amidst noisy support for the nomination, the Chairman said that Nichols should be heard, but first intimated that he could not and would not undertake the responsibilities of being President. He was very conscious of the honour they wished to confer on him, but could not accept it. Nichols then said:

> I have nothing against Brother Harris; but he is not
> sufficiently known . . . I have no one else to propose,
> only our President should be a man of influence and
> well known.

Harrison then called on the meeting to signify approval of his motion by standing, and the whole assembly rose. Harris was elected amid loud and long-continued cheering. His acceptance speech was punctuated by cheers, applause and assurances of prayer. He pleaded his inadequate qualifications for the office, but he was not a coward. He would not be overcome by opposition, but he was overcome at the moment. He hoped that on cooler judgement they would not regret their decision. He concluded, to vehement applause, by saying:

> I will do my best. Let me make you all presidents in
> your various localities, and go forth, feeling that you
> are all equal with your head, and that we are one in
> the Lord.

OFFICERS, TRUSTEES AND GENERAL COMMITTEE

The following were elected:

James Wild as Treasurer
Edward Cresswell as Honorary Secretary
Henry Reid (Scarborough), Dr Melson (Birmingham),
Edward Brooke (Huddersfield), Robert Swan Stanley (Newcastle),
Thomas Gurney (London), Richard Matthews (Barrister-at-Law) as
Trustees, and, as members of the General Committee:

Pearson, Matlock Green
Gandy, Spitalfields
Cope, Birmingham
Walker, Halifax
Hansom, London
Wood, London
Volkman, Spitalfields
Sharman, Sheffield
Keed, Lynn
Curnock, Bristol
Johns, Newport
Nelstrop, Pontefract
Palmer, Belper
Davison, Sunderland
Cluett, Wolverhampton
Nichols, Gt. Queen St.

English, Deptford
Knight, Gt. Queen St.
Flatman, Downham
Blake, Exeter
Dabb, Southwark
Lovely, London
Jameson, Gt. Queen St.
D. H. Harris, London
Russom, Bristol
Smithson, York
Unwin, Sheffield
Hurst, Ilkeston
Crockford, Rochester
Towne, Melton Mowbray
Bourne, City-Road

Three more resolutions brought the first Aggregate Meeting to the final votes of thanks. Two of these resolutions dealt with the nature and purpose of the Aggregate, and the arrangements for the following year's meetings. They show how strongly preachers of that time felt about their need of each other's help and support in the Christian life and the preacher's calling:

> In order to sustain and increase the deep affection and spiritual union reciprocated here these two days between the brethren, it is desirable that we hold an aggregate meeting of Local Preachers annually, and that our main object then be the spiritual elevation and improvement of the brethren, in order to secure which, arrangements be made for special religious services; and further, that the next meeting be held at Birmingham, this time next year.

The next aggregate meeting be held for three days, and that the third be entirely devoted to spiritual and religious services.

The last resolution established a procedure for appeals from members to be heard. Votes of thanks to those who had entertained delegates in London, and to the President for his able conduct of the proceedings, were then agreed, and Aggregate closed with the singing of the Doxology.

After tea, the majority of the brethren went to Wesley's City-Road Chapel to receive the Sacrament of the Lord's Supper. The service was conducted by six ministers, and the newly-elected President, William Harris, led prayers. The report ended with the statement:

Many brethren have been permitted for the first time in their lives – but not, we hope, the last – to meet their fellow-labourers in the wide field of British Methodism.

APPENDIX TO CHAPTER 10

In the following list names are shown as they appear in the record of the 1st Aggregate Meeting – very few had Christian names or initials included. The style 'Brother' was almost invariably used. The figures denote the number of times a man contributed to the discussions, if more than once.

C   denotes elected to Committee. (13 others were also elected)
Tru   denotes elected a Trustee. (5 others were also elected)
Pr   elected President
Sec   Secretary
Tre   Treasurer

The Names and Circuits of Those Who Spoke in the Inaugural Aggregate Meeting

Circuit (or town)	Names
1. Bakewell	Pybus
2. Barnard Castle	Atkinson (2)
3. Barnsley	Taylor
4. Bath	Luckman
5. Belper	Summersides (8)
"	Palmer C
6. Bilston	Hackett
7. Birmingham E	Read (Reid) (2)
" W	Dr J. B. Melson Tru
"	Edward Cope C
8. Blyth	Patterson
9. Boston	Hubbard
10. Bristol N	Tucking (Tuckey)
"	Curnock (3) C
11. Burnley	Ingram
12. Cambridge	Barton (2)
13. Derby	Topham (3)
14. Denby Dale	Peace
15. Deptford	IsaacEnglish (2) C
16. Downham	Flatman (4) C
17. Edinburgh	Mackay
18. Ely	D. Gunton (er?) (3)
19. Exeter	Saml. Blake (2) C
20. Gravesend	Brumwell
21. Halifax	Shaw (4)
22. High Wycombe	Taylor
23. Huddersfield	Midgley
" 1st	Jephson
" 2nd	Pogson (2)
24. Houghton-le-Spring	Cooke
25. Leamington	W.Heritage (2)
26. Leicester	Warner
27. Leeds 1st	Cheetham
28. Leyton	Tagg
29. Liverpool N	Riley
" 4th	Ellison (3)
30. Launceston	Gill
31. London 2nd	Nichols (9) C
32. London 4th	Parker (2)
33. London 6th	Hanson
34. London 7th	Ed Cresswell Sec
"	Potter
35. London 8th	Jn Harrison (5)
"	Wm Harris Pr
"	Chivers
36. Hinde St	Mann
"	Grosjean
"	Jas Wild (2) Tre
37. Hammersmith	Lovely C
38. Pimlico	Bowran
39. Spitalfields	Brown (2)
"	Illingworth
40. Lynn	Keed (3) C
41. Loughton	Shaw
42. Matlock	Francis
(Cromford)	Pearson (4) C
43. Melton Mowbray	J. Towne (4) C
"	Stamford
44. Midsomer Norton	Kinnaird
45. N'castleStaffs	W. Lawton
46. N'castleTyne	Taylor
47. N Walsham	Burchan
48. Norwich	Eggmore
49. Oxford	Banbury
50. Pontefract	Nelstrop C
51. Preston	Margerison
52. Richmond	Jos Harrison
53. Rochester	Crockford C
"	Ladd
54. Sheffield	Unwin (9) C
"	Collier
"	Sharman C
55. Sheerness	Skey (2)
56. Sunderland	Davison C
57. Swaffham	B. Hardy (6)
58. Sydenham	Harding
59. Tadcaster	Pearson (7)
60. Wednesbury	Horton
61. Wolverh'pton	Cluett C
62. Woolwich	Farrier
63. York	Smithson (6) C
64. Isle of Man	Saml. Johnson (2)
65. ?	Kennett
66. ?	Orchin

WESLEYAN METHODIST LOCAL PREACHERS' MUTUAL AID ASSOCIATION.

Report of the Proceedings

OF

THE FIRST AGGREGATE MEETING

OF

LOCAL PREACHERS,

FOR

THE FORMATION OF A MUTUAL AID ASSOCIATION,

Held in FREEMASONS' HALL, London, Oct. 3rd & 4th, 1849.

TOGETHER WITH

DR. MELSON'S SERMON,

PREACHED BEFORE THE BRETHREN IN GREAT QUEEN STREET CHAPEL;

AN ACCOUNT OF THE SERVICES IN CITY ROAD CHAPEL;

AND AN

Explanatory Address by the Committee.

LONDON:

AYLOTT AND JONES, 8, PATERNOSTER ROW;

AND ALL BOOKSELLERS.

1849.

Front cover of the Report of the First Aggregate Meeting

A Tribute to Francis Pearson

Readers:

Narrator (female)   Joseph Marsden (male)

Wm. Harris (male)   Francis Pearson (male)

Elizabeth Pearson (female)

Part A

In August 1889, a letter appeared in *The Local Preachers Magazine* from a recent past-President of Wesleyan Reform Union, William Marsden. He was the son of Joseph H. Marsden, who is referred to in the letter, and he recalls his father's conversation with Francis Pearson forty years earlier:

> On Monday 21st May 1849 they met in the house of Mr Marsden, a cottage at the bottom of Stony Way, Matlock Green, when the following conversation took place:

Mr Pearson: Friend Marsden, I thought today what a glorious thing it would be if all we local preachers could have a meeting.

Mr Marsden: Yes, it would be a glorious thing; but, if we could meet and form a society for the relief of poor, afflicted and aged local preachers, that would be still more glorious.

Mr Pearson: That would be a splendid thing but I don't think it practicable.

Mr Marsden: Not practicable! Why? It only requires an effort and it could be accomplished. And you would not easily get a meeting unless you had some specific object to place before it.

Mr Pearson: Do you think the editor of *The Wesleyan Times* would insert a letter proposing such a thing?

Mr Marsden: I have no doubt about it, for he suggested something of the sort in a leading article not long since.

As a result of this conversation, **Francis Pearson** wrote the first of four letters to *The Wesleyan Times*, headed 'To the Local Preachers in Connexion with the Wesleyan Methodist Societies', in which he said:

> Honoured Brethren . . . My object in addressing you is to suggest the propriety of us, as local preachers, assembling together for the purpose of exchanging friendly salutations and greeting each other with fraternal regards. Our meeting together would strengthen our faith and consolidate us into one great brotherhood. It would nerve us for fresh toils and enterprises, and whilst no harm could result from it, incalculable good might be the necessary consequence.

The ensuing correspondence led to the convening of the first Aggregate meeting, when an assembly of over 600 local preachers decided to form the Mutual Aid Association and adopted resolutions to guide the officers and committee in drawing up its rules.

PART B

The Wesleyan newspapers of the last week in September 1849 carried an advertisement which began:

> GENERAL WESLEYAN METHODIST LOCAL PREACHERS MUTUAL AID ASSOCIATION
>
> The Aggregate Meeting will be held on Wednesday and Thursday next, the 3rd and 4th of October, 1849, in Freemasons' Hall, Great Queen Street, Lincoln's Inn-Fields, to commence each day at nine, A.M., precisely.

It went on to give details of services arranged in connection with the meeting, and concluded:

> The brethren will be expected to bring their Circuit Plans and Society Tickets with them.

Some six hundred assembled, in response to this advertisement, for the opening of the proceedings. **William Harris**, who had chaired the planning committee, was at once elected to the chair. His opening speech began thus:

> My dear brethren, I have to claim your indulgence. I am not insensible of the honour intended to be conferred upon me. I have not sought it, and I feel that I am undeserving of it . . . I should have been better pleased if an elder had been chosen. If God spares me, I shall get older; and I think that whatever age I may attain to, I shall never lose my desire for the welfare of my brethren in Christ, and especially for my brethren as Local Preachers.

He then dwelt on the work of preaching and on the bond that existed between them as preachers because of their call to that work. He continued by emphasising the duty, laid upon them by the Gospel they preached, to care for the poor and needy amongst them. Calling attention to the inadequacies of public provision in this respect, he referred to those in the company who were actively involved in that provision as Guardians or overseers of the poor. Moving on, he said:

> I will give you a brief sketch of what has been done. Many of us had for a long time thought that something ought to be done in our various circuits. But we wanted a head to have the matter brought out. Early in this year a brother, whose voice you will presently hear – Francis Pearson . . .

The Chairman's voice was drowned by **tremendous cheers**. When he was able to continue, he said:

> Brother Pearson wrote a letter, which appeared in print. That letter was read and approved by scores and hundreds; The object of it was to urge the importance of calling the Local Preachers together. A second letter urged the formation of a Benevolent Fund. Brother Pearson received correspondence from all parts of the kingdom and determined on inviting a meeting at Birmingham.

Harris summarised the further action which had resulted in the present assembly, and then concluded his opening address as follows, but with a thinly-veiled reference to the controversies by which Wesleyan Methodism was torn apart at that time:

> One word more; we have prepared a series of resolutions, which will now be submitted to you. Calmly consider them; suggest any improvement or addition, if you please; and let me beg that, as I am called upon to preside, you will assist me in this office by close adherence in all your remarks to the objects now before us – there are topics I would not have you refer to . . . Let us show the world that we know what is our business – and that we have the ability to do that business.

Francis Pearson then rose to propose the first resolution, and was received, as the record puts it, 'with expressions of the **warmest affection**, which were some minutes before they subsided'. He was at last able to speak:

> Mr Chairman, and my dear brethren – I feel this morning at a loss to find words to express the feelings that exist in my soul. I am undeserving of the very flattering reception you have given me, though it conveys to me your kindness and love. It has been observed by the Chairman that I was the first to bring this matter before the public, through the medium of the newspapers; but while it just happened to be me who brought it forward, it appears to have existed in your hearts for years and years before.

> How it came into my mind to publish it, I do not know. I hope it was the Spirit of the living God, as I feel sure it is he who has put it into yours to make this society a blessing to the Local Preachers themselves, to the whole Church of which we have the honour to be members, and I trust also to the world at large. The necessity for societies similar to this is universally acknowledged, while the making of provision for the poor is one of the great scriptural duties of our holy religion.

He recounted in detail the experience of a poor local preacher in his own circuit, who was unable through illness to work, and who died through lack of food. Francis Pearson had, by special request, conducted that man's burial. Everyone seemed convinced that recurrence of such things should be prevented. He went on:

> Another result will attend the formation of this society – we shall become united – not merely in our various circuits, but through the length and breadth of the land . . . Let our first meeting be a memorable one – let us do something for the poor.

These remarks were greeted with shouts of **Hear! Hear!** and by loud cheers, so Pearson concluded by saying:

> You, my brethren, are satisfied about the propriety of that – it is quite clear and evident. I will therefore content myself by just moving this resolution, which is –
>
> That this society be called 'The Wesleyan Methodist Local Preachers Mutual Aid Association'.

The gathering worked throughout the two days, dealing one by one with a score of resolutions; at the end of the second day it came to the election of officers and committee. The name of Francis Pearson was proposed to be President of the Association for its first year; many seemed ready to second the nomination, but were unable to do so on account of continued **general acclamation**.

Pearson approached the Chairman, and, in a most determined manner said, 'I cannot.' Seeing that it was useless to urge the matter on him, the Chairman rose and requested the assembly to hear him. Pearson said:

> I hope the brethren will believe me when I say, that, as far as the advancement of the society is concerned, I will put forth all my exertions; but I can no more fill the chair than I could sit upon the Queen's throne. Whilst I could go down upon my knees to thank you for the honour you are so anxious to confer, I am bound to declare emphatically that I must respectfully decline it.

A delegate called out, 'Does Brother Pearson positively decline?' to which Francis responded, 'I really must.' Another delegate then proposed the election of William Harris as first President. He demurred, saying that he had done his best as Chairman but he could not hear of being President.

One of his London colleagues expressed the view that Harris was not well-enough known, and that the President should be a man of influence. The meeting however, insisted on having him. In a suitable display of modesty and reluctance, he felt they had been carried away by their kindness and hoped they would not repent of the honour they had conferred on him.

[Francis Pearson declined nomination for the Presidency on three further occasions, but his initiative in bringing about the formation of LPMAA was commemorated a hundred years later by the tablet in Wensley Chapel, near Matlock.]

*NB: Conclude with the sentence in brackets when part B only is being used. When all parts are being used, do **not** use the bracketed sentence above, but proceed from '. . . the honour they had conferred on him' straight to part C.*

Part C

But 1849 was a time of turmoil in the Wesleyan Church, and any association of laymen, especially local preachers, was regarded with suspicion by Wesleyan authorities as likely to be concerned with reform and the securing of more power to the laity. Less than a year after the formation of LPMAA, the Superintendent of the Cromford Circuit gave notice to the Local Preachers Meeting that he would bring charges against Pearson at the Leaders' Meeting, where the minister had authority to declare someone expelled from membership.

Whilst these charges were pending, Pearson's wife, Elizabeth, wrote to him (when he was away on business) a most moving letter:

Elizabeth Pearson:
> My Dear Frank,
> I hear charges are to be brought against you at the next Leaders' Meeting. My dear husband, I can only

recommend you to keep your own conscience clear in the sight of God, and then you need not be afraid what any man or number of men can do to you. May the Lord direct you in all these proceedings! Do all with a single eye to his glory.

Pearson was duly expelled, a fate shared by a number of early leaders of the Association. He and his family moved to Birmingham, where Elizabeth died in 1858, aged 34; her body was buried in the Key Hill Cemetery there.

This is the man commemorated by the plaque in the chapel at Wensley near Matlock. He and his wife worshipped in that chapel from 1845 to 1850, and Francis preached there frequently during that period. He declined nomination for the Presidency of LPMAA four times, affirming that he had done nothing deserving of the honour, and that there were others far more worthy.

Notes for Guidance on using this 'Tribute to Francis Pearson':

(1) It can be used in its entirety – in which case observe the italic note at the end of part B.
(2) Part B alone can be used to focus the part played by Pearson in the 1849 Aggregate Meeting.
(3) A shorter tribute to him can be achieved by using parts A and C only.

Parts A, B and C of the text have been arranged to make these three alternatives conveniently possible.

Sources:
The Local Preachers Magazine, August 1889 and *The Wesleyan Times,* June 1849
Report of the Inaugural Aggregate Meeting (October 1849)
Local Preachers' Meeting Minutes, Cromford Circuit, September 1850.
The Local Preachers Magazine, August 1858.

*The audience shoule be invited to provide the **'tremendous cheers'**, *'warmest affection', 'Hear! Hear!' and 'general acclamation' where indicated in the narrative.*

11

Struggles in the 19th Century

An Atmosphere of Unease
Controversy Over The Local Preachers Magazine
Re-appointment of the Editor • Membership Rises – and Falls
Who Shall Be Members ? • Money
The Story of 'Grandfather Johnson'
The President's Bible • Tribute to the First General Secretary

AN ATMOSPHERE OF UNEASE

The second Aggregate Meeting (Birmingham, October 1850) decided that the Association should publish a magazine, and appointed the Honorary Secretary, William Harris, as Editor. The first issue appeared in January 1851; annual bound volumes have been preserved, and the magazine is the principal source of information for the early history of LPMAA. No other records appear to have survived from decades before the 1870s. The Editor introduced the new publication in a short preface, and continued with a substantial summary of *The Rise and Progress of the Association*, which incorporated the first Annual Report of the Committee. Clearly the founding fathers were well aware of the difficult circumstances (see chapter 4), in which the organisation had been established:

> The critical nature of the times has operated in preventing many from joining the Association. . . . The attempt to form such an Association was regarded with suspicion and distrust. Their motives were misunderstood, if not misrepresented.

When in November 1851 the magazine reported the proceedings of the 3rd Aggregate Meeting held at Sheffield in October, similar observations were made:

> Rising as it did, amidst connexional disquiet and disaster, the avoidance of any allusion to contemporaneous events, at its meetings, was simply an impossibility.

The principal public event in connection with the 1851 Annual Meetings was presided over by John Ratcliff, a prominent citizen of Birmingham. He was an active figure in the Mediation movement in Wesleyan Methodism, and later a Trustee of the Association. A few weeks after the Aggregate Meeting, he chaired a Mediation meeting in Birmingham Town Hall (reported by *The Wesleyan Times*, 10th December). This meeting supported a 12-point declaration on authority, democracy, government and reconciliation in the Wesleyan Church. It was attended by several prominent LPMAA men, amongst them Isaac English (past-President) [see Appendix to this chapter], William Carter (President) and James Wild (Treasurer). Others present included W. Nelstrop, J. Unwin, R. Carter and J. Towne, all of whom served as President later in the 1850s. The Association's leadership clearly favoured reconciliation rather than revolution, but this did not protect its members from expulsion on the ground of involvement with reform activity.

In the course of the Sheffield meeting the Honorary Secretary made a suggestion with a prophetic flavour, the erection of alms-houses for poor old local preachers. It was nearly half a century before this idea was implemented, but at the 1851 public meeting the Chairman started a subscription list with the promise of £100. This was matched by a similar promise from James Wild (honorary treasurer), and augmented with a £50 promise by another member. However, the Annual Report of the Committee for 1851-52, presented to the 4th Aggregate at Huddersfield in October 1852, contained this statement:

> Notwithstanding the generous offers . . . the Committee have not thought it right to take any action in reference to the building of almshouses. They have no doubts but that in many places land might be obtained by gift, but, until they had obtained the sanction of a vote of the aggregate meeting, they did not feel that they were in a position to act. They doubt not that, when the scheme shall be taken up, many instances of generosity will be added to those already given.

The idea lay fallow until the generosity of David Barr and his colleagues made it possible at the end of the 19th century (chapter 13).

Three issues dominated the struggle of the Association to consolidate its existence and expand its work in the first twenty years of its life:

(i)   increasing its membership
(ii) the policy and purpose of its magazine
(iii) obtaining money for its philanthropic work

The first two of these were prominent at the 1852 Aggregate. Membership matters predominated on the second day, but the magazine occupied a large part of the first day's sessions.

CONTROVERSY OVER *THE LOCAL PREACHERS MAGAZINE*

The scene for the debate was set by the Report of the Committee the previous year. After stating that the decision of the previous year's Aggregate to have a magazine, published monthly, had been complied with, the Report continued:

> How far it has answered the expectation of the members it is not for your committee to say; but that it has tended greatly to advance the interests of the Association, they are bold to affirm – the many instances in which donations have been sent, and honorary members added, clearly traceable to perusal of its contents, encourage them to hope that it will not be allowed to fail for want of support, but receive increased circulation – that it may be made not only the medium of conveying intelligence respecting our progress to a greater number of persons, but ultimately to be a source of revenue.

There had been some ill-informed or even malicious criticism of the magazine's finances. The Report therefore pointed out that a loss on the first year was inevitable. Few publications had been launched on such a small budget. A footnote clarified the position:

> It having been insinuated, by parties who are jealous of our success, that those who promised money last year have not kept their word, and that £150 have been taken from the sick funds to keep up the magazine . . . The promise of £200 was not made by individuals, but by a vote of the Aggregate Meeting,

and it was intended to be raised by donations from individuals, and collections in the Branches. Of that sum, £74-19s-6d was sent in previous to the Report being read, and a sovereign has been received since then. We think this is creditable in the infant state of the Association.

The footnote explained that the Editor had been empowered to borrow from the Treasurer at 5 per cent interest. As the Association had not paid for advertisements, the Magazine had in effect given a large sum to the Association. This did not, however, disarm the critics. The magazine was not then included in the subscription, but was sold separately to any who would buy it, and not all members did so. There were those who saw every penny of the deficit as an erosion of the funds intended to relieve distress, and who were prepared to contest this misuse of resources. The 1852 Report had this to say:

> The Committee rejoice that the magazine has not been allowed to perish, as some persons wished and prognosticated that it would. To its advocacy of the cause, and reporting of our operations, many instances of liberality are distinctly traceable; of the £600 and upwards received, as free subscriptions, donations and collections, much is undoubtedly attributable to its influence. But while they know that the Association is indebted to the magazine, and feel that it would be difficult to carry on the Association without such an organ, the committee deeply regret that its circulation is not more extensive and feel persuaded that the efforts of friends have not been so decided as they might have been, or by this time it would have yielded a handsome revenue.

It would have been no surprise when a delegate (Edwin Benson, Birmingham, later of the Wesleyan Reform Union, its President in 1865 and 1885, and President of LPMAA in 1877) asked outright how much the magazine had lost in the year. This triggered a long debate on magazine financing, which soon expanded into the whole area of magazine policy. Increasing the circulation was a prime concern, both to improve the revenue and to extend awareness of the Association and its work. There was general agreement that a magazine was a necessary 'part of our apparatus' as one speaker put it, continuing, 'There needs no discussion; the magazine must go on.'

Disagreement arose over editorial policy, however, and whether articles related to the current controversies in Wesleyanism harmed or strengthened the Association. A local delegate, George Mallinson (Huddersfield), was reproved by the President for endorsing the vigorous rebuttal by the Editor of recent articles in Wesleyan publications. Benson expressed the view of those who believed it was detrimental for the magazine to take note of factions in the Wesleyan church:

> Many of the leading articles of our magazine
> . . . have been leading us to the contending parties –
> reform on one side, Conference on the other, and
> moderation in the middle.

He wanted the Editor to distance the magazine from the Connexional controversy, and concentrate on things pertinent solely to the proclamation of the Gospel. The President pointed out that the difficulty arose from the existence of two hostile parties; this had effectively driven the Association and its editor to support the Mediation movement. The Committee's report had drawn attention to a particular example of malicious misrepresentation in *The Watchman* (the establishment newspaper), to which the President and Honorary Secretary had replied. Their letter was not published!

RE-APPOINTMENT OF THE EDITOR

Discussion then moved on to the appointment of the Editor, but continued in reality to be about the contents and policy of the magazine. The re-appointment of William Harris was proposed, but even the seconder entered reservations: 'I approve of the editor . . . but I do not approve of some of the articles.' Harris did not lack for support, and an early speaker (Mallinson again) said:

> With regard to our magazine – for it is our own, and
> if we have not that or something better we shall
> suffer – I must say I never saw anything more
> moderately conducted in my life.

Another delegate said he had talked for twenty years of a Local Preachers Magazine, and hailed with pleasure the publication of the one connected with this Association, but wanted the editor to refrain from including articles on the current connexional disturbances. A number of speakers then debated the literary quality of the magazine, including Benson and Pearson, both of Birmingham, and the ex-President, W. B. Carter, of Nottingham. The former were displeased; Benson spoke of the character of our literature being of a meagre kind, Pearson described it as 'not equal to the times'. Carter defended the magazine:

> ... that the magazine has been marked by inferiority of literary characteristics is a proposition which I deny with all my heart . . . There is no religious periodical issued of pretensions similar to this magazine, or superior to it!

Isaac English (Deptford), a past-President, commented: 'Finding fault with the literary character of the magazine, and with the editor, is unkind and unjust.' There was far from unity and harmony on this question; compromise was necessary. Thomas Chamberlain (Windsor), a future honorary secretary and President (1856) put it this way:

> As there is diversity of mind, so will there be diversity of opinion. . . . If every brother will say, 'I will do all I can for the magazine' – if he can write, and will write – there will be no want of anything.

Collier (Sheffield) argued that the true course lies in the middle, not withstanding what had been said about 'moderation'.

> It is complained that this magazine gives offence. Why, our whole existence is a rock of offence. You cannot please those who will not be pleased. Let the truth be spoken.

Isaac English had already defended the editor personally, referring to his combined labours as editor and honorary secretary. Several speakers had upheld his right to defend himself and the Association when attacked by official Methodist publications. The general thrust was 'It is our responsibility because it is our magazine.' Finally, before the vote was taken, Meikle (Holmfirth) expressed 'unqualified approval of the editor's conduct,' describing him as 'one of the most eloquent and intelligent men amongst us'. Harris was re-appointed editor without dissent.

In a speech after the vote, Harris summarised his own and the Association's predicament. 'First-rate critics ought to be first-rate contributors,' he said, and passed on to the different opinions about the state of the Connexion.

> We are part of 14,000 men who are recognised universally as the backbone of the Connexion . . . I thought it would be better for the local preachers to be informed as to what was taking place in the Connexion.

He agreed that some of the articles in the magazine leaned towards the moderate movement, adding that these were the men and the measures to bring peace. He thought it in unison with the Association's own position and character.

> We are united not merely for supporting the sick and the aged, and for burying the dead, but . . . with a desire to bring all parties together.

In this William Harris again spoke with a prophetic voice – LPMAA *did* bring together local preachers of several of the separated strands of Methodism, well before the major Union of 1932. He pointed out that the majority of their supporters were identified with the moderates. He concluded by affirming,

> The great principles developed in these articles will live when conference, reform and mediation will be forgotten.

But it was a long time before these differences *were* forgotten, and the Mutual Aid Association continued to be affected by them.

MEMBERSHIP RISES – AND FALLS

As the reform movement began to lose momentum in the middle 1850s, some of the reformers entered into discussions with the Wesleyan Methodist Association. These concluded with the formation of the United Methodist Free Churches in 1857. Those reformers who could not accept even the modest elements of connexionalism in the new body came together two years later as the Wesleyan Reform Union (1859). During this period membership of LPMAA peaked at 2,648 local preachers (1854) and 532 honorary members (1855), then declined steadily to 1,667 and 381, in the two categories respectively, by the middle 1860s. Active consideration was therefore given to ways of increasing membership. There is no information about the numbers of members from the Wesleyan body and from the reformist churches. However, such indications as there are (see Harris above, and Towne below) suggest that a disproportionately large number belonged to 'reform' congregations. The concern was predominantly, therefore, how to increase membership amongst local preachers who remained within Wesleyanism. They probably numbered between 10,000 and 12,000 after the expulsions and secessions; there was obviously scope for recruiting new members.

The Aggregate Meeting of 1858 (Birmingham) was urged by Read, of the host city to elect a 'Conference brother'(ie a loyal Wesleyan) as President for the ensuing year. He felt sure this would have a favourable influence on the future of the Association. The impression was abroad that LPMAA was a reform institution. This impression, being incorrect, should be removed. Read believed it would be by the course he recommended. He therefore moved the election of John Towne (Melton Mowbray). James Wilde (treasurer) seconded; he believed the election of Towne would hasten the day when adherents of Conference would admit they had done local preachers an injustice and would unite with them in promoting the benevolent aims of the Association.

Several members spoke in favour of Towne, but there was some opposition. Jebson deplored the introduction of questions of 'Conference' and 'Reform'. There was an understanding, even a commitment, to recognise Francis Pearson's worth by electing him President when the Society met in Birmingham. Benson agreed with this, and reminded the meeting that although a large proportion of their Presidents had been elected from the Conference body, the use of Conference chapels had still been repeatedly refused. The General Committee had received letters from both Birmingham Superintendents refusing use of the chapels in their Circuits on Aggregate Sunday, one of them in abusive terms. Pearson, who, as has already been noted, was a modest, almost self-deprecating man, declined nomination for the fourth time, and Towne was elected.

Encouraged no doubt by the tone of the Aggregate debate, Towne sought to use his position as a loyal Wesleyan to increase support for LPMAA. The establishment newspaper, *The Watchman*, published a letter from him addressed to 'Members of the Local Preachers Mutual Aid Association in connection with the Wesleyan Conference'. In it he exhorted them to 'labours more abundant' that their society might prosper in both its spiritual and temporal condition. He pointed out that 'the larger number of brethren dependent upon the funds of the Association belong to ourselves'. This appears to imply that the Wesleyan preachers who joined LPMAA were more likely to be the less well-off, whilst those who left or were expelled from Wesleyan Methodism, many becoming reform preachers, were generally more prosperous.

The adverse effects on the Association of dissension between the parties dominated the later sessions of the 1858 Aggregate. Some believed this to be the cause of lost membership, party spirit having infiltrated the Association. One delegate argued that the difficulty in obtaining Conference chapels and support was that LPMAA was identified with the opposite side. They should meet in a neutral place, not in a Reform chapel as they were now doing. Some even spoke of splitting into two societies, one for the Conference party and one for the Reformers, because the spirit of dissension was too frequently manifest amongst them. A united front would obtain more support and confidence, but division would be inevitable unless there were some changes.

WHO SHALL BE MEMBERS?

The basis of membership, as well as increasing the numbers, was an ongoing topic of concern in LPMAA throughout its early years. This extract from the second day's debate at the Huddersfield Aggregate of 1852 conveys the conflicting opinions:

> **Field (Doncaster):** Suppose a person belonging to the Wesleyan Methodist Connexion, and a local preacher, enters the association, and, after he has done so, should leave the Wesleyan Methodist Church in disgust at the Conference, or from other causes, would he, there not being a branch of the Reformers in his circuit, if he were to join the Primitive Methodists, be entitled still to avail

himself of the privileges and immunities of this society?

The President (Wm. Nelstrop, Pontefract): Certainly not.

Field: This is important to us, as there are many standing aloof until after this Aggregate meeting. I differ from the President, and do so on the 56th rule, which says - 'If a member, from any cause whatever, except immorality, ceases to be a local preacher, but desire to continue a member, the members of the association in his own circuit shall consider his case and immediately report their decision to the general committee. If the decision of the general committee be in his favour, he shall continue a member: but if against him he shall have a right of appeal to the aggregate meeting .'

The Honorary Secretary: Bro. Field is right. And I think the President is in error. Each case must be considered on its own merits.

The President: My conviction is that, where a local brother who is a member of this association, leaves or is expelled from the Wesleyan community, and joins another church, he excludes himself from this association.

Pearson (Thorp Arch) (not Francis Pearson): His going to another church was never taken into consideration when that resolution was adopted. It was understood that the only disqualification should be downright immorality; as to whether he joined the Ranters or any other Christian Church, he was left to his own choice.

The President: I made my statement from conviction as to the objects of the association, and I am borne out by the designation of the society itself. I am aware of the circumstances alluded to by Brother Pearson; to meet such a case, the aggregate meeting passed the resolution which appears as a footnote to the second rule –

'That the words "Wesleyan Methodist local preachers" and "accredited local preachers" occurring in the rules shall not be taken in such sense as to exclude those persons who, in the present afflicted state of Methodism, are connected with the branch societies.'

According to this rule these parties are entitled to remain amongst us so long as they do not unite themselves to another church; as soon as they do that they cease to be members.

A Delegate: I know a member of this association who is a preacher amongst the Primitive Methodists.

Field: Then there is greater privilege given to a man who ceases to be a local preacher altogether than to one who becomes a member of another church?

Jebson: I have heard this question mooted, discussed and settled several times; it was understood at London and Birmingham that a member ceasing to be a Wesleyan local preacher, and uniting with another church, by such act severed his connection with this association. I shall contend that the rule be maintained intact, or else that we throw open the door to receive local preachers of all denominations . . . There is no case for which this rule does not provide, and I certainly shall support it being maintained in its integrity, for I shall regret the day when this association shall lose its distinctive character.

Pearson (Thorp Arch); May I ask in what position those members are placed who are denominated Reformers?

The President: The footnote explains that.

Pearson: What difference is there between a man going into the Primitive Methodists and his identifying himself with the Reformers?

The President: A very great deal.

The Honorary Secretary: This is the practical evil complained of. Many brethren who have been cast off from the Methodist society have it not in their hearts to run and join the Reformers, and would rather wait and try to get back again. They would like to join this society, but they say, 'Your rules say I must identify myself with the Reformers, or we won't have you.' Again, they might be disposed to unite with the Primitive Methodists, the New Connexionists, or any other branch of the Christian church, but our rules say, 'If you do that you cannot remain a member of this society.' This is an important matter; if brethren would turn their attention to it, I think they would be acting quite in accordance with the original object of the association.

A Delegate from Manchester: We have a good brother who has recently left the Wesleyan body through disapprobation of its proceedings, and on the grounds of expediency he has joined the Wesleyan Association, under the impression that when the present agitation has subsided all parties may come back again. This brother has been a member of this association from the beginning, and we think it would be very hard to exclude him.

Isaac English quoted an instance where a brother had removed to an area where there were no Reformers, and had attended the Baptist chapel and taken sacrament with them. It would be painful to expel such men; some discretion must be used.

Skey (Queensborough) said there were no Reformers in the Isle of Sheppey, and wished to know, supposing he was expelled from the Wesleyan body, what he should do.

Smith (Knottingley) felt that if men were expelled under such circumstances he ought not to give another penny to the association.

Knaggs (York) said that some time ago a young brother removed from York into a part of Oxfordshire where there was no Wesleyan Methodist body, but being an indefatigable labourer in the cause of Christ, he had joined the Primitives. He was still retained on the books of the York branch, and he wished to know what, under the circumstances, they were to do.

The ex-President thought the answer to the question might be found in the 56th rule. Those cases should be reported, and considered by the general committee, from which there was right of appeal to the aggregate meeting.

Mallinson submitted that they must maintain their Wesleyan character; if they did not they would lose the support of a great many honorary members.

MONEY

Although these differences continued to afflict LPMAA and to impede its development through the 1850s and 1860s, its beneficent objectives were pursued and some interesting initiatives taken to sustain and extend them. Subscription income from a static or declining membership was insufficient to meet even modest levels of benefit during sickness, *and* the payment of grants upon death to meet funeral costs. There was a strong body of opinion in favour of increasing benefits and of extending their coverage to include unemployment and old age. Support was also expressed for bringing dependants (in addition to widows) into the scope of the scheme. These improvements could only be brought about by raising additional money through collections, charitable donations, and voluntary efforts, and considerable energy was diverted to these activities from the late 1850s onwards. It is salutary to realise that many Methodist local preachers in the second half of 19th century depended on this kind of provision for such material support as they needed in order to continue their preaching work.

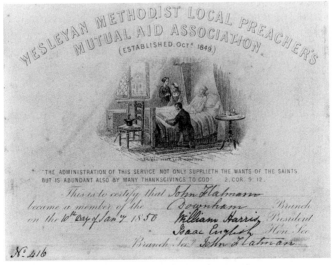

The earliest known Membership Certificate

The Aggregate Meeting of 1854 (London) addressed some of these issues, deferring for three years a proposal to reduce the burial allowance from £8-0-0 to £6-0-0, and resolving in the following terms to make allowances to elderly members:

> Any members being 70 years of age, and in necessitous circumstances, may make application . . . to the Committee of his Branch, to be placed upon the list of super-annuitants; if this application be approved, it shall be recommended to the General Committee, who shall allow him a weekly sum, not exceeding 4s, their discretion being guided by the state of the funds, and the amount obtained by free contributions.

The report of the Committee to the Aggregate Meeting the following year (1855, at Bristol) picked up and commented upon this matter. It described the Association as 'an institution of mixed character', having the characteristics of a self-supporting friendly society (in which members provide for their own needs in sickness) and some of the peculiarities of a benevolent society (through which charitably-minded individuals contribute to the needs of others in necessitous circumstances). The report continued:

> That portion of the demands upon our funds for the support of the superannuated, which to any other Friendly Society would bring speedy ruin, is the chief glory of our Association, and forms the foundation of our appeals to the Christian public. The sums allowed for the funerals of deceased members are also much too large for the rate contribution; but here again we take in the benevolent principle, and our honorary subscribers furnish us with the means of decently burying our dead.

Statistical returns for that year showed for the first time a small reduction in the number of members – 2,408 benefit members; 156 local preacher honorary members; 376 other honorary members – a total of 2,940 (2,954 in 1854), whilst the numbers receiving sickness benefit and the number of death grants paid both reached the highest number since LPMAA began, 433 and 58 respectively. At 98, the number receiving superannuation benefit was only slightly fewer than the 104 reported two years earlier. No-one doubted that the good work must continue. The only way to ensure it continued was to pray for divine blessing on it, and to put the need before fellow-Christians in new and imaginative ways.

Individual members, as well as officers and committees, played their part. One member gave up shaving and grew a beard, giving the money he saved to the Association; another solicited a penny (1d) from congregations for every sermon he preached, not surprisingly gaining the nickname 'The Penny Preacher' as a result. The election of John Towne, a loyal Conference man, to the Presidency in 1858 has already been noted; he initiated the production and distribution of special collecting cards, asking that all members and supporters of LPMAA who were willing to accept one should obtain not less than one shilling via each card before the next Aggregate meeting. His scheme produced £329-15-9d.

The gradual decrease in membership continued, however, and concern about the adequacy of the funds to meet future obligations increased. The President of 1863, James Arundale, made a special appeal for a sum of £2,000 to provide 4s weekly to aged annuitants. [This target would have been the equivalent perhaps of £500,000 or more at late 20th century prices.] The next President took over the appeal, but the total only reached just over £1,000 by the end of the second year. The full sum was not reached until after the 1867 Aggregate Meeting. Another special effort [described in more detail in chapter 18] was the organising and holding of a major bazaar in connection with the Aggregate Meeting of 1860, held at Exeter Hall, London.

THE STORY OF 'GRANDFATHER JOHNSON'

1860 was also the year when a notable figure in LPMAA mythology first appeared. 'Grandfather Johnson' was an imaginary story, based on typical examples of early LPMAA beneficence. It was first published in *The Local Preachers Magazine* in May 1860 as the work of an anonymous author, Alma. He was later identified as Philip Parker, an early stalwart of the Association, who had been a member of the Arrangements Committee for the first Aggregate Meeting and was soon elected to the new body's General Committee. Like many of his contemporaries he was deprived of his membership in the Wesleyan Church – and thus of his standing as a Wesleyan local preacher – because of his involvement in the Reform Movement. He continued to serve LPMAA until shortly before his death in 1895, having been closely associated with the publication and distribution of *The Local Preachers Magazine* for a quarter of a century from the early 1860s.

'Grandfather Johnson' was very soon reprinted as a 'penny pamphlet' and sold for the Association's funds, but its wider purpose was to inform readers about the work of Mutual Aid. It was re-published in 1891 as a Service of Song, including hymns for choir and congregation; members attending the 1892 Aggregate Meeting were exhorted to promote its use. A few copies were specially bound, for presentation to various people, including past Presidents. One of these copies has survived. Whilst the whole tract is far too long to reproduce here, a few extracts give the essence of the story and some impression of how the Association functioned in the beginning:

> *[James Johnson was born in the house he now occupied, his widowed daughter Jane and her family living with him.]* Before he had reached his twentieth year he had begun to preach. When about twenty-five years of age, his father and mother having passed away, he took to the paternal home her *[his wife, Emily]* who was to be his companion and friend till death. She was a helpmeet for him in his work as a local preacher, always ready to help and encourage him. There was no frown on her countenance, and no murmur issued from her lips when he had to take a long journey on the Sabbath to fill his appointments, and be away frequently for eighteen hours together. After the death of Emily *[her mother]*, Jane became her father's housekeeper.
>
> *[When Jane married she and her husband made their home with her father, but her husband died when their three children were only a few years old. Grandfather Johnson's small earnings kept the family for a while.]* For two years they struggled on until his earnings ceased altogether through sheer inability to work, occasioned by increasing infirmity and age. One thing after another was parted with to procure bread and pay the rent. Still they shrank from application to the parish, from the certainty that this would bring about the separation which they both dreaded. At last their circumstances became desperate, and the father, unable any longer to burden his daughter, determined to seek a refuge in the Union.
>
> *[The decision was made a matter of prayer. The children became aware that 'Grandfather must go', and even*

offered their few pence of savings if it would prevent this happening.]

Jane was calm as she superintended their frugal breakfast on the last morning. The latch of the door was lifted, and the district postman entered. 'Good morning, James; I have a letter for you'. The letter, bringing light and joy to this family, was from the General Secretary of the LOCAL PREACHERS MUTUAL AID ASSOCIATION, conveying the intelligence that the Committee at its last sitting, on the recommendation of the Branch, and in consideration of the high character and fifty years' labour of JAMES JOHNSON, had unanimously resolved to allow him the maximum annuity of four shillings per week.

The duties of the day ended, the family had just gathered together. 'There is Mr Frank, grandfather!' The next moment James was at the door to let in JOHN FRANK, Secretary of the Branch. 'O, Mr Frank,' said Jane, 'if you knew what that letter has done for us and what we are indebted to you and our kind friends. I am sure we shall never be able to make adequate return.' 'Return! don't mention it; long may your father be spared to you, and were he to live fifty years to enjoy this annuity the Methodist people would still be in his debt. However, to business. I have brought you, my old friend, your first month's instalment towards the debt we owe you. Goodnight,' said John, seizing the old man's hand.

'Let me see what we have here,' said Grandfather Johnson as he proceeded to undo a small packet John had placed in his hand – ONE SOVEREIGN, with an intimation that his first month was five weeks. 'What a providence,' said Jane; 'it is exactly the amount I wanted to put us straight with our landlord.'

So simple and clear were many of the needs that the Association tried to meet in the 19th century. Philip Parker's story must have had a wide appeal, or it would not have been re-published thirty years later.

THE PRESIDENT'S BIBLE

One further event in the early history of LPMAA must be included – the introduction of the President's Bible in 1862. The inscription in the Bible records the decision:

WESLEYAN METHODIST LOCAL PREACHERS MUTUAL AID ASSOCIATION

The Annual Meeting held in Becket Street Chapel, Derby 1862. Resolved:
That a Bible be purchased for the use of the President for the time being.
That the autograph of each President be written therein.
And that it be formally presented to each President on his taking the chair from his predecessor.

At that time all past-Presidents, except Isaac English [see Appendix to this chapter] were still alive and able to sign it. His signature was cut from a document, and pasted in the correct position.

TRIBUTE TO THE FIRST GENERAL SECRETARY

This chapter cannot conclude without some recognition of the man who, as its original General Secretary, administered the Association's affairs for the first 23 years of its existence. As substantial reference is made to him in chapter 25, two brief extracts from a poem 'On the Death of Brother Edward Cresswell' (*The Local Preachers Magazine*, November 1872) are given here:

> When the fund for local preachers was designed,
> Among the first was he to aid the cause.
> His counsels, ever wise, and never noisy,
> Were given to make this fund for mutual aid
> Like to an angel, going round the churches
> To bless the sick, the aged, and the mourners
> He gladly bore the burden of its work
> For twenty-three long years; . . .
>
> His ready pen no more shall neatly make
> Its careful entries in his well-ruled books;
> Nor send instructions to the local agents;
> Nor cautious counsel; nor encouragement;
> Nor dictum of Committee; nor resolve
> Of annual meeting.

APPENDIX TO CHAPTER 11

Isaac English became Honorary Secretary at the end of 1849, when Edward Cresswell was appointed General Secretary (the salaried office). At the Aggregate Meeting of 1850 he was elected President and William Harris took over the Honorary Secretary position. English was a class leader and continued to meet members of his class who had been expelled from Wesleyan membership. He also preached on some occasions to 'Reform' congregations, subsequently being summoned to answer charges at a Leaders' Meeting. Following this he was removed from the office of class leader and transferred himself to the Reforming cause. He died in November 1855, aged 61, only a few days after attending a Reform Committee and dealing with some Mutual Aid Association business. [Since 1997 the President's Bible has only been 'presented' for a few moments at the Aggregate Meeting. A copy of Holy Scripture is presented to each newly-inducted President as a gift from the Association.]

12

Relations with Methodism to 1907

The Place of Laymen in Wesleyan Methodism
The Effects for LPMAA
Some LPMAA Leaders of This Time - Waddy, Stephenson, Kilner
The Non-Wesleyan Branches of Methodism.

THE PLACE OF LAYMEN IN WESLEYAN METHODISM

In 1871 Rev John Holt Lord, then Superintendent of the Leeds Brunswick Circuit, compiled what were called 'biographical memoirs' of Edward Brooke, Esquire, one of the original Trustees of the WMLPMAA. He used the opportunity to express some views, which he had formed during 30 years in its itinerant ministry, on the institutions and practice of Wesleyan Methodism. This period spanned the Fly-Sheet controversy of the 1840s, the formation of LPMAA, and the Reform Movement of the 1850s. In chapter 6, on preaching, he made several observations about local preachers:

> Methodist has just cause to think well of her lay-preachers . . . the local preachers of Methodism need no apology . . . To her lay-preachers Methodism has done scant justice in the past; whilst of generosity she has been strangely and culpably neglectful. In but few circuits is anything like systematic training attempted.

> . . . when prematurely worn out, as not seldom happens, from the continuous strain of seven days' labour, no adequate provision has existed for the relief of the necessitous. There seems, however, in these respects to be the dawning of a better day.

The 'dawning' of that 'better day' was clearly discernible in the early 1870s. By then many of the issues which had riven Wesleyan Methodism in earlier decades of 19th century were resolved or were well on the way to resolution. This was encouraged by the development of parallel Methodist denominations, some of which had entered into or were moving towards a form of union. The characteristics of an evangelistic movement had become less marked, those of an institutional church more prominent. The quarrels over ministerial training, which had resulted in secession forty years previously, had abated. The controversies over the exercise of connexional authority, which had led to membership breakaway before that had also diminished.

One important matter remained to be tackled – the place of lay members in the formation of connexional policy: their admission as full members of Conference. This was necessary so that it might be representative of the whole Church, not solely of the ordained ministry. Part of the pressure for this move followed from increase in the numbers of well-to-do laymen, often successful businessmen, who were prepared to give substantial sums of money for the support of the ministry and for the building and maintenance of chapels. Some were local preachers, a few were members of LPMAA, and as the century progressed towards its end many more joined the Association and played an important part in its life and work.

Four particular initiatives were taken between 1873 and 1883 which had a bearing on this:

(i)   Action to achieve minimum educational standards for local preachers
(ii) The creation of a Representative Session of Conference.
(iii) The establishment of a Connexional Fund to aid Necessitous Local Preachers
(iv) Recording, by annual return, the number of local preachers.

The first of these related in an interesting way to the policy for the training of ministers, which was well-established by the early 1870s. A committee was appointed by Conference to review the Wesleyan Theological Institution. Its lay members included Samuel Waddy, Q.C. M.P., who had served as President of LPMAA in 1870, William H. Stephenson, later to become the first man to serve twice in that office (1883, 1895) and W. W. Pocock, President of LPMAA in 1875.

The Committee reported to Conference in 1873. The Minutes record that 'Conference cheerfully accedes' to the Committee's request to appoint a committee to ascertain what can be done to assist local preachers in preparation for their work. The report stressed the particular reason for this recommendation – it is from among local preachers only that candidates for the ministry are drawn. That reason would probably persuade many who were not concerned whether local preachers had any systematic preparation for their work, or who preferred they did not lest it gave them ideas 'above their station'. Perhaps the eminent 'locals' on the Committee were shrewd enough to realise that possibility, and worded the proposition accordingly.

In the following year Conference instructed Superintendents to give attention to young men who might become local preachers. They would be required to reach satisfactory standards in an examination on the Catechism and in the Elements of English Grammar. By 1876 these instructions were amplified. No candidate could be admitted as a local preacher until he had read John Wesley's *Standard Sermons* and *Notes on the New Testament*, and had passed an examination on the leading doctrines of Christianity as explained therein, with definitions and scripture proofs. A period of twelve months' probation [on trial] was required. A theology class in each Circuit was recommended, a course of study being drawn up by the tutors of the Theological Institution. Conference recognised the continuing importance of the class of non-accredited preachers known as Exhorters.

Meanwhile the second of the four initiatives mentioned above was under active consideration, and in 1878 a Representative Session of Conference with laymen and ministers together came into being. The all-ministerial Conference, with the Legal Hundred as its core, continued as a pastoral session.

The third initiative connected with the Wesleyans' concern about the place of laymen in the church followed closely on this. In 1879 Conference approved the investing of a sum of £8,000 from the Thanksgiving Fund, the interest to be used for the assistance of necessitous local preachers. Two years later the Thanksgiving Fund Committee, which included S. Rathbone Edge (LPMAA President 1889) and Samuel Waddy as a treasurer, sought instructions from Conference about the persons to be responsible for investing the £8,000. The 1881 Conference appointed Trustees (including Waddy), and a Committee (which included Waddy and Pocock) to oversee the distribution of interest. Finally, in 1882, a committee was set up to consider the registration of Local

Preachers. It reported the following year. Conference then took the fourth of the initiatives listed above, and called for the numbers of local preachers (and class leaders) to be recorded annually. The first returns (1884) showed 14,453 accredited Wesleyan Methodist Local Preachers.

THE EFFECTS FOR LPMAA

So, in a space of ten years, the Wesleyan Conference did what was necessary to recognise the place of laymen and especially of local preachers in the organisation and polity of the church. This made it possible for its leading laymen, many of them local preachers, to play a full part in its activities. Amongst other things this meant that they more readily identified with other local preachers in LPMAA. In 1870 LPMAA membership had reached only 1,715, a figure including those from the United Methodist Free Churches and Wesleyan Reform Union. Probably about half of them were Wesleyans.

The table below shows how the number of Benefit Members (local preachers) grew over the next 30 years. The 1900 total represents about half of all local preachers in the four Methodist denominations then eligible to join. There was also a steady increase in the numbers of Honorary Members over the same period. Many of them were affluent Wesleyans who supported LPMAA with a minimum annual donation of one guinea, which reflected the growing recognition of the Association in the late 19th century. (Honorary Member figures include some local preachers who chose to pay the higher subscription.)

Year	1870	1880	1890	1900
Benefit Members (LP)	1715	2659	4563	7835
Hon: Members	446	796	1608	2861

All this seems far removed from the situation in the middle of 19th century, when Wesleyan Methodism had experienced damaging tensions, and LPMAA was struggling to establish itself as an effective channel of support for preachers. A few sentences from an article in *The Methodist Magazine* of August 1852 help to emphasise the contrast:

> . . . we have been forced into the conclusion that the real question now at issue is between a pastoral church-government and one vested in a sort of lay-aristocracy . . . the usurpation of an authority which God has vested in the Christian Pastorate, and which is essential to the due and faithful discharge of pastoral duty.

After paying fulsome tribute to class-leaders and local preachers in general, the writer refers to some members of these bodies who have been

> . . . the promoters of strife; have agitated peaceable Societies into a frenzy of unholy excitement; and have misled thousands of simple-minded people into ruinous plans of organised mischief . . . For what have hundreds of Leaders and Local Preachers confederated to agitate the masses of Methodism?

A footnote asserted that the origin of the agitation was known, as were the pretences under which it had continued. The main article stated that the real object of the agitators has long been apparent – to degrade the Wesleyan pastorate, and to exalt themselves. A little later, using the phrase 'revolt against pastoral authority', the writer underlines his own and official Wesleyan opinion and disapproval of what was happening:

> The claim of discontented Leaders and Local Preachers is an equality with the regular pastorate of Methodism . . . They demand . . . to share the pastoral authority equally with the ordained and separated ministry . . . Can this claim to co-pastorship and ministerial equality be conceded?

Needless to say, the answer of *The Methodist Magazine* article's author was 'No.'

SOME LPMAA LEADERS OF THIS TIME

Reference was made earlier in this chapter to the part played in connexional affairs, during the 1870s and 1880s, by a number of local preachers who were active in LPMAA. Men like Samuel Waddy, William Stephenson, Wesley Pocock and Rathbone Edge all graced the presidential office during those decades, and there can be little doubt that their standing in the Church contributed greatly to the acceptance of the Association by rapidly-increasing numbers of local preachers, and its widespread recognition in Wesleyan Methodism.

Samuel Waddy, distinguished lawyer, Member of Parliament, son of the Manse, is often seen as the man around whom this change of fortune first began to appear. He was the eldest of the ten children of Rev. Dr Samuel Dousland Waddy, sometime Governor of Wesley College, Sheffield, and President of the Wesleyan Conference in 1859. Dr Waddy was Superintendent minister of Gold Street Circuit, Northampton, from 1831 to 1834, so Samuel junior spent three years of his early life there. Later he studied at his father's college, and graduated BA (London) in 1850 at the age of 20. After becoming a local preacher he offered as a candidate for the ordained ministry, but withdrew before the process was complete.

Called to the Bar in 1858, and attached to the Inner Temple, he subsequently represented four different constituencies as a Liberal Member of Parliament, serving a total of 17 years in the House of Commons. He was appointed a County Court Judge and officiated in this capacity at Chester and Sheffield. He continued to be in great demand as a preacher; it was something of an attraction for non-churchgoers when the judge who had presided in Court during the week was preaching in a local Methodist chapel on Sunday. This is the man to whom was attributed the statement:

During the week I am an advocate and a judge, but on Sunday I am a simple witness to the saving power of Christ.

His active membership of a number of Wesleyan committees has already been mentioned, but neither this nor his political and legal work prevented him from continuing with theological and biblical studies. Shortly after publication of the Revised Version of the New Testament (1881) he secured permission from the University Presses to use the text in his book *A Harmony of the Four Gospels in the Revised Version*. He also wrote a hymn paraphrasing the 23rd Psalm which compares well with more familiar metrical versions. [See Appendix to this cbapter]

```
IN MEMORY OF
SAMUEL DANKS WADDY K.C.
COUNTY COURT JUDGE AND
RECORDER OF THE CITY OF SHEFFIELD
AND A MASTER OF THE BENCH OF
THE HONOURABLE SOCIETY OF THE INNER TEMPLE.
BORN 27TH JUNE 1830.
DIED 30TH DECEMBER 1902.

THROUGHOUT A DISTINGUISHED CAREER AT THE BAR,
IN THE HOUSE OF COMMONS AND ON THE JUDICIAL BENCH
HE MAINTAINED AN UNSWERVING LOYALTY.
TO THE CHURCH OF HIS FATHERS.
HE SERVED WITH CONSPICUOUS ABILITY AND ZEAL
IN MOST OF THE OFFICES OPEN TO LAYMEN
IN THE WESLEYAN METHODIST CONNEXION
AND WAS ONE OF THE FOUNDERS OF THE METROPOLITAN
CHAPEL BUILDING FUND AND A MEMBER OF THE FIRST
REPRESENTATIVE SESSION OF CONFERENCE.
HE WAS A LOCAL PREACHER FOR 54 YEARS
AND PRESIDENT OF THE LOCAL PREACHERS'
MUTUAL AID ASSOCIATION IN THE YEAR 1870.

HIS CHILDREN INSCRIBE THIS STONE TO HIS MEMORY
IN LOVING RECOGNITION OF ALL THEY OWE TO
HIS WISE COUNSELS, NOBLE EXAMPLE
AND UPRIGHT LIFE.
```

Memorial Tablet in Wesley's Chapel to Samuel D. Waddy

Samuel Waddy's connection with LPMAA began in 1869, when he had been a local preacher for a number of years. Influenced perhaps by the attitude of the Wesleyan establishment, of which his father was part, towards unofficial lay activity he had been critical of the Association and of those who joined it. The following year's Aggregate Meeting was due to be held in Northampton; local tradition has it that a Northampton preacher, who had known the lawyer when he was a small boy, made a special journey to his chambers in London in order to enlist his support for Mutual Aid. In this he was successful, and Waddy was almost immediately appointed to the General Committee. The following year (1870), at Northampton, he was elected President. This is recorded in the memorial tablet to him in Wesley's Chapel. He served LPMAA for some years as one of its Trustees.

William H. Stephenson, a Newcastle-upon-Tyne man, was elected President in 1883, when the Aggregate Meeting assembled for the first time in that city. Like Samuel Waddy some years earlier, he had been educated at Wesley College, Sheffield, during the time that Waddy's father was Governor. Stephenson was a fourth generation Methodist and a successful businessman, who was deeply involved in the civic and public life of his city. He was also active connexionally; his membership of the Committee to review the Wesleyan Theological Institution in the early 1870s, along with Waddy and Pocock, has already been noted.

Stephenson was born on 15th May 1836, the family home then being at Throckley House, Newburn. His father had established a brick-making business in which William and his brother Charles John were later involved. William became Chairman of W. Stephenson and Sons, one of nine company chairmanships which he held during his life, including Throckley Coal Company (of which he was the founder), Newcastle and Gateshead Gas Company, and Tyne Tees Steam Shipping. He was also chairman of Newcastle Commercial Exchange and of the Tyne Improvement Commission, the latter from 1901 (in which year he was knighted) until his death in 1918.

His public life began with his election as Councillor for the Elswick Ward of the city in 1867 when he was 33. He was Chairman of the Finance Committee for more than 20 years, and served seven terms as Mayor and Lord Mayor of Newcastle, including 1883 and 1895, the years of his two LPMAA Presidencies. In the latter year, as Chairman of the Visiting Committee, Alderman Stephenson and his wife laid foundation stones at St. Nicholas Hospital. He endowed libraries at Elswick, Heaton and Walker, and gave the statue of Queen Victoria in Cathedral Square, Newcastle.

In Methodism, William Stephenson was a prominent member of Elswick Road Wesleyan Church, and amongst other things was on the committee for New Benwell Mission, where the first building was opened in 1881. Ten years later he contributed substantially to the cost of a further building there, in memory of his recently deceased sister-in-law, Charlotte Bond. As the century drew to a close, he offered to finance a new chapel at Benwell, which was opened in the Autumn of 1899. His distinguished record of public service and business success was recognised by the award of a number of honorary degrees, and by the city making him an Honorary Freeman. With men of this calibre and high esteem in business and public life, as well as within the Church, now willing to identify themselves as local preachers with the

Mutual Aid Association, any lingering animosity towards the body soon declined.

When the LPMAA Aggregate met in Newcastle in 1895, the Stephensons played a full part. Their home, Elswick House, was (to borrow a phrase from the fourth Gospel) 'a house with many rooms', and they entertained eleven guests. In addition to Stephenson himself, who was to begin his second Presidential year at that Aggregate, there were five past-Presidents, including Waddy and the outgoing President, John Bamford Slack, two who served as President in the next few years, as well as five other delegates. Slack became the Association's Honorary Secretary for three years from 1902. William Skinner, also a guest of the Stephensons in 1895, succeeded him in that office, serving until 1921. A weekend house party of that size and composition must have been a memorable experience.

William Kilner was another leading wealthy Wesleyan layman who served LPMAA as President in the later 19th century. He came from another part of the country and a very different background from either Waddy or Stephenson. He was the third son of John Kilner, who founded a glass-bottle manufactory at Dewsbury, Yorkshire, in 1844. The industry was greatly helped by abolition of the glass-duty in the following year, and by 1847 Kilner and his sons had been able to build 'The Providence Glass Works' at Thornhill Lees, only a few miles away. In 1850 the eldest son, Caleb, moved to London to manage a warehouse and the firm's exporting business, but by 1864 ill-health compelled him to relinquish this responsibility.

Examples of the 'Kilner' preserving jar

His brother William came from Yorkshire to take his place. The business prospered as technical improvements were made in the processes and products, and the volume and value of exports increased. The firm is most famous for its patent preserving jar, but it manufactured bottles for aerated and alcoholic beverages, for sauces and pickles, medicine and perfume bottles, sodawater syphons and infant feeding bottles. By 1889 its exports of common glass bottles alone reached nearly a million hundredweights, with a value approaching £500,000.

It was out of this success that William Kilner was able to contribute to the building of several chapels in the Finsbury Park Circuit: Gillespie Road; Winchmore Hill; Southgate; Newgate; Willoughby Road. He was not only recognised for his financial generosity, but was much-valued as a local preacher (for 45 years) and as a class-leader. He was one of the first laymen to be a member of Conference and from 1878 to his death in 1893, aged 67, he was a Conference representative twelve times, as well as serving on district and connexional committees.

It is not surprising that the funeral service of a man so well-regarded by Methodism should be, as *The Methodist Recorder* (24th August 1893) reported it, 'largely attended'. There were clergy of several denominations, and a number of senior LPMAA colleagues. Some had preceded him as President (Samuel Waddy Q.C. M.P.; Russell Johnson, also at that time Honorary Secretary), and others followed him (J. Calvert Coates; Thomas Snape, M.P.). John Harding, General Secretary since 1883, was amongst others present. The Superintendent minister, Rev. John H. Grubb, had officially concluded his three years in the Circuit ten days earlier, prior to moving to a new appointment, and referred to this in his oration:

> I little thought, when I closed my ministry here, that I should be detained to take part in a memorial service of so solemn a character. Mr William Kilner belonged to a class of Wesleyan Methodists not common in these days. From early life it was his privilege to live in a religious atmosphere, and to experience its benign influence. It fell to his lot to commence business life at the tender age of eight. His conversion took place at the age of fifteen. He began to preach, and with such acceptance that in due course [1848, *aged 22*] he was received on 'full

plan'. Young Kilner had to preach his trial sermon before ten of his brethren at the early hour of seven o'clock on a Sunday morning. Thus he started on a career of great spiritual usefulness, growing in the love and respect of his brethren, until in 1888 at Nottingham he was elected President of the Local Preachers Mutual Aid Association.

Mr Grubb went on to summarise William Kilner's work in London Methodism and in the Connexion. Before the final expression of sympathy and assurance of prayer to Mrs Kilner and her five sons and a daughter, he referred again to LPMAA, observing that the Association had lost a generous benefactor and a lifelong friend. The interment took place in Highgate Cemetery (in which the body of Karl Marx is also buried).

THE NON-WESLEYAN BRANCHES OF METHODISM

These then are some of the men who represented the Mutual Aid Association in Wesleyan circles during the later part of 19th century. They helped it to achieve a recognition that would have seemed unlikely, if not impossible, during the early decades of its existence. More and more local preachers joined, financial support from Methodist congregations grew, the numbers of members and dependants receiving financial help and the total value of that help increased. LPMAA began to enjoy the connexional sunshine as never before. Just after the turn of the century (year 1902-03) its income exceeded £20,000 for the first time, total membership reached 11,812 including over 8,000 Local Preachers and over 3,000 honorary members, payments for sickness, annuities and death benefits amounted to £14,735, and 647 Local Preachers and widows were receiving annuities, the highest number recorded up to that date. It is well that this was the case, for within the next ten years the Association, in common with all Friendly Societies, would have to face major changes resulting from new directions in public policy. Consideration of these must wait until chapter 15, but it can be noted now that LPMAA would have found it far more difficult to adapt to substantial extension of state aid for sick and elderly people if it had not gained general acceptance and support in the church.

There are other elements in the relationship of LPMAA with Methodism up to 1907. From the beginning, its basis of membership had been a matter of debate and discussion. The decision to interpret the rules so as to retain in membership the many local preachers who either left or were expelled from Wesleyan Methodism in the early 1850s made a prolonged period of strain inevitable. The Association saw itself, however, as inclusive rather than exclusive. When the Reform Movement crystallised in the formation of the United Methodist Free Churches (1857) and the Wesleyan Reform Union (1859) local preachers of both denominations were made eligible for membership. By 1872 there was a feeling that the name of the Association should be amended to reflect this, by deleting the word *Wesleyan* from its title. The Aggregate Meeting of that year rejected a motion to make the change. In spite of LPMAA's self-perception as a microcosm of Methodist unity, if not union, the same Aggregate also deferred consideration of a proposal that local preachers of the Methodist New Connexion should be eligible for membership.

In 1891 a formal request to admit local preachers of the New Connexion was referred to past-President Samuel D. Waddy, Q.C., for a legal opinion. He advised that there was no insuperable legal objection, but warned that the possibility of legal proceedings from members hostile to the proposal made the move very undesirable. When the admission of Methodist New Connexion local preachers came to Aggregate in 1893, the following resolution was carried by a large majority:

> That while expressing its sympathy with the local preachers of the Methodist New Connexion, and its great interest in their work, this Aggregate Meeting regrets that the financial and other difficulties in the way of admitting them to benefit membership with the Association are so serious that the proposal cannot be entertained at present.

Since 1872 the Rules of LPMAA had specified that they could only be amended every third year, so that 1896 was the next opportunity to consider the extension of membership to Methodist New Connexion preachers. The resolution this time said:

> That this meeting having received the recommendations of the General Committee to accept the local preachers of the Methodist New Connexion as eligible for benefit membership of the Association upon the payment of the sum of fifteen

hundred pounds (£1,500), and considered the correspondence which had passed between the Rev. George Packer – the President of the Methodist New Connexion – and the General Committee, hereby agrees to the inclusion of the Local Preachers of that Connexion in the Association upon such terms, and that the Rules of the Association be altered accordingly.

The record concludes:

This resolution was carried unanimously with much enthusiasm and the Doxology was sung.

The last major extension of the membership and beneficence of LPMAA, until the Union of Methodism in 1932, came when the Methodist New Connexion, the United Methodist Free Churches and the Bible Christians amalgamated to form the United Methodist Church in 1907. As described above, local preachers of the UMFC and the MNC were already eligible for membership of LPMAA and it was not therefore a difficult matter to bring in the preachers of the Bible Christian tradition. The precedent of 1896 was followed, and an agreed sum of £3,000 was paid by the Bible Christian denomination to secure right of membership for its local preachers, some 300 of whom joined LPMAA within the first year.

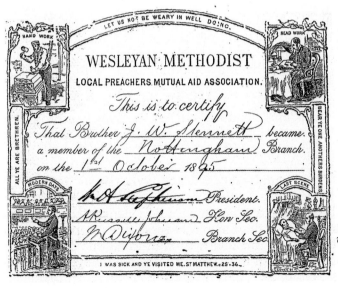

A Membership Certificate of 1895. The four corner pictures show how the role of LPMAA was perceived in the late 19th Century.

APPENDIX TO CHAPTER 12

Judge Waddy's hymn was included in the 1904 Methodist Hymn Book (Wesleyan), set to a tune called 'Ansdell'; neither the hymn nor the tune have been retained in subsequent hymn-books, but the words are given below, and the tune 'St. Merryn' (MHB 420) – with the slightest alteration at the beginning of the first and second lines – fits and suits them well.

Jesus my Shepherd my want shall supply:
Down in green pastures he makes me to lie;
He leads me beside the still waters of rest;
My soul he restores to the fold of the blest.

If from his paths I am tempted to stray,
He guards me from sin, and guides in the way;
I walk undismayed through the valley of dread,
Where darkness and death gather over my head.

Evil I fear not , for with me thou art;
Thy rod and thy staff, they comfort my heart;
Thou spreadest a table, in sight of my foes;
My head thou anointest, my cup overflows.

Goodness and mercy shall follow me still
All my life long, as my course I fulfil;
Then, Saviour, for ever, in heaven above,
With thee I shall dwell, in the home of thy love.

In the book about *The Waddy Family* by the late Rev. J. Leonard Waddy (a great-nephew of Judge Waddy), which is an important source of information about his great-uncle's life, there is reference to his having something to do with establishing the right of Non-conformist ministers to use the title 'Reverend'. David Walmsley, himself a former President of the Association (1968), a lawyer and leading citizen of Northampton, has investigated this matter in view of its unusual nature and relevance in the life of an important LPMAA figure of the past. A Wesleyan minister, Rev. Henry Keet, living near Epworth, was refused permission by the incumbent of Owston Ferry parish, Rev. George Edward Smith, to place a stone over the grave of his daughter which described her as 'the daughter of Rev. Henry Keet, Wesleyan Minister'. In June 1875 the Lincoln Diocese Consistory Court had upheld Smith's refusal, but this was overturned on appeal before the Judicial Committee of the Privy Council the following year, on the ground that the word 'reverend' is not a title of honour or dignity; a person prefixing the word to his name does not thereby claim to be a person in holy orders. A leading ecclesiastical lawyer of the day, Dr A. J. Stephens Q.C., appeared for Rev. Henry Keet. David Walmsley suggests that Samuel Waddy as

   (i)   a well-known lawyer himself
   (ii)   a prominent member and local preacher of the Wesleyan church
   (iii)   a member of Parliament for a nearby constituency

was probably asked to advise informally on the case, and secured the services of the best people to argue it. Although a layman and a local preacher, he was not willing to see the ordained ministry denigrated, and used his best offices to assist Methodism in establishing the right of its ministers to use the customary title for their calling.

13

Homes for Retired Preachers
(19th Century)

*The Need Identified • David Barr's Initiative
His Early Life, Business Career and Public Service
The Plan Fulfilled*

THE NEED IDENTIFIED

In the Association's early years it was impossible to tackle the provision of homes (or almshouses) for aged local preachers. Resources were insufficient for such expense if the more pressing needs of some members for weekly subsistence were to be met (see chapter 11). It was not at first possible even to consider the payment of superannuation allowances to elderly members who were too frail to work. The subscriptions of members would do no more than meet the necessary cost of benefit payments during illness or injury, and funeral grants when members died.

There was, however, an underlying awareness that the level of benefit the Association could afford was often only enough to cover the rent of a cottage, with little over for food and other necessaries. The idea persisted that one day something could and would be done to make a limited amount of rent-free accommodation available for those in greatest need. This chapter looks at the story of how, in the closing years of 19th century, a group of LPMAA members, realising the Association could not yet undertake this task, pursued it as a private project.

DAVID BARR'S INITIATIVE

The driving force behind the enterprise came from David Barr, J.P., a leading Wesleyan layman, a successful business-man, and a prominent public figure in Birmingham from the 1870s. He was one of many who, in various parts of the country, used their success and the wealth that it brought to serve the Wesleyan

Methodist Church, their fellow-citizens, and their brothers and sisters in Christ. Others, including William Kilner (of Yorkshire and London) and Alderman W. H. Stephenson (of Newcastle-upon-Tyne), are mentioned in chapter 12. They, like David Barr, were called to the Presidency of the Association in recognition of their achievements. Barr had been a local preacher for over thirty years before his active interest in the Association was kindled. He records in his autobiography that this happened as a result of attending the public meeting in Carr's Lane Congregational Church, Birmingham, in connection with the Aggregate Meeting of 1890.

He had been compelled to retire from business and to reduce his public commitments when only 48 (in 1879) through ill-health. He recovered sufficiently to be able to take up new business activity and seek fresh opportunities of service when in the late fifties. The Mutual Aid Association was the field in which he found those opportunities. He was elected to serve on General Committee in 1892. Through regular attendance at its meetings he became aware of the nature and extent of the hardships endured by many of his fellow-preachers. In particular, he realised that the payment of rent for house or cottage left insufficient, from the benefits paid by the Association, to meet other essential costs. As there was no likelihood of the WMLPMAA being able to deal with the problem, David Barr put his concerns and intentions into a letter to *The Methodist Recorder*. It was published on 19th December 1895. The key paragraphs were:

WORN-OUT LOCAL PREACHERS
(from Mr David Barr, 117 Hagley Road, Birmingham)

I want to brighten the eventide of some of our old local preachers, and if a few friends will assist it may easily be done. By the help of the Local Preachers Mutual Aid Association and the Necessitous Local Preachers' Fund, many of the brethren and their widows are kept from dying in the workhouse, but at present the utmost that can be given to husband and wife in time of need is 8s per week. To those that are past work and have no other income that is barely sufficient to keep them from starvation after house rent is paid.

What I want to do for such is to build a few neat cottage homes in a pleasant, healthy and central locality near a Methodist chapel, where they can enjoy the means of grace as long as they are able, with a reading room and social room attached, where they can also have fraternal intercourse to relieve the monotony of old age. I am told by an experienced architect that neat little cottage homes, including cost of land for a garden, may be built for £100 each, so that for a very moderate sum provision could be made for ten or twenty married couples.

If possible I should like sufficient money invested to yield a revenue to keep the property in repair, and supplement their income by special dole in times of urgent need. The entire scheme may be accomplished with a fund of about £3,000.

To such, especially, as owe their all to village Methodism, I appeal with confidence, and if I receive the promise of definite help, which I fully expect, I will at once take steps to organise the scheme and make such arrangements for settling the property on trust - and placing it under such control as the donors may approve.

The editor of The *Methodist Recorder* supported the thrust of Barr's letter with these observations, preceding a report of a meeting on Saturday 7th December of LPMAA General Committee.

Mr David Barr has made a proposal which seems to us both sensible and opportune . . . A sum of £3000 would suffice to do all that is immediately necessary. Mr Barr offers £200 by way of beginning. This is precisely the kind of good deed many men of means are glad to do. Everybody will agree that, if done at all, it ought to be done quickly. To let it drag on would not be gracious; to do it straight out of hand, as a Christmas gift to our dear old local preachers who have borne the heat and burden of the day, would be taken as an act of loving kindness shown to all the brethren, whether they actually need the benefaction or not. We shall be glad to publish a subscription list, or in any other way within our powers to further so excellent a suggestion.

BARR'S EARLY LIFE, BUSINESS CAREER AND PUBLIC SERVICE

At the time of David's birth (18th March 1831) the Barr family lived in the village of Fillongley, six miles north of Coventry and twelve miles east of Birmingham. He therefore planned that the preachers' cottages should be built there. His early life had led him through several occupations and places. At age 12 he worked as a baker's boy in Coventry, then with his elder brother as a shoemaker, and after that as a railway porter at Staveley during which time he contracted, and recovered from, smallpox. His only major spell away from the Midlands was from 1848 to 1851, when he secured an appointment (by advertising his services in *The Methodist Magazine*) as secretary and cashier at an hydropathic centre, near the Wesleyan Theological College in Richmond, Surrey. It was here that David Barr, as a late teenager, acquired some of the fundamental business skills that underlaid his success in later life, and enabled him to serve the Association and his needy fellow-preachers.

On returning to the Midlands he worked as a commercial traveller and married the daughter of a prominent Wesleyan layman, J. H. Newey (a 'hooks and eyes' manufacturer). Newey was strongly opposed to reform in Wesleyanism. Barr then developed a successful property-management business and became a director of the Birmingham Freehold Land Society, and Treasurer and Vice-Chairman of the Wesleyan and General Assurance. This had been formed by some Wesleyan laymen in the 1840s as the 'Wesleyan Provident Society', to provide sick-pay and funeral grants, with the intention of keeping young men away from benefit societies connected with public houses. The word 'General' was introduced later to allow members of the public to join.

His public work included Chairmanship of the Aston Local Board of Health, membership of the Aston School Board, and, significantly for the present story, he was elected a member of the Board of Guardians of the Poor for Birmingham. In Methodism he served as both Society and Circuit Steward, was representative to Conference seven times, and was a local preacher in the Belmont Row and Islington Circuits. His call to preach had come early in life. He came On Trial in the Coventry Circuit after returning from Richmond, and was fully-accredited before moving to Birmingham in 1854.

THE PLAN FULFILLED

As a result of his letter to the *Methodist Recorder*, David Barr received substantial and widespread support for the scheme. Donations came from Wesleyan ministers (Hugh Price Hughes; F. Luke Wiseman), from an M.P. (Rt. Hon. Sir Henry Fowler), from supporters all over England and Wales, and from abroad. A Trust was formed to manage the project, consisting of eleven Wesleyan laymen (six of whom were J.P.s) and a retired minister, Rev. William Harris, who as a layman had been first President of LPMAA. He had left the Wesleyan church in the 1850s to join the reform movement, subsequently becoming a minister, and was given the honour of laying the principal commemorative stone at Fillongley. Two other trustees served later as President of the Association, John Barnsley and David Barr himself. John's father, Thomas Barnsley, and David's son, A. H. Barr, were trustees.

Arrangements were made for the foundation stone-laying ceremony to take place on Saturday 27th August 1898. It may have been David Barr's personal standing in the business and civic life of Birmingham that caused the Birmingham *Daily Gazette* to take notice of the event. Advance information appeared in the issue of Tuesday 23rd August and a full report of the proceedings on Monday 29th August. The latter is particularly interesting as it gives some account of the speeches made at the after-tea meeting. Some extracts from the *Daily Gazette* reports are included as an Appendix to this chapter, to show how people perceived poverty and philanthropy at the end of 19th century. They also reveal some of the religious and social concerns of that time. It will be noticed that LPMAA is described, at most points in them, as a 'society' rather than an Association.

Building work proceeded rapidly, and by the early summer of 1899 (the Jubilee Year of LPMAA) the cottages were completed and the first seven occupants were in residence. The Aggregate Meeting of that year was held in Birmingham, John Barnsley, one of the trustees of the Fillongley Cottage Homes being elected President. It was arranged for a group of delegates to make a pastoral visit to them on Tuesday 13th June, the last day of the Aggregate.

[The Aggregate Meeting of 1993 was also held in Birmingham. It was therefore possible for a group of delegates on

Sunday 13th June, exactly 94 years later, led by the President, David Mitchell, with hosts and friends totalling 70 people, to visit the cottages (now in private ownership). There was a short act of thanksgiving for the vision of our fathers in the faith.]

The Fillongley Preachers Cottages today

Foundation stone, showing the name of William Harris, first President, with David Mitchell, President of 1993.

The aged preachers who lived in the Fillongley cottages in 1899 expressed their gratitude for the provision made for them by David Barr and the trustees in an illuminated address:

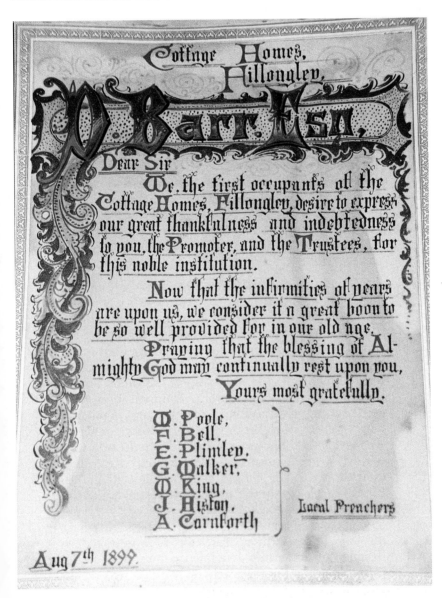

APPENDIX TO CHAPTER 13

HOMES FOR AGED LOCAL PREACHERS
(Birmingham *Daily Gazette*, 23 August 1898)

Saturday next is to see the formal inauguration of a scheme which has for two years occupied the attention of a few kindly hearts in Birmingham. It embraces the provision of a group of cottage-homes in which local preachers, worn out in the service of God and humanity, may pass in peace the eventide of life. A local preacher springs, as a rule, from the humblest walks of life, and in the course of his self-denying labours is obliged by constant demands upon his generous instincts to dip deeply into his small income. Small wonder is it that when old age makes impossible a continuance of his daily toil he who has given freely of his time and money for the good of others should suffer the pinch of poverty and be obliged in the end to seek the shelter of the workhouse.

For fifty years now the Local Preachers' Mutual Aid Society has done its utmost to spare preachers this last indignity; its annual gifts now amount to £10,000 distributed amongst 600 veterans of the pulpit. It has been the means of making glad many a home which otherwise would have been desolate. But the increasing demands upon the funds render it impossible to allocate to any claimant more than 8s per week, a sum which, after the rent is paid, is barely sufficient to keep body and soul together. It was while dealing, as a member of the Committee, with the applications made for help from this quarter that Mr David Barr, of Beech Lanes, Birmingham, one of the staunchest Wesleyans in the Midlands, conceived the happy idea of providing cottage homes for the decayed preachers. Mr Barr foresees that, with all care for rent removed, a disabled preacher may live fairly comfortably on the help which the Local Preachers' Mutual Aid Society is able to give. It is hoped that philanthropic Methodists in other parts of the country may be led to do something in the same direction. Already, indeed, a similar scheme seems to have found favour in Nottingham.

Locally a start is being made in a humble way. It is proposed to build seven self-contained cottage homes as a first instalment. With characteristic generosity Mr Barr has provided a site of half-an-acre in the healthy and pleasant district of Fillongley. This site commends itself in several ways, but its chief recommendation is that it is contiguous to one of the prettiest little village chapels it is possible to find. Here the occupants of the homes may find, without going far afield, the spiritual consolation which in days gone by others have received through them. In addition to the site, Mr Barr contributed £200 in cash towards the cost of the buildings. Mr A. H. Barr has given £100, and Rev. W. Harris, Mr C. Heap (President 1896) and Mr Thomas Barnsley have each contributed an equal sum. The site has been conveyed to a trust composed of a dozen well-known Methodist leaders, and the deed confers the right of nomination to one of the homes upon each donor of £100. Aged or necessitous local preachers (or local preachers' widows) in *any of the Methodist bodies* are eligible for election. [Philanthropy was not to be constrained by ecclesiastical boundaries.] If the scheme does not work to the satisfaction of the trustees, power is reserved in the deed to sell the property by public auction, and pay over the proceeds to the treasurer of the Local Preachers Mutual Aid Association.

HOMES FOR WORN-OUT PREACHERS
(Birmingham *Daily Gazette*, 29 August 1898)

Fillongley fits in exactly with Tennyson's conception of

> A sleepy land, where under the same wheel
> The same old rut would deepen year by year.

It is not altogether surprising, therefore, that the inhabitants should remain absolutely uninfluenced by the fact that in their midst a movement is being started from which great and far-reaching results are anticipated. Here, amid all that is reposeful and pleasant, the promoters of the cottage homes for aged local preachers, described in the 'Daily Gazette' the other day, have decided to make a start. Briefly stated, the idea is to erect seven self-contained cottage homes, where worn-out local preachers may end their days free from the care of rent, and with the advantages to be derived from the companionship of godly men.

The memorial stones of the new homes were laid on Saturday, and though Fillongley itself was not deeply moved by the event, there was sufficient enthusiasm on the part of Mr Barr and friends who accompanied him to justify the assertion that the movement is assured of success. Copious showers of rain made it desirable that the ceremony out of doors should be cut down to the shortest limit; the company afterwards sought shelter in the pretty little Wesleyan chapel close at hand, and the movement was fully discussed. The Rev. W. T. Wardle Stafford explained how it had originated in the kind heart of Mr Barr, who had long taken a keen interest in the temporal as well as the spiritual welfare of local preachers. He referred to the local preachers of today as a standing protest against sacerdotalism in every form, and said that Methodism owed a good deal more to this class of men than people were sometimes prepared to admit. The Rev. W. Harris, as President of the Local Preachers' Mutual Aid Society [the report is misleading here – Harris had been the first president, in 1849] naturally welcomed the scheme, and said he rejoiced to find the feeling growing that those who served God and their fellows should not, in their old-age, be obliged to seek the shelter of the workhouse. Mr Barr followed with a description of the work done by the Local Preachers' Mutual Aid Society.

A second meeting, held after tea, was especially noteworthy by reason of the fact that the chair was taken by Mr Joseph Blackham, a Churchman, whose liberality of mind has won for him the esteem of all the countryside. Mr Barr gave some further information anent the scheme, pointing out that the relief which the Local Preachers' Mutual Aid Society was able to give meant little more than starvation by the time the rent was paid. It was not supposed for a moment that the thing would end with the seven cottage homes at Fillongley, for the feeling was growing throughout the country that to let men starve who had done Methodism such good service throughout their lives was nothing less than a disgrace to the church. Mr Barr announced that he could already see his way to £856, but the contract had been signed, and he was personally liable for £1,255. That there was abundant sympathy with the movement was made apparent by the announcement that the collection made during the afternoon totalled up to £83 odd. In his genial optimism Mr Blackham looked forward to the day when old-age pensions shall have made it unnecessary for aged workers of any class to resort to the workhouse. He went on to refer to Nonconformity as a bulwark against Romanism, and said that in the present day there was more need than ever that Nonconformists and loyal Churchmen should stand together against the common enemy.

[This closing remark typifies sentiments often expressed in Protestant circles in the late 19th century.]

Section Three

CHANGE IN THE 20TH CENTURY

There is a sense in which the 20th century began in 1896 – in that year four things happened which changed the pattern of life significantly. They were:

- Publication of the first popular daily newspaper (following the rise in public literacy resulting from the Education Acts of 1870 and 1880)
- Transmission of the first radio signals
- The first public moving film show
- The lifting of speed restriction ('Red Flag' Act) on motor vehicles

The full impact of these developments was not experienced until the 1920s, but growth of mass media and motor transport became the distinguishing marks of the first half of the century. Simultaneously, the state was becoming more involved in the lives of its citizens by provision of services and social benefits, whilst the Christian Church found its worshipping congregations decreasing in number and size. Above all, the country was at war for ten of the years from 1914 to 1945, which had far-reaching effects on economic and social life. Change, in both attitudes and institutions, characterised this period. The Local Preachers Mutual Aid Association, like all organisations, was affected by these changes. This was the era of the expanding state and the contracting church.

143

14

The Fillongley Retirement Homes (continued)

To David Barr's Death • Problems After the 1914-18 War
An Approach to LPMAA • The End of the Cottage Homes.

To David Barr's Death

When David Barr was inducted to the Presidency of
LPMAA at the Aggregate Meeting at Bradford in 1906, three of the
occupants of the Fillongley Cottages were grateful for the
opportunity to attend. Although the project was not the result of an
official LPMAA policy intiative, it was close to the hopes of many
members, several of whom were directly involved as Trustees. *The
Local Preachers Magazine* included reports on the cottages from time
to time in the early years, in respect of both the financial position
and the occupancy.

The first meeting of the Trustees after the cottages were
occupied took place on 7th August 1899 under the chairmanship of
Thomas Barnsley. The illuminated address from the tenants
(mentioned in the previous chapter) was received, and the meeting
also noted that a sum of £217-18-2d was still needed to meet the full
cost of the project. Conditions of tenancy were agreed, and the
application of W. Poole for a tenancy was approved in place of
another applicant who had ceased to be a local preacher. By the
time of the Annual Meeting of 1901, held on 21st March,
Rev. William Harris (one of the original trustees) had died, and it
was resolved that the Superintendent Minister of the Birmingham
Islington Circuit should be a trustee in his place. Thus began a
formal link with Methodism that proved significant at a later date.

Some changes in occupation of the cottages were reported,
and a payment of £5-0-0d per annum was agreed for the services of
a local doctor to provide medical attention for the tenants. Finally
the conveyance of some additional freehold properties from David
Barr to the Trust was accepted. These would provide income to

meet rates, repairs and taxes on the Cottage Homes. The terms of the conveyance provided that if the scheme ceased, this additional property should be sold to support local Methodism.

The following year the balance due to the treasurer was still in excess of £200, and the Trust was now faced with the need for exterior re-painting of the cottages. A letter was received from the 'inmates' (a term used to describe folk who lived in a workhouse) expressing gratitude for their comfortable dwellings, Christmas gifts, and Mr Barr's regular visits. It concluded 'Yours obediently . . .' At the meeting in 1904, the Superintendent Minister took the chair. The other trustees present included David Barr, A. H. Barr and Lt. Col. John Barnsley. The annual financial statement showed the following:

Income		Expenditure	
Rents	£56-16-8d	Doctor's fee	£10-00-0d
Donation	6-10-0d	Rates, etc	5-08-4d
		Repairs/painting	13-18-4d
		Insurance	1-11-6d
	£63-06-8d		£30-18-2d

This left a revenue balance of £32-8-6d for distribution to the tenants to supplement any other income they had. At this meeting David Barr conveyed property in St. Helens to the Trust, which was currently leased to the Wesleyan and General Assurance, thereby providing additional income for maintenance of the Preachers' Cottages. The next year's meeting was chaired by John Barnsley, and one G. H. Gibson was elected a trustee, taking over the Secretaryship from A. H. Barr, who relinquished that office through ill health. David Barr made a further donation, of £25-15-7d. A Primitive Methodist local preacher from London was offered a vacant tenancy, and was joined in another tenancy the following year (1906) by James Dixon, United Methodist Free Church preacher, who is recorded in the minutes as having been a member of LPMAA for 22 years.

1910 was a sad year for the Fillongley Cottage Homes Trust, and for the tenants of the cottages, as on 9th March that year David Barr, the promoter of the enterprise, died. His last preaching appointment had been at Raunds, near Northampton, a year earlier. He had been present at the Covenant Service at Sandon Road on the first Sunday of January. On 12th March the funeral service took place there, followed by interment in Key Hill Cemetery (see footnote to chapter 7). Rev. R. A. Mitcheson Brown, as Chairman of the Fillongley Cottage Homes Trust and Superintendent Minister, gave the address, referring to the deceased's energy, toil and ability, which had gained him positions of honour and trust in commercial and civic life. He had loved work, enjoyed life and been a stalwart defender of the best traditions of Methodism, having held nearly every office open to a layman. The Annual Meeting of the Cottage Homes Trust later in 1910 appointed David's son, A. H. Barr, as Treasurer in succession to his late father.

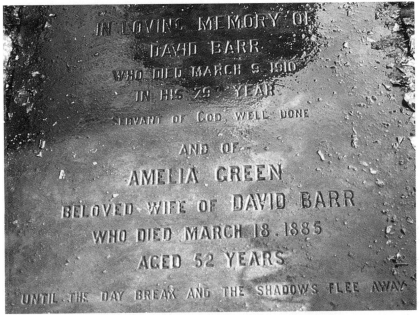

The Barr family grave (Key ~Hill Cemetery)

PROBLEMS AFTER THE 1914-18 WAR

By this time national Old Age Pensions had been introduced, and each tenant was paying a weekly rent of 4s-4d. The Trust therefore received additional income of 30s per week. In 1915 note was taken of the increase in the cost of living due to the war, and there is the first reference to the supplying of coal to tenants. Repairs were postponed because of the war. There appears to have been no further minuted meeting until March 1920, well after the conclusion of hostilities. The Superintendent

Minister, Rev. E. I. Lyndon, Sir John Barnsley, A. H. Barr, A. G. Buller, and G. H. Gibson (Secretary) were present; two important matters received attention. One was the impact of Old Age Pensions on the work of the Trust, and it was decided to liaise with LPMAA over this. The other was the appointment of new trustees. In due course nine were appointed, including G. Morley Edwards of the Barr family business, D. Gordon Barnsley, F. W. Amphlett, Henry Garner and A. E. Leeson, all well-known in Birmingham Methodism.

Monument on the Barnsley family grave (Key Hill Cemetery)

The 1921 meeting approved the use of the Reserve Fund (£144) to meet the cost of the postponed repairs. Seven applications were considered for a vacant tenancy, which was allocated to J. E. Tregurtha, of Aysgarth. A possible sale of the St. Helen's property, which was deteriorating significantly, was also discussed.

This sale was finally effected in 1927, at a price of £1,125, the proceeds being invested in 5 per cent War Stock. Other problems, which ultimately proved insoluble, were beginning to affect the Trust's affairs. Repairs costing £325 in 1925 left a balance on the reserve account of only £63-14-4d. There were changes in the office of Treasurer in 1923, 1925 and 1926, further deaths reduced the number of trustees, and it was proving more difficult to find tenants for cottages as they fell vacant. The meeting of the Trust in 1925 decided to write to W. J. Back, then the senior Honorary Secretary of LPMAA, to seek his help in securing nominations for two vacant homes. It appears that national Old Age Pensions were making it possible for more folk, including local preachers and their dependants, to continue living in their own homes during retirement. A further decision was therefore made, to initiate consultations with A. H. Barr about the possibility of handing the Cottages over to LPMAA.

By 1927, the Trust had an adverse balance of £89-15-3d, and although a local preacher from Walsall Wood had recently taken up a tenancy, it was decided to advertise vacancies in Methodist newspapers. During this period of difficulty the Trustees had been assisted by regular gifts of between £20 and £35 annually from A. H. Smith in South Africa, a relative of the late David Barr. In 1929 they wrote to him asking for money towards the building of a washhouse. They also agreed to offer a tenancy to a Baptist, in order to obtain rent income from an otherwise empty cottage. Nevertheless, the bank overdraft remained high, reaching £92-11-6d in 1930. One of the tenants, Mr Reynolds, undertook to act as rent collector. He was receiving an allowance from LPMAA, but this was deemed not to conflict with the established policy that tenants could not continue to occupy a cottage if they were receiving 'outdoor relief'.

During the 1930s the difficulties intensified. Electricity supply to the cottages was a high priority, but the capital outlay could not be met. A special meeting of the Trust in June 1932 resolved to sell some or all of the cottages, though this decision was rescinded before it could be implemented. Further help from Mr Smith in South Africa, some rent increases, and the sale of £125 worth of stock made clearance of the overdraft possible in 1933, but more repairs and improvements created a fresh overdraft of nearly £200, which could only be liquidated by the sale of stock in 1934. The Trust had a small credit balance in each of the next two years, and the coal allocation to the residents (not now 'inmates') was increased from 8 to 9 hundredweights. By the beginning of 1938 two of the longest-serving trustees (Amphlett and Gibson) had died. A detailed report on the current situation was prepared by the honorary secretary of the time, B. K. Parry, at the end of that year.

This began with an unequivocal statement of his intention to resign from his position: 'I am far too busy with other voluntary work to be able to continue.' The substance of the report, however, suggests a situation with which he might not have wished to be associated any longer. He had visited the preachers' homes a score of times during the year and was thus able to report on the problems from first-hand knowledge. First of them was water supply and sewage disposal. Local Authority pressure was anticipated in respect of both. The adequacy of the well to meet increasing demand, especially in dry years, was in doubt, and the need to link the Cottage Homes to a sewerage system, then being constructed in the area, would arise eventually. The Secretary also drew attention to the urgency of proceeding with the installation of electric lighting on safety grounds. He pointed out that to implement these improvements the Trustees would have either to borrow heavily or to make inroads into revenue-producing capital. The report referred also to the need to spend substantially on some of the Trust's other properties.

On residents, the Secretary mentioned the good work being done at the village chapel by one particular local preacher. He noted that the widow of another was receiving a weekly allowance of 7s 6d from LPMAA, but then stressed the difficulty of finding new tenants. Advertisement in *The Local Preachers Magazine* had attracted only one suitable application. Consequently two cottages were occupied by non-Methodists, who were not eligible for financial help from either LPMAA or the Necessitous Local Preachers' Fund. He doubted whether it was legal for them to have been offered tenancies, and questioned the future need for the Preachers' Cottages, in the light of National Insurance Schemes and the activity of LPMAA. The whole position of the Trust in the enormously changed conditions of the time should therefore be seriously discussed.

Mr Parry recalled that there had been a proposal some years ago to ascertain whether LPMAA would take over the Trust. The anomalous position of the Fillongley Chapel as a remote outpost of the Birmingham Islington Circuit, once large and wealthy, was also highlighted and its possible transfer to a Coventry or Nuneaton Circuit anticipated. The care of local preachers living in the Cottage Homes would then no longer be the concern of the Islington Branch of LPMAA.   Copies of the report were being sent to the Superintendent of the Circuit, and to Messrs G. Morley Edwards and L. E. Harper, the only trustees whose addresses he had. He would hand the Minute and Account Books to Mr Edwards, and was prepared to attend the next meeting of the Trust to give any further information required.

Before any action was taken on these matters war broke out, and the affairs of the Fillongley Cottage Homes Trust appear to have gone unrecorded throughout the war years.   A single auditor's certificate of February 1949 covers the years 1940 to 1948. The usual items of income and expenditure were included, with an exceptional extra payment (£8 per annum) for war damage insurance contributions and, in 1948, a donation of £100 to the Fillongley Chapel Trustees. It appears that the Fillongley society had been neglected during the war. Following the agreement of the Islington Circuit Local Preachers' and Quarterly Meetings, consultation with the Superintendent of the Coventry Circuit resulted in the transfer of the chapel and the membership to Coventry in June 1946.

An Approach to LPMAA

From this point, if not before, it was inevitable that the Cottages would be sold and the Trust wound up.   The chairmanship of the Trust remained with the Islington Superintendent, who under the Deed was ex-officio a trustee, but since the transfer of Fillongley Methodism to the Coventry Circuit he wished to see the matter brought to a speedy conclusion. After the transfer to Coventry, a leading LPMAA figure from that circuit, Charles Weatherall, accepted appointment as Treasurer to the Cottage Trust in 1950.   He served as President of LPMAA in 1952-53.   One of his colleagues on the Association's General Committee as well as on the Fillongley Cottage Trust was Miss Lorna Shirley Smith, of Birmingham, only the second woman to serve on General Committee and the first to have been nominated for the Presidency, although not elected.   They were both very much involved in the negotiations between LPMAA and the

Cottage Trust about the possibility of the Cottage Homes being taken into the work of Mutual Aid.

Through the 1950s, attention was directed almost exclusively towards property matters, in anticipation of eventual disposal of the cottages and the Trust's other properties. Heavy repair bills led to an overdraft of £334 by 1952. This had risen by 1954 to £491 as a result of the building of modern lavatories. In February 1956 the Trust met and decided to sell the property; the proceeds (under the provisions of the Trust Deed) would be received for the Local Preachers Mutual Aid Association. The situation was complex, however. Four of the cottages were let at 12s 1d per week rent to tenants who had been accommodated after the Coventry air-raid in 1940. These enjoyed the protection of Rent Acts. The other three cottages were occupied rent-free under the terms of the Trust. One was occupied by a very elderly local preacher, and the other two by widows of local preachers. The concern was that any purchaser would probably turn out these three, who were not protected tenants, in order to sell the cottages with vacant possession or let them to other tenants.

In a statement to LPMAA, the Trustees expressed strong feeling that they should transfer the cottages to the Association so that the local preacher and preachers' widows could be looked after. Charity Commissioners' approval would be needed but legal advice was that this would most probably be given. The suggestion was also made that all three might be accommodated in one of the (then) three Mutual Aid Homes, leaving the way clear for the sale of the whole property. The Secretary of the Trust (H. C. Holt, Esq., of Cartwright & Son, Chartered Surveyors, Auctioneers and Estate Agents, Coventry) wrote to Miss Shirley Smith setting out reasons why LPMAA should accept the cottages. He enquired specifically whether the Association would accommodate the three unprotected tenants if the properties were sold. His services were available if LPMAA accepted the properties and subsequently wished to dispose of them.

Correspondence then passed between the General Secretary of LPMAA and the Fillongley Trust's Solicitors (Shirley Smith and Son, the firm headed at that time by Miss Shirley Smith's brother). The Association's Finance Committee was given opportunity to inspect the original Fillongley Trust Deed, but the Solicitor pointed out that the decision to wind-up the Trust had been made and that the Trustees could only act within the terms of the Deed. LPMAA had to decide whether to take the properties as they were, with the tenants. If the decision was made not to do so, the Trustees would be obliged to sell at auction, leaving the three unprotected tenants at risk of eviction.

An additional minor difficulty existed in the form of the Trust's bank overdraft (see above). It was unclear whether the Association would have to accept responsibility for this. The matter was considered at a meeting of the Finance-Sub Committee on 9th April 1956. Both Charles Weatherall and Lorna Shirley Smith wrote to the General Secretary prior to the meeting to supply information about the Cottages and the occupants. Two were members of LPMAA, the third a widow annuitant. Incidental comments in their letters reveal some of the tensions of the time:

> I think it would be disastrous if Bro. Reynolds and Mrs Calow were turned adrift. It's about time some of the members of Mutual Aid Homes Ltd got a realistic view of the Association and the increasing difficulty of presenting its claims. (C. Weatherall)

> It would be so bad for the name of the Association if after all our protestations of care for the aged in general, we were harsh to three in particular. Our detractors would make such a lot out of it!!! (E. L. Shirley-Smith)

THE END OF THE COTTAGE HOMES

Following the Finance Sub-Committee meeting, the General Secretary circulated a report of its deliberations to all members of the Finance and General Purposes Committee, with recommendations that the Fillongley Trust be asked to sell the properties by auction, and that they should be bought at the auction for Mutual Aid Homes Ltd. Several Finance and General Purpose Committee members raised objections to this course of action, expressing concern about establishing precedents, pointing out the need to consider carefully and not rush, questioning legal obligations and the role of the Charity Commissioners, etc. Miss Shirley Smith observed that in the original deed David Barr had provided for all eventualities except two world wars! She strongly favoured proceeding immediately. The matter was considered by

General Committee, and by 3rd May the General Secretary was able to advise the Secretary of the Cottage Homes Trust that the Association was ready to purchase the cottages at auction, for the sake of the three occupants for whom it had some reponsibility.

By the Autumn the property was still unsold, but the situation had changed in that one of the tenants had died and it was thought that a second had moved to other accommodation. The Honorary Secretary reported to the General Committee on 13th October 1956 that he had received no communication from Mutual Aid Homes on that subject. He advised the passing of a resolution affirming the Committee's agreement to the sale of the properties by auction. There would have to be satisfactory arrangements for the sole remaining tenant, and a limit to the amount of bank over-draft for which the Association would be responsible.

It was not, however, until 7th February 1959 that General Committee could be informed that the sale had been completed, and final accounts were then accepted. The thanks of the Committee were conveyed to Miss Shirley Smith and her brother for their help in bringing the business to a satisfactory conclusion. Charles Weatherall advised that he had despatched a cheque for £2972-3-4d from the Fillongley Trust, and a letter of thanks was sent to him and his co-trustees for their patience and assistance. The cheque was received on 3rd March 1959, and for LPMAA the matter was closed.

The proceeds from the sale of the Fillongley Trust's other properties were later paid to the Methodist Church Trustees. At three further meetings the Trustees agreed the winding-up arrangements, received Charity Commissioners' approval for the transfer of their assets and responsibilities to the Superintendent and Circuit Stewards of the Coventry Circuit and disbanded the Trust (16th June 1960). Charles Weatherall and Lorna Shirley-Smith were present at the final meeting, so that through some of its leading members, LPMAA was involved at the end as at the beginning of the Fillongley saga.

15

The Effects of Public Policy

New Days – New Ways • Before 1914
National Insurance and LPMAA • The Inter-War Period;
The 'Post-Beveridge' Era.

NEW DAYS – NEW WAYS

The history of the Fillongley Local Preachers' Cottage Homes, summarised in the two preceding chapters, illustrates well how philanthropic enterprises of any kind had to adapt their activities to social, economic and political changes in the first half of the 20th century. Expectations also played an important part in the process of adaptation. What had been acceptable in 1900 was less acceptable by the 1930s; after the 1939-45 war expectations in all areas of life were totally different from those of half-a-century earlier. Fillongley can be seen as a microcosm of all this, and similar influences were at work in the history of LPMAA during the same period. Social change, economic progress and developing public policy all affected the way the Association evolved to meet the needs of its members and their dependants. The role of the State expanded, and the general level of prosperity increased steadily.

In the last quarter of the 19th century many Friendly Societies were, in effect, paying old-age pensions to eligible members in the form of long-term sickness payments. This liability had not been taken into account in determining subscription levels. [LPMAA was helped to meet this outlay by the donations of Honorary Members, and by collections at meetings and services.] It was recognised that there were growing numbers of old people who did not have any means of support and who had to turn to the local workhouse. Various ideas were put forward, both by individuals and official committees, to deal with the situation in which many Friendly Societies therefore found themselves. Many of their members could not afford the higher subscriptions necessary to provide an annuity as well as sick pay and a funeral grant. The suggestions made fell into three main categories:

(i)   that people should be required by law to contribute towards a pension
(ii) that State aid should be available to everyone who wished to contribute for a pension
(iii) that the State should assume total responsibility

For some years Friendly Societies, co-operatives and trade unions opposed State involvement, fearing that it would undermine their role and loosen members' control of their savings. This delayed the introduction of state pensions in this country. (They already existed in some countries; for example, New Zealand, Denmark, Germany). However, the need for this kind of provision was being noted and talked about publicly; for example, the Birmingham *Daily Gazette*, in its coverage of the Fillongley Cottages stone-laying ceremony on 27th August 1898, reported the reference to old-age pensions by Joseph Blackham (see Appendix to chapter 13).

Friendly Societies had been given some support by an Act of 1894, which authorised Guardians of the Poor, when considering applications for relief, to disregard benefits up to 5s (25p) per week paid by Friendly Societies. This amount, equivalent perhaps to one-eighth of an average week's wage at that time, would have gone some way towards necessary living expenses. Associations like LPMAA were well aware that it would not meet the whole cost of living. David Barr's perception of this, as explained in the Fillongley Cottages chapters (13 and 14) was what motivated him to initiate the provision of rent-free accommodation for aged local preachers.

BEFORE 1914

At this time, several prominent Wesleyan laymen were Members of Parliament, chiefly as Liberals. Their party was committed to a range of social policies which, when implemented, changed dramatically the context in which Friendly Societies operated. Their concerns also extended more widely. John Bamford Slack (LPMAA President, 1894) was elected Honorary Secretary in 1902. The following year he was unexpectedly returned to Parliament as Member for Mid-Hertfordshire and relinquished the Honorary Secretaryship in 1904. During his short Parliamentary career he promoted a Bill to enfranchise women, asserting that voting was not a privilege but a right. It did not reach the Statute Book, and its objective was only partly achieved in 1918, an indication of how far ahead of his time he was. He was knighted in 1906, having lost his seat in the General Election of January that year. His party was, however, returned with a large majority, and embarked upon a programme of far-reaching social legislation. Amongst other needs addressed were those of working men who did *not* have Friendly Society or trade union support, but inevitably this affected men who were members of such bodies.

A Royal Commission to consider the operation of the Poor Law had been set up in 1904, before the return of a Liberal Government in 1906. It did not report until 1909, but its work encouraged both the public expression of views about poverty, its causes and cure, and the collection of information on the subject. The Liberal Government did not wait for the Commission's Report, but presented Bills to Parliament dealing with what it perceived as the most pressing needs. Some of these related particularly to the care and education of children, but in 1908 legislation was enacted to provide an old-age pension of 5s per week for people aged 70 and over. This came into operation at the beginning of 1909. Pensions were paid out of taxation, there being insufficient time to create the administrative structures for a contributory scheme; the matter was judged too urgent for delay.

It was also to be means tested, and it was this provision that made Old Age Pensions significant for friendly and benevolent societies such as LPMAA. Having exercised an active concern for the needs of its members in old age for over half a century, the Association approved of State support for the elderly poor. It was, however, keen to ensure that any members who were eligible for an Old Age Pension should receive their entitlement in full. As Friendly Society benefits were taken into account in assessing a pensioner's means, an LPMAA annuity might result in a member losing some or all of the old-age Pension and thus be no better off.

This situation was in effect a signpost for the way the Association would move in the 20th century. Previously the principal aim had been to ensure that no member would need to seek poor relief or admission to a workhouse, or at death be buried in a pauper's grave. From 1909, when state-funded pensions became available to people over 70 years of age, the emphasis gradually shifted towards meeting needs with which public provision did not deal adequately. In *A Goodly Fellowship* Harold Buss summarised the immediate action that was taken:

> All the Branch secretaries and annuitants were circularised and where necessary the Association's allowances were reduced in order that the full amount of the national pension might be claimed.

The consequence, in the first year, was a reduction of nearly £1,000 (approximately 10 per cent) in the total amount paid in annuities, but some increase in sickness benefit to younger members soon absorbed this saving. More significantly, it was quickly realised that, even when state allowances met essential material need, the needs for personal support, practical help and pastoral care were just as great as ever. These needs were recognised as a continuing component of mutual aid, and members were urged to provide them, as officers of Government departments could not do so. This concept was explicit in the arrangements for the payment of benefits to other large groups of people under the next major piece of social legislation.

The National Insurance Act of 1911 became effective at the beginning of 1912. Part 1 of this Act dealt with benefit payments related to ill-health and disability, and these were made through Friendly Societies, trade unions and insurance companies, collectively termed Approved Societies. Their tried and tested methods were preferred as the avenue for paying health insurance benefits, because they provided a more personal, caring service than the State could give. The difficulties this presented for LPMAA are examined below. Part 2 of the Act introduced compulsory unemployment insurance for workers in a number of basic industries. The cost of benefits under both parts of the Act was met by contributions from workers, employers and the State. Lloyd George guided Part 1 of the 1911 Act through Parliament, and Winston Churchill Part 2, making Britain the first country to have unemployment insurance.

NATIONAL INSURANCE AND LPMAA

As soon as the Bill was presented in Parliament it was apparent that a difficult decision would confront the Mutual Aid Association. It did not identify with the fierce opposition expressed in some quarters to the whole concept of the extension of State welfare provision, but could not avoid some anxiety about its effects on the Association's work, indeed on the basis of its existence. The situation and its outcome are fully described by Harold Buss in chapter 6 of *A Goodly Fellowship*. The core issue was the place of Approved Societies in the scheme. To become 'approved', and thereby the channel through which its members would receive their benefits, LPMAA would have to come under the provisions of the Act. The 1911 Aggregate Meeting debated the desirability of this course of action, although shortage of time and the importance of the matter precluded an immediate decision. It thus became the only Aggregate in history to be adjourned, in order to resolve the question at a later date.

The date for the resumption was eventually fixed for 9th March 1912. The General Committee met twice after the National Insurance Act came into effect on 1st January, to decide its advice to the Aggregate and approve the necessary resolutions for submission to the reconvened meeting. On 18th January the Honorary Secretaries recommended that the Association should not seek to become an Approved Society under the Act, but should continue so far as possible in its present form. An amendment to form an Approved Society was rejected, after prolonged debate, securing support from only one-third of members present. On 17th February the Committee agreed resolutions to be proposed at the Aggregate Meeting, the most significant being the necessary discontinuation of the category of Benefit Member. Existing Benefit Members would continue to enjoy their privileges (subscription rates and benefits), but no new Benefit Members could be accepted. In future, local preacher members would be called Ordinary Members and be able to receive benefit only by proving need, not as a right in virtue of membership.

The Aggregate heard the arguments in favour of this course of action from the Honorary Secretary, William J. Back. Government control, administrative complications, competition with other Approved Societies, and the effects of State regulation on voluntary advocacy and charitable giving were all presented. The amendment to form an Approved Society was moved, as in General Committee, by A. J. Cash, of Derby, a lawyer who later represented the United Methodist Church in negotiations leading to Methodist Union. The amendment was again defeated. Members of LPMAA were encouraged to join an Approved Society in order to receive State benefits when eligible, but only a small number left the Association. An interesting addendum to this part of Mutual Aid history is that it was not until 1993, after the last surviving Benefit Member had died, that all reference to that category was removed from the rules.

THE INTER-WAR PERIOD

The first half of the 1920s was unusually busy with General Elections. On 15th November 1922 a Conservative majority was returned to the House of Commons, on 6th December 1923 the Conservatives remained the largest party but did not have a majority over the combined Liberal and Labour seats, and on 29th October 1924 the Conservatives regained the control they had held before the 1923 election. The Mutual Aid Association's leaders kept a close watch on these developments, as well as following the fortunes of the many local preachers who stood as candidates on behalf of the several parties. A brief reference in the July magazine report of the 1923 Aggregate indicates the particular ground of this interest in the political affairs of that time:

> The limitations of the Old Age Pensions Act were keenly felt, but . . . attempts to obtain the removal of the restrictions have not been successful.

In the January 1924 magazine William Back (then sole Honorary Secretary) commented in his *Obiter Dicta*:

> It may be that the political changes consequent on the results of the election will lead to some modification of the Pensions Act, for at least the Liberal and the Labour Parties are pledged to a change. Such a change is overdue, not in the way of a larger pension, but in enabling philanthropic societies . . . to do more without jeopardising the full State pension . . .

The editor's observations on the political scene the following month were made under the title 'The Triangle Parliament'; he referred also to Methodist local preachers in the nation's leadership. In March he was able to comment optimistically on the probability of the removal of the income limit upon pension eligibility, thus enabling the Association to increase its help to elderly members. To do this would require an increase in resources. This focused attention on the effect of the 'Envelope

System' of giving, then being widely-adopted by Methodist congregations. It resulted in reduced contributions to LPMAA when only the 'loose cash' element of collections was given to the Association.

The long-awaited change in old-age pension arrangements was announced in the Budget in the Spring of 1924. By late summer the Bill was through Parliament, and the Honorary Secretary commented in the August magazine that although the income limit had not been removed, the higher level meant the Association could increase its grants. Also, some members who could not have applied previously would now be able to do so. He was concerned lest the impression might be given that the Association would be able to reduce its expenditure. The opposite was the case, and in September he emphasised again the need to use all possible avenues for increasing membership and income. In October he drew attention to the need for greater expenditure on the pre-1912 category of Benefit Members who were needing more help through age and sickness. Under an Act of 1925 contributory pensions were introduced, payable to an insured worker at the age of 65 and, should the situation arise, to his widow. This also provided that at the age of 70 transfer would be made to the 1908 non-contributory scheme, and the means test under that scheme was discontinued.

THE 'POST-BEVERIDGE' ERA

Price inflation during the early months of the 1939-45 war led to the introduction of supplementary pensions to protect the purchasing power of old-age pensioners. The implications for LPMAA were similar to those that followed the introduction of old-age pensions in 1908. A limit of 7s 6d (37p) was set for weekly allowances from Friendly Societies if a pensioner was to remain eligible for the full supplementary pension. (This limit was later raised to 10s 6d.) LPMAA had to comply, but naturally looked for alternative ways of meeting members' needs which would not prejudice their entitlement to State aid. The idea of giving single lump-sum grants to meet specific need, for example, the provision of urgently-needed domestic equipment, replacement of worn-out footwear or clothing, or a contribution to the cost of a convalescent holiday after illness, was adopted. The 1943 Aggregate Meeting, at Nottingham, approved the rule-change needed to allow this new method of support. Other changes made dependent relatives of deceased members, in addition to widows, eligible for assistance. The amounts payable to Benefit Members were also raised – 1,600 of them were still alive, having been in membership of LPMAA before 1912.

While the Association was developing this response to the introduction of Supplementary Pensions, the Beveridge Report on Social Insurance and Allied Services was published (late 1942). Some details about Sir William Beveridge, the background to and the results of the Report are given in Appendix 2 to this chapter. Although it was not warmly received by politicians or by his fellow civil servants, it caught the public imagination, and proved to be a major influence on the social legislation of the immediate post-war years (Appendix 1). The Acts of 1946 provided, on a compulsory and contributory basis, for unemployment, sickness and disablement benefits, and for universal old-age pensions. The Poor Law was abolished and National Assistance, later called 'supplementary benefit', was introduced to replace it in 1948. The involvement of voluntary associations in the administration of State benefits ceased, and Approved Societies were discontinued.

It is not surprising that, following this massive extension of public support for unemployed, sick and retired people, LPMAA and similar bodies experienced a gradual decline in the numbers needing traditional forms of financial help. This was emphasised by the eventual disappearance of the pre-1912 Benefit Members and by the continuing slow decrease in the membership of the Methodist Church and in the number of local preachers. In the Centenary Year (1949) there were nearly 1,400 beneficiaries, and local preacher membership was just over 13,000. By the late 1990s these figures had fallen to about 100 and 8,000 respectively. There were, of course, nearly another 100 members and dependants resident in the five LPMAA Homes (see chapter 33). What did appear was that when need arose it was just as serious as it always had been, but that the causes were now often quite different.

Younger preachers facing difficulties stemming from unemployment or family breakdown, some in middle age confronted with redundancy, others afflicted with disabling illnesses and needing more help to cope than is available – these are examples of need for which LPMAA has been able to provide personal and financial support. This has sometimes enabled the preachers concerned to continue serving as preachers.

The Association continued to keep a watchful eye on changes in public policy and the implications for its beneficiaries. This is illustrated by events in 1974, when the officers wrote to the Minister for Social Security about the effect of the very small amount of other income that was disregarded for the payment of supplementary benefit. The amount of the disregard was increased to £4 towards the end of 1974. The General Committee, ever prudent, took £1.50 as an initial guide-line, approving allowances up to £4 in special cases. This has, of course, been considerably increased to take account of continuing inflation and further changes in Social Security regulations over the years.

The latest change in public policy is to enable and encourage people to live in their own homes to an older age, rather than seek residential care away from their families, friends and neighbourhood. For LPMAA this is opening up opportunities for personal mutual aid on a 'live-at-home' basis, leading to residence in an LPMAA Home when, but not until, that becomes the only meaningful option.

APPENDIX 1 TO CHAPTER 15

Some of the More Important Social Legislation and Reports of the First Half of 20th Century

Before 1914:
1908 Old-Age Pensions Act (non-contributory; means tested) 5s per week maximum for people over 70.
1909 Report of the Commission on Poor Law published. Recommended development of other forms of aid, and phasing out of Poor Law, with Local Authorities taking over Poor Law administration in the interim period. (This was enacted in 1929, Boards of Guardians of the Poor ceasing from that time).
1911 National Insurance Act.
       Pt. 1 – Health Insurance (sickness and disability benefit, et al) covered all workers earning less than £160 p.a. Men could receive 10s per week, women 7s 6d, for up to thirteen weeks, then 5s per week for thirteen weeks more. Administered through Approved Societies (i.e. Friendly Societies, trade unions, and similar bodies).

Pt. 2 – Unemployment Insurance (Britain was the first country to introduce this) applied to seven most vulnerable occupations, cost being shared between workers, employers and the State. A minimum of 26 weeks' contribution gave 15 weeks' unemployment pay at 7s per week.

Between the Wars:
1919   Income limit for health insurance raised to £250. [By 1939 this had been further raised to £420. Almost all workers were then included, but not dependants.]
1920   Unemployment Insurance Act. Extended coverage to all workers except domestic servants, civil servants, and farm workers. In 1921 dependants were included.
        [Later Acts introduced transitional benefits to avoid poor relief, and made them means-tested and administered by Local Authorities. An Unemployment Assistance Board became responsible for transitional benefits, in place of Local Authority Public Assistance Committees.]
1925   Widows, Orphans and Old Age Contributory Pensions Act. Provided 10s per week for the insured and widow at age 65. At 70 transfer was made to the non-contributory scheme of 1908, but without means test.

After 1939:
1940   Supplementary Pensions introduced because of war-time inflation. Administration was given to the former Unemployment Assistance Board, now simply Assistance Board.
1942   Report on Social Insurance and Allied Services (see Appendix 2, on Beveridge).
1945   Family Allowances Act (enacted before 1945 General Election). Applied to second and subsequent children.
1946   National Insurance Act and National Insurance (Industrial Injuries) Act. Provided, on compulsory basis, unemployment, sickness and disablement benefits, and old-age pensions. Approved Societies discontinued.
1948   National Assistance Act. Abolished the Poor Law, and created a National Assistance Board. (National Assistance was later re-styled 'supplementary benefit'.)

APPENDIX 2 TO CHAPTER 15.

Sir William Beveridge and the Inter-Departmental Report on 'Social Insurance and Allied Services'.

William Beveridge was born in India in 1879, his father being in the Indian Civil Service. William was educated as a boarder at schools in England, including Charterhouse, from which he went as an exhibitioner to Balliol College, Oxford, in 1897. After graduation and a brief period studying law in London, he was awarded a prize fellowship at University College, Oxford, becoming a Batchelor of Civil Law in 1903. This was followed by two years as sub-warden of Toynbee Hall, in East London, at a time when social problems were coming to the forefront of political thinking. During these years Beveridge came under the influence of Fabian socialists Sidney and Beatrice Webb, who later introduced him to Winston Churchill. He became convinced that social policies should be based on rigorous study of social problems, and in 1905 took a post as writer on this subject with a leading newspaper. Many of his articles concentrated on unemployment, arguing that a combination of labour exchanges and state insurance was the best practical solution to the problem. Much of his thinking was embodied in *Unemployment: a Problem of Industry*, published in 1909 shortly after he had been appointed by Churchill as his personal assistant at the Board of Trade, to work on the legislation which eventually formed Part 2 of the National Insurance Act, 1911.

Becoming a permanent civil servant in 1909, Beveridge held senior positions at the Board of Trade, the Ministry of Munitions and the Ministry of Food. He was knighted in 1919 and soon afterwards took up the Directorship of the London School of Economics, a post he held for 18 years, during which he developed it into a leading world centre for the study of social sciences. From 1926 to 1928 he was Vice-Chancellor of London University. Controversy and conflict had accompanied some of his activities in the Civil Service, especially during the 1914-18 War, and this continued in his academic career. He was committed to empirical methods rather than abstract speculation, believing that society's problems would be solved by discovering objective socio-economic laws. His strongly-held view that academics should not identify with political parties or ideologies was the root of his differences with some of his distinguished colleagues. In 1937 he left LSE to become Master of University College, Oxford.

By the outbreak of the 1939-45 War, Sir William had returned to the view he had held before 1914, that substantial state intervention was necessary to deal with social and economic problems, and he anticipated being appointed to a senior post in the direction of the nation's war effort. Eventually, in December 1940, he was appointed to such a position in the Ministry of Labour, but was very soon diverted to the chairmanship of an inter-departmental inquiry into social services post-war. He perceived this as an opportunity to shape the future of British society and consulted widely and deeply on issues such as unemployment, health care, poverty and the special needs of childhood and old-age. When it was published at the end of 1942, the report met with a cool response from both civil servants and politicians, but was so popular with the public that over 70,000 copies were sold in the first few days. Its imagery made a great impact.

Beveridge identified five 'giants', two kinds of freedom, three methods, three assumptions and six principles. Freedom, he contended, had been seen largely as freedom to do things – to vote, to speak, to worship, and so on. He wanted more emphasis on freeing people from things –hence the 'giants' of want, disease, ignorance, squalor, idleness. His methods were:

    (i) Social Insurance, to provide basic needs
    (ii) National Assistance, to deal with special cases
    (iii) Voluntary Insurance, to provide above basic level

All this assumed a National Health Service, universal children's allowances, and full employment. The underlying principles of the Beveridge recommendations were that both insurance contributions and benefits should be at a standard flat-rate, there should be unified administration (one Government department), that benefits should be at adequate subsistence level, the plan should be comprehensive, and the population classified by risk.

Although the Beveridge report on Social Insurance had not been well-received by politicians of any party, the thinking in it was a major influence on the social welfare legislation of the first post-war Labour Government. Sir William was created a peer in 1946, but did not hesitate to attack what he perceived as shortcomings in the legislation. He was very critical of the decision to exclude voluntary agencies (for example Friendly Societies), hitherto known as *approved societies*, from the administration of state insurance. In 1948 he published *Voluntary Action*, a vigorous defence of the role of the voluntary sector in social welfare, perhaps doubting the effectiveness of the welfare bureaucracy that his report had helped to create. [The same doubt motivated LPMAA members to maintain their Association and to adapt its provision to meet needs that fell outside the scope of the welfare bureaucracy.]

16

War and Peace

The War of 1914-18 • When Will It End ? • Between The Wars
War Again (1939 - 1945) • Peace At Last.

THE WAR OF 1914-18

The previous chapter reviewed the effects of developing public policy upon LPMAA. All voluntary societies engaged in self-help had to adapt to the legislation by which the welfare state was gradually created. The impact of world war was also of great significance for the Association, because of the loss of members in the conflict, and because of the acceleration it caused in the change of attitudes towards religion. These changes affected Methodism as a whole, and other branches of the Church as well. The expansion of the state and the contraction of the Church took place in parallel. The Report of General Committee to the last peacetime Aggregate (June 1914) focused this dimension in the following sentences:

> The Total Membership of the Association . . . is 12,185 – a Net Decrease of 223, or 1.8 per cent. Your Committee deeply regrets the necessity of reporting a decrease, but deems it only fair to point out that it coincides, and very closely corresponds, with the decrease reported by the Methodist Churches in their Connexional Membership; and, moreover, that the great number of Methodist emigrants [referred to earlier in the report] probably includes a larger percentage of Local Preachers, and young men who might be expected shortly to become Local Preachers, than is found in the ranks of the Home Churches.

When the first wartime Aggregate assembled (Plymouth, June 1915) it received the Annual Report of General Committee which repeated some of these points. The number of Benefit Members had decreased by 431, whilst the Ordinary Membership category had increased by only 274, resulting in a drop of 157 in total local preacher membership. Honorary Member recruitment (which may then have included some local preachers) had improved. The Committee alluded to the diminishing membership of the Methodist Churches and the continuing decrease in the number of local preachers, declaring the position of the Association to be 'not unsatisfactory', but went on to state:

> Not one-half of the local preachers in the three Churches which form the constituency of the Association have joined us . . . No young man should be admitted to Full Plan without being invited to join.

In other parts of the Report, the Committee struck a more positive and optimistic note, identifying LPMAA with all churches and charitable bodies who bear heavy burdens of anxiety and responsibility during war. In the light of the need to maintain the level of allowances to the Association's beneficiaries, it was possible to record with profound thankfulness to God and the Methodist people that :

> . . . fears of a largely diminished income were unwarranted, and that, notwithstanding the innumerable appeals, public and private, national, ecclesiastical, and philanthropic, and in face of heavy losses sustained in consequence of the War by many of our people, the income of the association has been substantially maintained, and the income from Public Collections considerably increased.

Doubtless this underpinned the decision, mentioned in the Report, that members of LPMAA who joined His Majesty's Forces should not be removed from membership if their subscriptions lapsed during the war,. The question of remitting any arrears which accumulated whilst on active service would be dealt with after the war.

Sunshine and shadow again characterised the Annual Report in 1916 The Aggregate Meeting was held at Liverpool, and assembled for a second time 'under the sombre shadow of War' as the Report put it. Nevertheless, it affirmed that LPMAA was 'more solidly grounded in the confidence and affection' of Methodism than it ever had been. It paid tribute to the progress of the work in the Liverpool District, acknowledging the diligent and successful labours of the local workers . As in the previous year, reference was made to the financial demands of the war effort and explicitly to the innumerable claims of war charities. The Committee was happy that its fears about possible adverse effects on 'Connexional and semi-Connexional funds' had proved groundless. The Association's finances were in a more satisfactory state than for several years in spite of continuing, if gradual, reduction in membership. On the linked issues of members and money two particular points were again emphasised:

(1) Thousands of Local Preachers are at this moment serving in His Majesty's Forces, and many hundreds of young men who might reasonably be expected, under other circumstances, to be entering our ranks are devoting their energies to the defence of their country.

(2) There are thousands of Local Preachers in our three Churches who have not yet joined the Association.

The Report went on to press the need for recruiting Honorary Members, whose subscription in those days was the customary charitable guinea (£1-1s), five times the Ordinary (Local Preachers) Member subscription. In many cases local officers had neglected to collect these guineas, and Honorary Members had thus lapsed. Whilst asking for greater care over this matter the Committee commended a plan which had been found useful in some Branches, the enlistment of ladies as collectors. When the Report turned to the payments side of the accounts, the importance of controlling expenditure was stressed:

> To this end the Committee urges the regular holding of Branch Meetings, to which all expenditure should be reported, and the effective maintenance of our system of Sick Visitation . . . This safeguard to our funds is one which it is most desirable to maintain, and, moreover, a system of regular Branch Meetings tends to promote keener interest in our benevolent work and to intensify the spirit of brotherhood which it is one of our objects to promote.

CONFIDENCE IN MUTUAL AID

Amongst the list of beneficiaries the annuitants, who accounted for well over half of all payments, now included two women local preachers. The growing number of widows included younger women with families, whose local preacher husbands had been killed in action. Mothers, whose sons had been their only support but were now in the Forces, were also receiving financial help.

WHEN WILL IT END?

In 1917, when the Annual Aggregate met in Wesley's Chapel, London, it received a General Committee Report which began, with sadness, by observing solemnly that:

> . . . for a third successive year we meet under the black pall of war. The world-shaking struggle has during the last twelve months even extended its devastating area as fresh nations have entered the lists. Hundreds of thousands of young and vigorous lives have been laid upon the altar of national sacrifice, and still we see not the end. Thousands of millions of sterling have been lavished upon munitions of war, and yet the limit of expenditure seems far distant. No home in these islands has escaped the touch of sorrow, or a least of anxiety . . .

This sombre note reflected the changed mood of the nation as war dragged on, but also indicated new emphases within LPMAA. There was an increasing number of members and dependants experiencing bereavement – parents who had lost sons, women left widowed having to care for young children. Also men were returning from the front not only with permanently disabling injuries but after faith-shattering experiences. The Association was grateful that it had the means to assist them financially, but it had also to meet their non-monetary needs for loving care and pastoral support. The essential ethos of mutual aid was put to the test.

Early in 1916 the magazine had included a translation of extracts from a Paris newspaper article which offered some comfort and consolation especially to the mothers, wives and daughters of servicemen who had been killed in action. Under the title 'Somewhere in France', it began:

> Weep not, mothers, for around the solitary crosses
> that mark the graves of your hero sons all France in
> arms keeps watch

and concluded,

> Weep not, you mothers, you wives, you daughters,
> though the days seem long and sad away from those
> spots of sacred soil whither your sorrows would bid
> you rush and mourn.

The Editor of the magazine at that time clearly felt that these sentiments would be helpful to bereaved women. They might also have been useful to officers and members of the Association as they sought to offer pastoral care to any whose sons, husbands or fathers had made the supreme sacrifice. In October of the following year the magazine carried two intimate, personal letters that were written by a former President of LPMAA, himself a senior army officer, and by his son before he was killed at the front. On learning of the death of the young Lieutenant Barnsley, the General Committee had sent a letter of sympathy to Brigadier General Sir John Barnsley (President of 1899). The reply from Sir John was, with his permission, printed in the magazine, along with extracts copied by Lady Barnsley from a letter written by their son in case he did not return.

> I am home on leave for ten days, spending the first
> hours of sorrow with my dear wife, and very sacred
> and precious they are. Will you please tell the
> Committee how grateful we are for the kind
> message of sympathy you sent us? Such letters are
> very helpful to us. We are passing through
> Gethsemane, but it is a comfort to be able to do so
> together . . . I had great hopes and ambitions for our
> dear boy. He was very good, absolutely fearless,
> with a simple piety which would have made him a
> useful minister. . . . I have seen enough in France to
> make me re-echo a thousand times your hope that it
> may soon be over, but I am afraid the way is a long
> one yet. I am returning to France on Monday. My
> feelings lead me to remain at my dear wife's side,
> but the brave woman says: 'You must go; Ken would
> say – duty first, carry on.'

The Sound of A Voice That Is Still.
(*Extract from Lieutenant Barnsley's Letter*)

As I write this, in a dug-out just behind the lines, I realise how little it means to me personally whether I even get out of this alive or not. If I have learnt anything out here, it is this – that it is really of no great importance whether we live or whether we die. If I live, then I see before me the prospect of much happiness, and, as I hope and believe, of some usefulness in the world. If I die, then I hope and believe there will be an infinitely greater happiness, and, most certainly, increased and continual opportunities of service. That is my belief as far as a future state goes. And so many friends have gone before me, that really the prospect of death is not terrible or even sad in the least . . .

A memorial tablet to Kenneth Barnsley was later placed in Sandon Road Chapel in Birmingham, where his family had been members of the congregation for three generations

These extracts from *The Local Preachers Magazine* during 1914-18 war help to show the impact of that international conflict on the nation and on men and women of faith, not all of whom came through their experiences with faith intact. Preaching during war was a great challenge. The Editor commissioned a series of short articles on *Preaching in War-Time*, saying in his introduction that the work had rarely been beset by greater difficulties. The preaching ministry was presenting problems of peculiar perplexity. In his own words:

> . . . for our mutual encouragement and help we have asked some of our brethren to set out what they have found of trial and joy in the work of that ministry in these times of shadow and sorrow.

William Greenhalgh, J.P., President of 1917, wrote that in the pulpit he tried to realise people's needs through their eyes. He found no cheap idealising of war, no blatant patriotism, but the determined mien of men and women terribly conscious of the world agony. The President-Elect, J. W. Hampson, referred to three new experiences: first, when his son had said, 'If we are worth fighting for, I must go.' It was the righteousness of the call that arrested him – the heroic found expression; it was an easy first. The second was when letters and field–cards ceased to come through and anxiety gripped his heart. The third experience was receiving the message that his son was in hospital in England, and waves of anxiety drowned the thunder and the guns.

These men spoke for thousands who shared similar experiences, but even in the later stages of the war the beneficent purposes of Mutual Aid were kept in focus. The Aggregate Meeting had endorsed a recommendation to increase weekly grants by 20 per cent during and for twelve months after the war. General Committee dealt with a large number of applications for these 'War Increases', to 12s per week (6s for widows). Nearly £10,000 was paid during 1917 in superannuation allowances to 727 local preachers and widows. Some unusual causes of need were identified during the war years. One member had been receiving a small income from relatives who worked a farm in France. When they had to leave the farm, the German army razed the homestead to the ground. The income ceased, and the Association then made a weekly allowance of 7s. It was possible to strike an occasional happier note, for example, when the Honorary Secretary was able in the magazine for November 1917 to congratulate George Lunn, J.P., on his selection for a third consecutive year as Lord Mayor of Newcastle-upon-Tyne. He was the second 'LPMAA man' to serve an extended term in that office.

Concerns engendered or emphasised by the war were, however, never far away. The 1917 Aggregate took note of the effect of military service upon both recruitment of local preachers into membership and active participation in the work. It was estimated that between 7,000 and 8,000 local preachers were serving in the armed forces; a similar number might have become preachers – and thus potential members of LPMAA – but for the call to military service. In total, out of some 26,000 local preachers in the three denominations covered by the Association, nearly 14,000 had not become members. It was lamented that so many held aloof from the visible bond of union, fellowship and co-operation amongst local preachers that LPMAA provided. These attributes have always been essential to the well-being, progress and very existence of Methodism.

The Honorary Secretary followed this up in the November magazine with an analysis showing that just over 40 per cent of

Wesleyan, barely 30 per cent of Wesleyan Reform Union, and only 28 per cent of United Methodist Local Preachers were in membership. His notes in December that year summarised some of the difficulties that the war had imposed upon LPMAA:

(a) The necessity of granting war increases to annuitants, exceeding £600 per annum.
(b) The serious handicap to the Association's work arising from the number of Branch officials serving in the Navy and Army.
(c) The decline in new members resulting from the number of young local preachers serving in the Forces.
(d) The increase in applications for sick pay and annuities, owing to injuries and illnesses suffered during the war.
(e) Difficulties in arranging deputations and Committee attendances because of reduced railway services.

Other problems might have been mentioned, but the note concluded with a tribute to the loyalty of District and Branch Officials, and gratitude for continued generous financial support.

The claims of military service when it became compulsory in 1916 nearly deprived the Association of its recently-appointed General Secretary. On 14th August of that year the Office Sub-Committee was advised that W. E. Noddings had been granted exemption until 3rd September. It was decided to appeal and ask for total exemption. In November it was reported that exemption had been extended for two months 'in the national interest'. On 15th February 1917 the Committee heard that an application for further exemption had been refused, but Bro. Noddings would not be called up before 22nd February. An appeal had been lodged; on 3rd March General Committee was informed that this had been successful, exemption from military service being granted to the General Secretary until the middle of May.

At meetings in May and September of 1917 the General Committee decided to appeal for further exemption, strongly urging the retention of Bro. Noddings 'in his present occupation'. On 27th October the Committee was advised that his exemption from military service had been extended to April 1918, in which month it learned that exemption had been granted until March 1919. By this time hostilities had ceased. This persistence in seeking to retain the services of the General Secretary during the war years reflects conviction about the importance of the Association's work. The effectiveness with which William

Noddings had fulfilled the duties of his office, since his appointment in 1914, was widely recognised. Without him, continuance of Mutual Aid through the war would have been much more difficult, if not impossible.

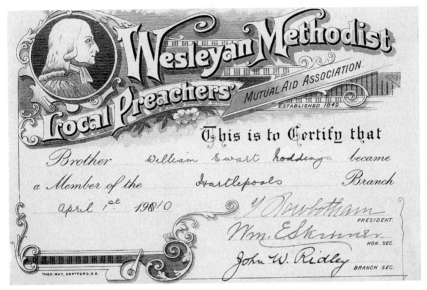

Membership Certificate of William E. Noddings four years before he became General Secretary. (His 'Note to preach' appears in Workaday Preachers, *p.71.)*

BETWEEN THE WARS

A small but historically interesting piece of business awaited the attention of the General Committee and the Association soon after the war was over. The existence of local preachers' Friendly Societies in various parts of the country before LPMAA was formed is described in chapter 5. This included brief reference to a society in Cambridge, which appears to have continued in existence through to the end of the 1914-18 war, though none of its records survive. By 1921 the Cambridge Society had decided to accept the offer of LPMAA to receive its members (numbering seventeen) into the Benefit Section of the Association's membership. The funds of the Cambridge Society (amounting to about £140) would then be transferred to the General Fund of the Association. General Committee was informed of this on 6th October of that year. At its November meeting it was reported that the transfer of the members and funds of the Cambridge Society to the Association had been effected. Arrangements had been made to inaugurate the new Branch on 1st December 1921.

The years immediately following the 1914-18 war saw the granting of royal patronage to LPMAA. The personal memories of William Douthwaite (President in 1921), who was instrumental in bringing this about, were the basis for the very full account in *A Goodly Fellowship* (pp.101-105). In January 1922 royal patronage was granted, donations of 10 guineas (£10.50) being received from both King George V and Queen Mary. *The Local Preachers' Magazine* was able to report this in February and to publish the royal letters in the March issue. Succeeding monarchs have continued their patronage, and the Association sends loyal greetings to its patron at the time of each year's Aggregate Meeting.

The cessation of hostilities in November 1918 had been greeted by everyone with relief and rejoicing, but also with the recognition that rebuilding life in the post-war period would not be easy. If it had been known then that within little more than twenty years Europe would be at war again, the will to undertake rebuilding might have been weaker than it was. In economic and political terms there could be no return to the 'status quo ante bellum'. The days of Britain's industrial supremacy were gone, and the political scene had been changed for ever by the strength of organised labour, particularly the Labour Party. Women over 30 were now enfranchised, and the election of the first woman M.P. (Lady Astor) in 1919 was in this context symbolic. The rebuilding of family life was sometimes difficult following long war-time separations. The loss of a million mainly young men left a whole generation of young women with diminished opportunities of marriage and motherhood.

Neither did the rebuilding of religious life prove to be easy. The decline of membership in all the Methodist denominations continued, reinforced by loss of life and loss of faith through war-time experiences. Indeed, it was in this context that the planning for and eventual implementation of Methodist Union took place. The implications of this for the Mutual Aid Association are considered in chapter 17, but the year of Union, 1932, was significant in other ways for society and for the nation. It was the last year before Hitler came to power as Chancellor of Germany, and was also the year when economic depression was at its worst, with unemployment exceeding 50 per cent in some parts of the

United Kingdom. It was the year of the first flight around the world, and of the first broadcast television programmes.

Sport, the arts and entertainment all had important events in 1932. Cricket was rocked by what became known as the 'bodyline' bowling controversy during the England tour of Australia. The London Philharmonic Orchestra was founded, the Windmill Theatre opened (with the subsequent public debate about nudity on the stage), and the first Sunday opening of cinemas was permitted. These exemplify the nature and extent of change during the inter-war decades. Some of the effects for LPMAA are examined in chapter 18. Expanding means of travel and communication, with growing diversity in opportunities for leisure activities were, however, soon overshadowed by the gathering of fresh war-clouds. By 1938 war in Europe seemed inevitable. By the beginning of September 1939 it had started.

WAR AGAIN (1939 - 1945)

Upon the outbreak of the Second World War problems of a different kind confronted the Association. General Secretary Noddings was still in post and remained so until after the war was over. In 1939 he had to deal with matters directly affecting Head Office and LPMAA records, rather than his own liability for compulsory military service. The country was being prepared through the summer of 1939 for the possibility of air attacks on major cities, especially London. Accordingly, the Association's Office Sub-Committee was summoned on 9th June to consider Air Raid Precautions. Shelters were being constructed in the basement of No.1 Central Buildings, Westminster, where documents could be stored. A new Deed Box had been purchased; a list of its contents and LPMAA investments was being issued to all Trustees. The Sub-Committee met again on 28th June, when it decided that a letter about the National Emergency should be sent to all Branch Secretaries. This would stress the importance of complete and accurate local records being available, in case the Association's books and records at Head Office were destroyed in aerial bombardment.

Meanwhile, the Honorary Secretary, acting at the request of the Trustees and the Office Sub-Committee, had secured the authority of the General Committee to deal with all necessary matters if war began, which it did on 3rd September. An Emergency Sub-Committee was formed; on 3rd October it approved the recommendation from the Office Sub-Committee that the Association's Head Office should be moved out of London. Staff and equipment were transferred to a rented house at Weybridge; the General Secretary went to live there, and the administration of Mutual Aid was maintained in difficult circumstances throughout the war. Lodging and travelling expenses were paid to staff who had to incur these additional costs. General Committee meetings scheduled for October, November (1939) and January (1940) were cancelled, and a meeting was called for 11th December in London. It confirmed arrangements for its future meetings and for the 1940 Aggregate. 'Normal' business continued, including the appointment of Richard Burnett as magazine editor following the death of Alfred England, and the re-appointment of the six LPMAA representatives to the Connexional Necessitous Local Preachers Fund Committee.

At General Committee meetings during 1940 further decisions resulting from war-time conditions were made. In accordance with precedent established during the 1914-18 war, the arrears of any members who were unable to pay subscriptions because of service in the armed forces were cancelled. Paper shortage and increased postal charges caused the magazine to be reduced to six issues per year. It was decided not to hold some meetings of the General Committee, partly because of travelling difficulties. In 1941 meetings were held only in alternate months and the size of the Aggregate Meeting that year was reduced by a half. A decision was made also to curtail its length.

PEACE AT LAST

Inevitably, as war ended in 1945, many members of LPMAA – like many ex-Service men and other citizens – hoped to go back and pick up life as it had been in the 1930s. This was, of course, impossible. The country entered a new political era, with a large Labour majority in the House of Commons, and public policy took a different direction. The cost of post-war reconstruction was massive, and as a generation grew up having no memories of 'before the war,' social and economic life changed rapidly. All branches of the Christian church and all Christian organisations had to recognise these changes as they began again to look forward and to plan their future. LPMAA took one or two tentative steps to re-shape its organisation; at the end of 1945, a General Purposes Committee was established by merging the Office Sub-Committee with three others: the Convalescent Homes, Connexional Relations and Centenary Handbook sub-committees. The logical combination with the Finance Committee, to form a Finance and General Purposes Committee did not come about until 1963.

The first post-war Aggregate met in Leeds only a month after the ending of conflict in Europe. The Assembly returned thanks 'to Almighty God for deliverance from great dangers'. Before proceeding to normal business there was a moving moment when a letter from the Channel Islands Branch was read. Those islands were the only part of the United Kingdom to have been under German occupation. The letter stated that members there had endeavoured to carry on LPMAA work as usual during the war. Subscriptions had been maintained and collections taken. They had nearly £300 in hand. A reply was sent from the Aggregate, rejoicing in the liberation of the Channel Islands and giving thanks for the courage and faithfulness of members there.

Two things dominated the Association's immediate post-war life. One was the conviction that Eventide Homes, or other appropriate form of residential care for elderly members, should become part of its provision as soon as it could be prudently undertaken. For the full account of how this was achieved readers are referred to *More Precious Than Rubies* (1989) by Alfred Gilliver. The other was its approaching centenary. This began to appear in official records as early as the Aggregate Meeting of 1945, which appointed a committee to investigate the possibility of producing a history of the Association 'to honour the illustrious founders of our movement and to commemorate the work of one hundred years'. The May-June 1947 issue of *The Local Preachers Magazine* included a note from the senior Honorary Secretary, F.Harold Buss, intimating that the General Committee had asked him to undertake this task and appealing for source material. The book, *A Goodly Fellowship*, appeared in the centenary year.

In September 1946 the General Committee was advised that the General Purposes Committee had appointed a sub-committee to consider the preparation of the handbook for the Association's centenary. The General Committee gave further attention to centenary matters in August 1947, when Harold Buss expressed the hope that celebration events would be held in many places throughout the centenary year. The Committee also acted on a recommendation of the General Purposes Committee and appointed a small sub-committee to consider the nomination of a suitable person as President for 1949, the Centenary Year.

This chapter has been concerned with the half-century which includes the 32 years during which William Noddings served LPMAA as General Secretary. It is fitting, therefore, to conclude it with some reference to the tributes paid to him on his retirement at the end of 1946. In January 1947 the editor of *The Local Preachers Magazine* published his own appreciation, its key sentence being:

> Through two wars, and during the uneasy armistice between, and so during a period of unrest and economic strain, he has upheld the traditions of our work and helped to carry them to even loftier levels.

The official resolution in the General Committee minutes refers to his

> . . . unfailing fidelity and devotion in the discharge of the duties of the office. As an advocate and administrator, he has done invaluable work; as a colleague he has been the soul of courtesy and brotherliness, and by his sterling character and graces of spirit he has commended himself to all who have known him.

He continued to serve LPMAA for some years afterwards, as a Trustee and therefore a member of General Committee, and as Secretary of the Mutual Aid Homes Company from 1948 to 1957. His retirement from the General Secretaryship of LPMAA, nevertheless, marked the end of an epoch.

17

Methodist Union and Afterwards

Preparation and Planning • The Methodist Church Congress;
Primitive Methodism's 'Lightning Effort'
The Local Preachers' Who's Who of 1934
Closer Relations – a Matter of Money?
LPMAA Considers Its Response
A Small Majority and Its Consequences;
The Correspondence Continues • The Internal Debate in LPMAA.

PREPARATION AND PLANNING

From very early in its existence, and regardless of its title, the Wesleyan Methodist LPMAA had embraced in its membership local preachers from some of the non-Wesleyan Methodist traditions. Before the end of the 1850s local preachers of the United Methodist Free Churches and of the Wesleyan Reform Union were in membership; in 1896 those of the Methodist New Connexion were made eligible to join, and in 1907 (upon the formation of the United Methodist Church) Bible Christian local preachers were brought in. The Association was in that sense a pioneer of Union, only Primitive Methodist preachers remaining outside it until the major Union of Methodism in 1932. Concern about the fragmented state of Methodism motivated LPMAA in 1887 to send a resolution to the Conferences of the several traditions from which its members came, urging action to achieve union. In 1918 the Aggregate expressed whole-hearted support for Union, although it did not come about until 1932.

In 1926 the three Conferences directed the officers of their respective Local Preachers Committees to meet in order to 'gather information and prepare plans for unification of the Departments'. They did so on 8th March 1927, together with the officers of the Wesleyan Necessitous Local Preachers' Fund, the Secretary of the Primitive Methodist Local Preachers' Aid Fund and the Secretary of the United Methodist Local Preachers' Fund. The Treasurer and General Secretary of LPMAA attended by invitation. Also present were Sir Robert Perks, later Vice-President of the 1932 Uniting Conference, and Rev. J. Aldom French, Secretary of the Methodist Union Committee.

Sir Robert suggested they should keep quite separate in their minds the matters of training for local preachers *and* of aid and financial assistance, referring to LPMAA as a powerful, popular and successful organisation. He anticipated Methodist Union being accomplished by September 1928. Much discussion, according to notes made by William Noddings (General Secretary, LPMAA), centred on the membership of the Association and its future place in Methodism. Even the possibility that the Methodist Conference might not allow collections for Mutual Aid after Union was mentioned. The meeting decided to send a letter to the General Committee of LPMAA urging two points:

(a) The receiving of Primitive Methodist local preachers into membership of the Association.
(b) The desirability of bringing LPMAA into closer relationship with the Conference.

THE METHODIST CHURCH CONGRESS

The enthusiasm of the Association for the unification of all branches of Methodism was recognised in an interesting and unusual way when the basis for Union was eventually agreed. As part of the preparations for implementing Union, two national assemblies of the three uniting traditions were held, one at Bristol in October 1929 and one at Sheffield in February 1931. They were known as the Methodist Church Congress, and were four-day events with formal delegate sessions each morning and afternoon, and public meetings in the evenings. Approximately 1,000 men and women attended. The emphasis in 1929 was on 'Methodism's Present Responsibilities', whilst the 1931 Congress was concerned mainly with 'Methodism's Message for Today'.

Amongst a large panel of distinguished speakers, the 1929 Congress heard the Presidents of the Conferences of the three uniting branches of Methodism speaking in turn from the same platform as the President of LPMAA for that year, Harry Dawson, J.P. Harry was a successful wool merchant in Bradford and had been active nationally in LPMAA for many years before his election to the Presidency. The fact that he was invited to share the platform with three current Presidents of Conference – surely the only layman ever to have that honour – was a particular tribute to Local Preachers and the Mutual Aid Association. The opening sentence of his brief address, reproduced here in full, indicates his own consciousness of this:

> It is my privilege as President of the Association to represent at this Congress 37,000 Methodist local preachers, each of whom claims to have been called by God to proclaim the simple gospel of his grace. We are not called to be orators, or entertainers – or even psychologists. We are called to be witnesses of the sure salvation we have found in Jesus Christ. I am authorised to say that this great company of men – and women also – is prepared to sustain the Methodist witness, not only in the town and village pulpits, but in the open air also. We are prepared to go anywhere. The local preachers of Methodism ask the Methodist people to use them and to stand by them. I believe that, if this cordial co-operation is assured in mutual confidence and in goodwill and in the fellowship of earnest, believing prayer, there will be a genuine revival of the work of God in all the Churches.

> Eighty per cent of the people of England outside the Churches seems a great problem. It is. But it is also a great opportunity. I am an optimist. Even in such a situation I have confidence in the all-sufficiency of God's grace in Christ. We have a message for the outsider, the same message our Methodist fathers found arresting and attractive. I think I may claim to know the working-men of Lancashire and Yorkshire; and I can assert that they are sick of the arrogant materialism of the day . . . What they want is what Christ came to give – peace of soul. They are waiting for professing Christians to obey the constraints of the love of Christ and thus to become his witness to their neighbours. We can never win others to Christ until we love them and by love serve them.

Primitive Methodism's 'Lightning Effort'

Three years later, the Uniting Conference formally inaugurated Methodist Union. There were important implications for local preachers, especially those from the Primitive and United Methodist Churches, e.g. authorisation to conduct Communion Services. This had never been the practice in the Wesleyan tradition, whereas it was accepted in Primitive and United Methodism. 'Dispensations' were granted to some PM and UM local preachers to continue presiding at the Lord's Supper, but those becoming local preachers after Union were rarely authorised to do so.

For LPMAA, however, the immediate issue was the basis on which Primitive Methodist Local Preachers might become eligible for membership. Following the precedents of 1896 and 1907, a sum was agreed between LPMAA and the PM Connexion, which Primitive Methodism paid to the Association to secure rights of membership for its local preachers. The page of the Primitive Methodist Year Book, 1932, bringing to the attention of its members this 'Lightning Effort' to raise the money, is reproduced here:

MUTUAL
AID
APPEAL

*Lightning Effort
to Raise*

£20,000

Mr J. LONGSTAFF, J.P.,
"Woodside,"
Grange Road, Fenham.
Newcastle-on-Tyne.

---

1. The Wesleyan Mutual Aid is a remarkably sound organisation and is splendidly managed.
2. Its capital is £147,000, of which £52,000 is specifically set aside for the payment of annuities.
3. During the 81 years of its existence the Association has distributed £812,000 in relief of distress, an average of £10,000 per annum. In recent years it has disbursed more than double that average amount.
4. 991 members or their widows received annuities in 1930, the weekly average allowance being 10s 6d for men and 8s 4d for women.
5. We are asked to pay a capital sum of £20,000 in

order that our Local Preachers may be eligible for membership. Assuming that amount is paid, our Local Preachers will be placed on exactly the same terms as present members as regards Entrance Fees, Annual Subscriptions, and Benefits.

6. It is extremely desirable that when Methodist Union takes place our Local Preachers should have the right to become members of such a splendid organisation, otherwise they will be placed in an invidious position as compared with Wesleyan and United Methodist Local Preachers.

7. The provision of £20,000 is, therefore, a moral obligation on the part of our Church.

[The story of this 'Lightning Fund' is told in some detail by Harold Buss in *A Goodly Fellowship*, pp.116-119. It is also referred to in *Workaday Preachers*, chapter 10.]   The assets of the Primitive Methodist Local Preachers' Aid Fund were transferred to LPMAA, which undertook to maintain the annuities being paid to some 200 ex-Primitive Methodist preachers. In the first two years of Methodist Union over 5,000 PM local preachers joined the Association. By the outbreak of war in 1939, out of approximately 34,000 Methodist local preachers, nearly 16,000 had taken up membership of the Mutual Aid Association. 1,367 were receiving regular benefit payments. There were a further 526 Life Members and 6,730 Honorary Members, some of whom were local preachers who had chosen to pay the higher subscription.

THE LOCAL PREACHERS' WHO'S WHO OF 1934

An interesting initiative with which LPMAA was associated in the post-Union years was the publication of a directory of local preachers in the Methodist Church. It was published by Shaw Publishing Co. Ltd., specialists in the compilation and publication of this kind of reference book, in co-operation with official bodies. A foreword explained that this, the first – and so far only – *Methodist Local Preachers' Who's Who*, had been prepared with the co-operation of the Connexional Local Preachers Committee and the Local Preachers Mutual Aid Association. The assistance of the two General Secretaries, R. Arthur Button and William E. Noddings was specifically acknowledged. Every one of Methodism's 36,000 local preachers received a questionnaire form; those who did not reply were circulated a second time, and if necessary a third and fourth time. Nevertheless, the book only included between 20,000 and 21,000 names. It is still, however, an interesting and useful source of information about Methodism's lay preaching resources at the time of Union, especially as many of the responses were from preachers who came into the work in the 19th century.

Rev. J. Scott Lidgett, who had been President of Conference in the year of Union, provided an introductory tribute to the work of local preachers and their place in Methodism. The LPMAA President of the same year, F. Harold Buss, contributed a brief history of the growth of local preaching. The preliminary articles also included a note about local preachers in rural Methodism. The Secretaries of the Connexional Committee, the Mutual Aid Association, and the Necessitous Local Preachers' Fund wrote about the role and responsibilities of their respective organisations. There was also a short explanation of the Commemoration Fund, established to meet the costs of amalgamating the three branches of the Methodist Church.

The main part of the book is, of course, the alphabetical listing – 570 pages of brief notes submitted by local preachers about themselves. This was followed by a supplement about Local Preacher training, studies and examinations, and information about officers and committee members of LPMAA. The Connexional Local Preachers' Committee at that time included amongst its 30 lay members and officers the current LPMAA President, four past-Presidents, a future President, the General Secretary of the Association, one of its Trustees (in addition to two of the past-Presidents who were Trustees), and two other members of the General Committee. This seems to suggest genuine cordiality between the two bodies as Methodist Union was implemented. The entries about individual preachers vary from one or two lines to fourteen or fifteen, giving personal information about each man and woman, their special interests, and Methodist and public offices held. It is noticeable that many were meticulous in listing their membership of LPMAA and offices held in Branch or District, whilst a number of entries include reference to service as a Guardian of the Poor.

CLOSER RELATIONS – A MATTER OF MONEY?

During the last years of the 1939-45 war, as signs of an end to the conflict began to appear, Methodism – like other branches of the church – started to consider the post-war situation. There would clearly be fewer local preachers; recruitment had declined significantly, whilst losses through the war had been at a high level. The Connexional Local Preachers' Committee addressed this concern, and focused on two related issues – recruitment and improved training. Both of these required increased funding, particularly the appointment of travelling tutors, then seen as a main element in achieving higher standards of preaching.

The resources available to the Local Preachers' Department were inadequate for this development. Rev. Fred Farley, Connexional Local Preachers' Secretary, was encouraged by his committee to seek an opportunity for explaining the position to the General Committee of LPMAA. A special meeting was held on 27th January 1944 to which Mr Farley (accompanied by two colleagues) was invited. The full text of his statement is included in the minutes of that meeting; the following extracts give the essence of the Connexional Committee's thinking, and the specific proposals that were put forward. Referring to the appointment of more travelling tutors, Mr Farley said:

> We were faced with the constantly recurring question of how to pay for it. Somebody suggested that we should ask Conference for a Sunday in all our Churches – Local Preachers' Sunday – to let us get our money by a direct appeal to the Methodist people. I resisted the idea on the ground that LPMA was already having a collection and that it would not be fair for us to ask the Circuits to give up two collections in one year. My Committee saw that this would be a great difficulty . . . Then somebody suggested that if the obstacle was the one Sunday per year why not approach Mutual Aid about it. . . .

He dwelt on the different functions of LPMAA and the Connexional Committee, the former to help local preachers in need, the latter to administer Conference Standing Orders. He pointed out that LPMAA membership is governed by the Standing Order stating the conditions for being recognised as a Local Preacher. There was, of course, reciprocal interest in each other's work, and the great spirit of fellowship which characterised LPMAA might be infused into the Connexional Committee's work. He continued:

> This is our proposal: It will be of immense value if we can have your support in propaganda; that would give us the chance we want of telling the Methodist people what we are doing and what we want to do. We could get that if you would take it up for us; the suggestion I want to bring forward is that one Sunday in the year should be regarded as a day when local preachers' affairs as a whole can be reviewed . . . what we ask is – will you share with us the Sunday's collection? Then you can advocate our work as well as your own . . . Go on, only on that Sunday you should include us in your appeal to the Methodist people and separate three-quarters of the collections for the Association and let one-quarter go to the Connexional Committee.

Mr Farley then advocated an annual conference of local preachers to be held in conjunction with the Aggregate Meeting, and concluded his remarks by inviting other proposals from the General Committee. On behalf of the Committee, the Honorary Secretary (F. Harold Buss) thanked Mr Farley for coming, and recalled that in the early years the Association received little sympathy and no help from the church, but now it enjoyed the affections of the Methodist people. Nothing should be done to impair that affection:

> If the Spirit of God can lead us to help you in the difficulties in which you find yourselves, I am sure it will be done, not only to profit your work, but to profit the Church of God and the Kingdom of Jesus Christ.

After a few questions, mainly for clarification of Mr Farley's proposals, he and his colleagues left the Committee, which then resolved to hold another special meeting for detailed discussion of those proposals. This was held on 23rd March 1944. Before then (1st March) a meeting of the Connexional Local Preachers' Committee had discussed the matter. According to notes made by the LPMAA General Secretary of the time, it was intimated that the proposals put to the LPMAA General Committee might result in £4,000 for the Local Preachers' Department. A ministerial member of the Connexional Committee then observed that it was not enough, as the work of the Department was ten times more vital than that of the Mutual Aid Association.

LPMAA CONSIDERS ITS RESPONSE

When the General Committee met, the Honorary Secretary indicated two ways in which the Association could assist the Connexional Committee financially if they and the Aggregate wished to do so. The first would be to follow Mr Farley's suggestion and agree a division of the collections. This would not require an alteration of the rules. The other way would be to amend the rules to allow the Association to make periodical grants to the Connexional Local Preachers' Department. Each course of action found support in the General Committee, as also did the view that neither should be followed at present and that the matter should await more precise details of the Connexional Local Preachers' Department's needs. Some speakers sensed the possibility of a move towards Conference control of the Association and urged that this be resisted. The position of the Wesleyan Reform Union members was also remembered.

The meeting was clearly influenced by Herbert Ibberson, who had recently completed his year of office as Vice-President of Conference (he served as President of LPMAA in the following year, 1945). He was a member of the Connexional Committee but Vice-Presidential duties had prevented him from attending it when the present matter had been discussed. His view was that the approach to the Association was wrong and that no consideration should be given to the proposals until a specific case could be made. He seconded a motion by A. J .Cash to this effect, which was passed with only one against. The possible amendment of Rules was to be on the agenda for a future meeting of General Committee.

At the General Committee meeting in Birmingham on 6th May 1944, the Honorary Secretary was able to report that a letter had been received from Mr Farley in response to the copy of the resolution sent to him. In this he gave his own estimate of the cost of the travelling tutors scheme and associated expenses, totalling £3350 annually. The Honorary Secretary reminded the Committee that mutual aid over nearly a century had been entirely the work of local preachers, whereas the Connexional Committee was composed of ministers and laymen, which was bound to affect its approach. He warned against any action which might lead to organic union with the Connexional Department, and urged concentration on the financial aspect of the situation. He had privately suggested to Mr Farley that the Association might stand aside every third or fourth year. [There may be the unspoken implication that congregations would then be in no doubt which aspect of local preachers work they were supporting on a given day.] Members discussed the suggestion, pointing out that Quarterly Meetings would have a role, and that loss of advocacy would be as serious as loss of money.

A Small Majority and Its Consequences

The outcome was the appointment of a sub-committee to explore the proposals of the Connexional Committee, including the possible amendment of Rule 3, defining the objects of the Association. At the end of November 1944 the General Committee received the report of the sub-committee, and resolved to recommend the following year's Aggregate to approve the addition to Rule 3 of these words:

> . . . and to assist financially in the training and equipment of local preachers.

Some unease was expressed at the General Committee in March 1945 about the proposed alteration, but it was decided to go forward and, if Aggregate approved, to send it to the Districts for consideration. When the recommended addition to the Rule was put to Aggregate in June it was approved, but by less than the two-thirds majority required for an amendment of Rules. If the matter could have been brought to Aggregate again in 1946 without unnecessarily abrasive public expressions of opinion, it might have secured the modest additional support needed to achieve the rule-change. However, when the result of the vote was reported in the *Methodist Recorder* (7th June 1945) as part of its coverage of the Leeds Aggregate, a flood of correspondence was initiated, which continued until late August of that year.

The first letter was from Sir George Knight, Connexional Local Preachers' Treasurer, who was to become Vice-President of Conference a few weeks later. His opening salvo stated:

It will be widely regretted that the LPMA at their Aggregate Meeting last week declined to adopt a proposal for a wider and wiser use of the monies they collect in our churches. Their few valiants who are putting off the armour are amply cared for. The Association has an accumulated reserve of more than £250,000.

These statements provoked some equally forceful counter-statements in succeeding weeks' issues, which in turn stimulated Sir George himself to return to the fray only a month later. His original letter went on to say:

> . . . Methodist people must be made aware of the complete range of facts about Local Preachers' affairs. The best way would be for LPMA to revise its judgement. The impoverishment which frets the Training Committee cannot continue while unnecessary collections are taken for a cause that does not need them.

That sentence alone would have been sufficient to call forth strongly-worded replies from many directions, and in the following week's *Recorder* (21st June 1945) the Editor included six letters, two supporting Sir George and four firmly opposing his views. The most substantial of these was from Harold Buss (Honorary Secretary of LPMAA), who tackled some of Sir George Knight's assertions directly:

> If 'impoverishment' is the correct word to describe the financial plight of the Department, it is not surprising that he should look to the other organisation in Methodism which serves local preachers to come to the rescue. But no evidence is afforded to show that the state of the Department's exchequer is as desperate as all that.

> Sir George speaks of the Association's 'few valiants' as being 'amply cared for'. The 'few' number more than eleven hundred, and 'amply' is a big word for an average allowance of seven shillings a week. This very modest grant is not our fault. In these days of rising cost of living, our beneficiaries would not be 'passing rich' if we gave double that amount.

Already the Association's recently amended rules are making greater demands on our funds and fresh extensions of our benevolent activities are in contemplation. So it is scarcely accurate to say that contributions of the Methodist church and people are 'for a cause that does not need them'.

I beg Sir George to believe that the Association's executive are anxious to find a way of practical help in the work the Department is doing. If there is 'friction' it is not on our part. But in view of our history and constitution, it is not so simple and easy as it may appear to make a 'wider' and, as he would have it, a 'wiser' use of our funds.

There were letters from two District Officers of the Connexional Local Preachers' Committee. One emphatically endorsed Sir George Knight's opinions, the other pointed out that LPMAA's financial reserves were mainly from legacies given specifically for its benevolent purposes. He regretted that Methodists were not equally enthusiastic about Local Preacher training. Another writer, an active member of the Association, was disappointed by the lack of vision evidenced by the decision of the Aggregate Meeting. Two letters expressed concern about the hint of control of the Association by Conference and about the jealousy of its magnificent voluntary work and efficient management shown by some Connexional officials.

The same week's issue of the *Methodist Recorder* included a report of the Connexional Local Preachers Committee, which had met on the day following Aggregate. Rev. Fred Farley had advised the Committee of the decision made at Leeds, and it was felt that steps should be taken to appeal directly to Methodism. The next week (28th June) the *Recorder* carried an article by Mr Farley in which he set out in detail the position of his department. He reviewed the events – including his own meeting with the LPMAA General Committee – that led to the equivocal vote in the Leeds Aggregate. Writing warmly of the way the Association had received him, he specifically disowned any intention or suggestion that LPMAA should be brought under Conference control. His final paragraph, however, disconcerted many LPMAA members. Having referred to LPMAA receiving £7,000 annually more than it needed, he concluded:

> ... LPMAA is now seeking for ways of expending its
> surplus income, not in response to needs that have
> been felt and expressed, but as an alternative way of
> disposing of its surplus rather than of acceding to a
> request of the Connexional Committee. Nothing
> was heard of these alternative benefits, such as
> convalescent homes, until the Connexional
> Committee placed its need frankly and almost
> suppliantly before the LPMAA.

There was a further selection of readers' letters on the
subject. One was fiercely critical of the Association and almost
abusive about the 'stale with age' members of the Aggregate
Meeting. Others reaffirmed the distinct functions of LPMAA and
the Local Preachers' Department, and the legal and moral barriers
to the diversion of funds from the benevolent purposes for which
they were given. There was also criticism of the lack of support for
the Department in many Circuits.

THE CORRESPONDENCE CONTINUES

By July some early contributors to the debate were catching
the editor's eye again. Others wrote to add weight to the argument
on either side, one contrasting the democratic nature of LPMAA
General Committee with the much less democratic nature of the
Connexional Local Preachers' Committee. Another related the
controversy to the new theological teaching embodied in the
current Local Preachers' textbooks. One writer suggested that
Mr Farley's idea of sharing a Sunday collection should be
implemented on an equal shares basis.

On 5th July the *Recorder* included an article by the current President
of LPMAA, Herbert Ibberson, former Vice-President of Conference
and an Honorary Secretary of the Connexional Local Preachers
Committee since Union. He said he would not feel happy if a
Connexional Department (particularly the Local Preachers'
Department) was to be wholly or mainly financed by an unofficial
body. Referring to the marginally insufficient majority in the
Aggregate Meeting vote, he expressed his certainty that:

> ... if it had not been for the precipitate action of Sir
> George Knight and Mr Farley, the necessary consent

> would have been forthcoming, after due explanation
> . . . What I fear now is that, by this action, many
> members of LPMAA who would otherwise have
> supported this appeal will withdraw their support.

Herbert Ibberson devoted the last part of his article to rebutting the assertions in the closing paragraph of Mr Farley's article in the previous week. He made it clear that the easing of Government limits on the level of Friendly Society allowances to annuitants was imminent. This would enable the Association to apply its funds more fully to the purpose for which they had been given. On the final point of 'expending its surplus income' (as Mr Farley had put it) the President observed that Mr Farley was not acquainted with the facts regarding the plan to provide Homes for Aged and Infirm Local Preachers. This had been raised both officially and unofficially a number of times, and had been fully discussed at the Nottingham Aggregate in 1943.

Both Sir George and Mr Farley were afforded space in the *Recorder's* Editorial Letter Box on 12th July to respond to Ibberson's article. The former did so quite briefly, but Mr Farley wrote a longer letter characterised by the same kind of discretions and courtesies that had marked some ministerial statements at the time of LPMAA's formation. He referred to other correspondence on the subject, concluding by apologising for his error over the matter of Homes for Aged Local Preachers.

By this time the flow of letters had diminished as different topics attracted attention, though three did appear in the *Methodist Recorder* issues of 2nd and 23rd August (1945). One questioned the constitutional right of LPMAA to have any money from collections, a matter not finally resolved by Conference until the late 1980s. The others were from two LPMAA sages, Walter Kirkham and Fred Ogden. The former pointed to the fact that many members of the Connexional Committee were LPMAA men, and suggested that further action on the current question should await the return of the younger men from war service. Fred Ogden wrote from the viewpoint of an ex-United Methodist preacher, whose ancestors had been active in the foundation of LPMAA, and recalled the pleasantry in his tradition with which LPMAA Sunday was always granted.

THE INTERNAL DEBATE IN **LPMAA**

It is not surprising that during this prolonged correspondence attitudes had hardened, and by the autumn of 1945 the Editor of *The Local Preachers Magazine* decided to promote an informed discussion on the subject in its pages. The September issue carried two articles, one by W. H. Kneen favouring co-operation, and one by Charles Wass opposing it. The Editor invited comments combining courtesy with enlightenment, saying that light rather than heat was needed. The response revealed as much difference of opinion within the Association as had been seen in the columns of the *Methodist Recorder*. One or two writers appeared in both publications, including Mr Farley himself. Altogether fourteen letters were published in the November 1945 and January 1946 magazines, after which the Editor declared the correspondence closed, making brief reference to 'the large number of letters received'.

Meanwhile the General Committee decided to take no further action in the matter, other than at its meeting on 14th December 1945 to amalgamate three sub-committees into one, designated the 'General Purposes Committee'. One of the three had been dealing with the Connexional Local Preachers' proposals, the others with Convalescent Homes and a Centenary Handbook respectively. This suggests that the Connexional relations question had become too prominent in the Association's collective thinking. It had now to take its place alongside other important matters such as the evolving policy on the provision of Homes and the forthcoming Centenary, then little more than three years away. It did, however, surface once more, in the Aggregate Meeting at Lincoln in 1946. The business on Monday afternoon, 3rd June, commenced with the following motion, proposed by the Honorary Secretary, F. Harold Buss:

> The Aggregate Meeting in response to the appeal of the Connexional Local Preachers' Department for the co-operation of the Methodist Local Preachers Mutual Aid Association in providing the necessary funds for the extension of its work, recommends that in all districts and Branches where the services are arranged on behalf of the Mutual Aid Association, request shall be made to the Quarterly Meeting or other Church Authorities by whose consent such services are held, that a proportion of

the collections may be allocated to the Local Preachers' Department. The Aggregate Meeting suggests that such allocation shall be in the proportion of four-fifths (4/5) to the Association and one-fifth (1/5) to the Department.

This was seconded by C. Ernest Snowdon, but an amendment was immediately moved by Emanuel Spence (Alderman, of Middlesbrough) and seconded by J. Clark:

That in view of the diversity of opinions expressed by the General Committee, this Aggregate Meeting is of the opinion that the best interests of the MLPMAA and the Local Preachers' Connexional Committee will be served by leaving the whole matter in abeyance.

After debate this was carried, and as the substantive motion, was then carried unanimously. A further motion, proposed by P. Izzett and seconded by J. H. C. Miller, sought to make some progress in the light of that decision:

The Aggregate Meeting having considered the appeal of the Connexional Local Preachers' Department, expresses its continued interest in the development of the work of the Department and its desire to facilitate in any practical way the raising of the necessary funds. In view of the forthcoming changes in the secretariat of the Department, the Aggregate Meeting proposes further discussion between representatives of the Association and the Connexional Local Preachers' Department in order to ascertain the immediate needs of the Department and the means by which the Association can help to meet those needs.

This also received unanimous support. Its particular interest lies in the mention of the forthcoming departure of Rev. Fred Farley from the office of Connexional Local Preachers' Secretary. His successor was Rev. Greville Lewis, but the aftermath of the events described in this chapter was such that very little real progress was possible for some years. Peaceful co-existence was the pattern. The Connexion was adjusting to the new and challenging circumstances of the immediate post-war period, whilst the Association's energies and attention were engaged in adapting to a rapidly changing social context, to the meeting of new needs, and the celebration of its Centenary in 1949.

These matters, together with Connexional relations, did however lead to the production of a memorandum to all District and Branch Officers in February 1948. Under the headings

- The Mutual Aid Association and the State
- Mutual Aid Homes
- The Association and the Connexional Local Preachers' Department
- What is the Way Out?
- Fruits of Service

this four-page leaflet presented the up-to-date policies of LPMAA, and emphasised the duties of District and Branch Officers to implement those policies locally. Having affirmed that neither the work of the Local Preachers' Department nor the work of LPMAA must be allowed to suffer, it concluded with a reminder of some words from the previous year's (1946) Annual Report about the Mutual Aid Association:

> . . . so much more than an organised charity, whose status can be estimated by scanning the returns of income and expenditure. Of far greater importance are the spiritual blessings it bestows – the strengthening of the bonds of fellowship among preachers, the joy of selfless service to others, mutual encouragement in the preaching of the Word, and the nurture of the graces of the Christian

18

Social Change and LPMAA

Yet More Change • Women in LPMAA • Life and Leisure
The Media Revolution • Education Into Religion.

YET MORE CHANGE

No organisation can avoid being affected by its social, political and economic context, and by the changes going on around it. It will either adapt and evolve to take account of those changes, or it will shrivel and eventually disappear. LPMAA has survived and continued its work over 150 years because it has faced changes and coped successfully with them. The impact of public policy in the 20th century is dealt with in chapter 15, and the effects of changes in Methodism in chapters 17 and 33. This chapter considers the effects of some other changes, no less significant, but not so easily identified. Changes in social attitudes and behaviour have inevitably affected the Association, especially since the war of 1914-18. Greater geographical, occupational and social mobility have all been stimulated and encouraged by:

- the expansion of popular education
- changing attitudes towards religion
- the growth of mass media
- increasing car ownership
- developments in the role of women

Apart from compulsory public educational provision, the origin of which is usually dated from the Forster Act of 1870, these are predominantly 20th century phenomena. As indicated in the Introduction to this Section, another significant year was 1896. The first transmission of wireless signals, the first moving film show, and publication of the first 'popular' daily newspaper, all took place in that year. The 'Red Flag' Act, which restricted the speed of powered vehicles on roads to that of a man walking ahead with a red flag, was abolished.

The Great War stimulated some of these changes further, for example, the development of motor transport and aircraft, the enfranchisement of women over 30 in 1918, and the acceleration of the drift from religion. The Edwardian decade, sometimes called 'The Long Garden Party', was characterised politically by contention over votes for women, by the growth of trade unionism and the Labour Movement, and by Home Rule for Ireland. It gave way after the war to the 'The Long Cocktail Party' of the 1920s and 1930s, during which these and other issues reached some kind of outcome.

The social context of religion and religious organisations had changed fundamentally, and it was necessary to find appropriate responses to the new situation. What was not appropriate was to consolidate existing structures and ways of working. This would have diverted enormous resources of time, effort and money away from the developments that were needed. People in general were more literate; they were better informed and more able to think about their lives; they had rising political aspirations and economic expectations, and were much less likely to adopt unquestioningly the values, attitudes and standards of older generations.

WOMEN IN LPMAA

Developments in the participation of women in LPMAA and its activities illustrate these changes well. At a public meeting in Huddersfield, in connection with the Aggregate of 1852, ex-President Isaac English said that they wished to see 'the ladies' amongst them. Though it was not expected that they should take part in the business proceedings of the Association, they could become Honorary Members, and thus give it their countenance and support. In the Association's first decades, funds for the basic financial support of sick and disabled members, and for death grants, were the overriding concern. 'The ladies' (mainly the wives of members, all male at that time) were seen as the obvious source of energy for the organisation of tea-meetings, sales of work, and other forms of money-raising activity. This was the normal perception of the role of women in an age when few of them had independent financial means, and had to rely on a husband for economic support. If they were to make any personal contribution to a cause it had to be by doing rather than by giving – hence the tradition of sewing meetings (vividly described by Arnold Bennett in *Anna of the Five Towns*, chapter 7), cake stalls and bazaars.

The outstanding example of this in early LPMAA history is the great bazaar held in connection with the Aggregate Meeting of 1860 in London. The idea was put forward early in 1859, and in June that year the General Committee appointed a sub-committee to make all the necessary arrangements. The specific need was for funds to support aged and infirm members, subscription income being sufficient only for sickness benefit and death grants. The confident hope was expressed that 'the ladies will exert themselves'; circulars were distributed urging the formation of local Ladies' Committees. Advertisements were placed in both major Methodist newspapers. The event took place in the Hanover Square Rooms, and yielded almost £1,300 pounds (equivalent to over £400,000 at late 20th century prices). Surplus goods enabled a supplementary sale to be held in Exeter Hall the following month.

It was more than 35 years later before consideration was given to the possibility of women local preachers becoming full members of the Association, with the same voting and benefit rights as men. Some consternation was caused in the Aggregate meeting of 1897 (at Plymouth) when the proposed rule-change was put. One member enquired whether ladies would then be allowed to attend Aggregate meetings, and another was horrified to realise that this meant they would take preaching appointments. The position was embodied in the Rules of the Association as reprinted in the Jubilee Year, 1899. Rule 2 (defining membership) specified;

> . . . Local Preachers who are members of the Wesleyan Methodist Connexion, the Wesleyan Reform Union, the United Methodist Free Churches, and the Methodist New Connexion. Women, who are duly accredited Local Preachers of the Churches referred to in this Rule, shall be understood to be entitled to all rights and privileges in the Association which are enjoyed by men.

Inconsistencies remained in other Rules, which still referred to 'brethren', 'wife', 'widow'! The same Rule 2 wording still appeared in the reprint of 1928, the year when all women over age 21 were enfranchised for Parliamentary elections.

There was a small but significant change of flavour at the Aggregate Meeting of 1923 (Hull) when the newly-inducted President, Alderman E. R. Lightwood, B.A. J.P., began his Presidential Address, 'Fathers, *sisters*, brethren'. There were several women delegates to that Aggregate, but a much more noticeable change came when it elected the first woman member of the General Committee. The change was emphatic, for she topped the poll in a field of 17 candidates for 13 places, ahead of five members offering themselves for re-election. Lady Alice May Newbald Kay, the wife of the M.P. for Pudsey, Sir Robert Newbald Kay, was already well-known as an LPMAA deputation preacher. She had served in that capacity in London only a few weeks earlier, and appeared in Lincoln, Grimsby and other Circuits in the first few months after election to the General Committee.

At the 1924 Aggregate (Bolton) she was one of the speakers at the principal public meeting, taking the growing power of women's influence as her theme. The report in the July magazine (pp. 212 and 213) refers to the charm, wit and power of her address. Following the convention of the time, she is described in the report as '*Sister* Lady Newbald Kay'. She spoke forcefully about the rights granted to women after the 1914-18 war, rights which had been refused to the suffragette campaigners before it. She saw women and men as complementary to each other, making specific mention of the opportunity women had to serve as local preachers, though they would encounter much prejudice. The Chairman, Sir William Edge, characterised Lady Kay's speech as 'moving, inspiring and eloquent'.

She had given a similar speech at Lytham St Annes Branch Anniversary meeting a fortnight before Aggregate, on 'Emancipation of Women, with its Relationship to the Christian Church'. Sir Robert, founder and head of a firm of solicitors in York, served as Lord Mayor of that city in 1924-25. Lady Alice – an accomplished musician – was praised (in an illuminated address, still displayed in the offices of Newbald Kay in York) for the excellence of her hospitality and entertainment as Lady Mayoress. These duties precluded her from regular attendance at the General Committee during that year. She died in 1960 in a Scarborough Nursing Home, having suffered from diabetes for many years.

Part of a photograph of the Aggregate Meeting, Hanley Bethesda, 1926.
Four women appear in this; there were only two others in the outer parts of the photograph.

It was not until during the 1939-45 war that a second woman member of the General Committee was appointed. She was Miss E. Lorna Shirley-Smith, of Birmingham, the District in which the Fillongley retired preachers' cottages were located, and with which she was connected as a Trustee (see chapters 14 and 23). Meeting in November 1944, the General Committee elected her to fill a vacancy in its ranks. This elicited the comment from the Honorary Secretary, in his *Obiter Dicta* in the magazine for January/February 1945, that 'it might not be a bad thing if more of our sisters were to join her on our executive body'. The same writer in *A Goodly Fellowship* (1949) p.73, observed '. . . even yet there are few who have dared to envisage the installation of a feminine President.'

That possibility came a step nearer at the following year's Aggregate meeting at Bournemouth when Miss Shirley-Smith was nominated as a candidate for the Presidency. In a straight contest with W. H. Kneen she received approximately one-third of the votes. Thus the Association was prepared for the eventual election of a woman President. Nearly twenty years later this distinction actually fell to Alice Nuttall, who became President at the Sheffield Aggregate of 1969. The office has been occupied by women in five subsequent years – 1981 (Hilda Sendell), 1986 (Mary Bevin), 1990 (Rita Sawyer), 1996 (Doreen Shuttleworth) and 1998 (Ruth Haines). Half a century after the Honorary Secretary's remark about more of our sisters joining the executive, approximately a quarter of the General Committee members are women. Many more are active as District and Branch Officers.

LIFE AND LEISURE

Earlier in this chapter reference was made to the important developments in communication which took place in 1896, laying foundations for the media and transport revolutions of the 20th century. Three decades on, the impact of these developments on society and social behaviour was being felt in all spheres of life, including the life of the Christian Church and its associated organisations. In the 19th and early 20th centuries most people had limited time, means and opportunity to pursue leisure interests and social recreation. As late as the 1930s the typical working week was still 50 hours spread over at least five and a half days per week, the working year was 50 weeks and the working life 50 years. Incomes were not generally sufficient for much expenditure beyond rent, and food and clothing for the family. Before the 1914-18 war, leisure facilities for the majority of people did not extend much beyond public houses and music halls.

In these circumstances the activities of the chapels offered some attractions. Many less-well-off people, whose homes were perhaps not very comfortable, could not afford to spend money on going out. Worship provided opportunity to pass an hour and a half in a warm, brightly-lit building, meet friends, enjoy some community singing, and be entertained by an orator who would enliven his address with some amusing anecdotes. The 14 year old John Hamer Shawcross, in chapter 6 of Howard Spring's novel *Fame Is The Spur*, records in his diary how the special preacher mesmerised the congregation at the Chapel Anniversary, and kindled in him a desire to become a preacher. As a means of using limited free time inexpensively, the occasional 'special events' when famous people came from other parts of the country, were even more attractive. Attending big assemblies to hear long speeches by eloquent speakers was an important part of social life in the Victorian and Edwardian eras. Like many other bodies, LPMAA promoted such events for its own purposes.

The annual Aggregate was the peak season for public meetings, and in the heyday of the Association several would take place before, during and after the business days. In 1906 when it met at Bradford, as well as fourteen open-air meetings and three love-feasts, five full-scale public meetings were held in major centres around the District. These were addressed by 19 leading speakers, including the President (David Barr), six past-Presidents, three who later served as President, and three overseas representatives. At three of these 'great gatherings', as the *Methodist Recorder* called them, the Mayors of the local boroughs presided.

THE MEDIA REVOLUTION

By the mid-1920s, however, things had changed – 'the wireless' was finding its way into many homes, public cinematograph entertainment was easily available, and motor transport in the form of charabanc travel brought inexpensive days-out within reach of more and more people. Public meetings to hear outstanding orators declined in popularity, in the political and educational realms as much as in the religious sphere. There were only three such events at the 1926 Aggregate (Hanley Bethesda United Methodist) having between them a mere eight speakers. Little more than a further decade passed before a single public meeting with one main speaker became the norm.

The Association was not slow to adapt to the changing situation. If people were less inclined to come to traditional events, other means of communication had to be sought. Dr T. E. Nuttall (President 1925-26) was the first representative of LPMAA to make use of a broadcast medium. The Senior Convener of Birmingham District, Arthur E. Deed, explained in *The Local Preachers Magazine* in March 1926:

> General Committee visited Birmingham on 16th and 17th January. It occurred to our District President and myself that it would be a good idea to arrange for the address at the usual Studio Service broadcast from 5IT, the Birmingham Station of the BBC, to be given by Dr Nuttall. Arrangements were duly made, and it was my privilege to accompany him to the Studio and read the Lesson (Parable of the Talents). This, I believe, was the first occasion on which any of our Presidents have had this privilege, and means that he was addressing an audience of anything from 100,000 to 250,000 people.

The magazine also contained the text of the President's broadcast address, in which he derived from the parable a pertinent message on 'Negligence' – neglect of God's gifts means that we shall lose them. Since that time, LPMAA has made opportunities for Presidents and other representatives to broadcast on radio and television. Recordings exist of some of these broadcasts. In 1969 the Aggregate service at Millhouses Methodist Church in Sheffield (led jointly by the President, Alice Nuttall, and the immediate past-President, David Walmsley) was broadcast on both media. The use of radio and television has sometimes proved challenging; for example, when only five minutes have been available to someone accustomed to developing a theme over twenty minutes, or when the broadcast has taken the form of a brisk interview by a radio DJ!

EDUCATION INTO RELIGION

This was the title of a book by Professor A. Victor Murray, Vice-President of Conference, 1947. In it he identified five elements of a growing Christian experience. There is, he said, something to know, something to feel, something to choose, something to do, something to belong to. These were some of the important influences on Christian organisations, and the Church itself, in the post-1945 years. Opportunities for learning, for choice, for employment and leisure activity, and for belonging to groups with shared interests, all expanded. This presented a challenge, if not a threat, to people who were accustomed to finding their fulfilment in a Christian setting.

The Methodist Church and its associated organisations had to recognise these influences and address their challenge. The Local Preachers Mutual Aid Association had emerged from the difficulties described in chapter 17, and whilst planning for the celebration of its centenary in 1949 began to develop new policies and programmes. These developments are described in Sections V and VI of this book – 'Continuity and Change' and 'Living Memory and Present Hope'. Before that, however, a few chapters (Section IV) are devoted to the local activities of LPMAA in Districts and Circuits under the title 'Our Roots Are Our Branches'.

Section IV

OUR ROOTS ARE OUR BRANCHES

The majority of members of the Local Preachers Mutual Aid Association have never held national office, never had opportunity to serve on national committees, never been able to attend the Aggregate Meeting. Their active involvement in the Association has been in their local Branch, or possibly in District events. For most members, the only times when they have been caught up in the life of LPMAA as a Connexional body have been when the General Committee or the Aggregate Meeting has visited their District. Hence these chapters, which remind us that without its local manifestation – its membership in the Branches – there would be no Association.

Sadly, records in some Districts are incomplete, or even non-existent, apart from current minute books. When former secretaries have stepped down from office past records have not always been handed on. Much knowledge of LPMAA activity has similarly perished when a present or past office-holder has died. In other Districts, records and memories have been better preserved, and have enabled someone to prepare a contribution for this part of the book. Some Districts have remembered with pride members from their Branches who have become national figures in the Association; some have recalled experiences when the Aggregate or the General Committee met in their area; some have been able to focus on very local matters, typifying the work in many Branches over the years.

[Far more information has been received from a few areas than could possibly be included. This was unavoidable for a reasonable balance to be achieved, but some of this material has found a place in other sections. One or two Districts hope to produce a booklet about their own history.]

LPMAA In:

Chapter	19	The North	Chapter 23	The West Midlands
Chapter	20	Yorkshire	Chapter 24	Eastern England
Chapter	21	Lancashire	Chapter 25	The Home Counties
Chapter	22	Wales	Chapter 26	The South and West

19

LPMAA in the North

The most northerly part of LPMAA, as of Methodism itself, is Scotland and the Northern Isles. The Association's membership there is numerically small and geographically scattered; this restricts Branch activity. One Branch officer intimated that the majority of LPMAA members in his area had joined whilst living in England! Nevertheless, one recent President was able to visit Scotland and reported an encouraging response. Correspondence with members 'north of the Border' shows that they appreciate being remembered.

Newcastle-upon-Tyne's outstanding LPMAA personality, William Stephenson, has a prominent place in the story of the Association's relationship with Methodism in the later years of the 19th century (see chapter 12). He was the first man to serve twice as President of LPMAA (1883,1895). In each of these years the Aggregate Meeting was held in Newcastle and he was Mayor, or Lord Mayor, of the city, a position he occupied seven times altogether. The Newcastle-upon-Tyne District has entertained the Aggregate Meeting on seven occasions, most recently in 1986 – jointly with the Darlington District. The General Committee's last visit to the District was in April 1998, when the President had the pleasure of presiding 'on home ground'. The members in this most northerly of the English Districts have always taken a lively interest in the affairs of the Association. A good example of this is the persistence of some of its leading members during the late 1950s in pressing LPMAA to extend its beneficence to all local preachers and dependants, regardless of membership. (This actually came about in 1961, as explained in chapter 32).

Geography has dictated that Cumbria's main centres of population – Barrow, Carlisle, Whitehaven and Workington – are on the periphery. Even today isolation by distance and the weather affects, *inter alia*, the work of LPMAA. The usual methods of travel – on foot, by horse and trap, train, bus, bicycle and, eventually, car – were, of course, available. However, the hazards of reaching appointments in this area of mountains and valleys are illustrated by the plaque erected on Irton Fell in the Whitehaven Circuit:

In memory of William Malkinson,
Wesleyan Local Preacher.
Died here suddenly. Sunday February 21st 1886.
'Be ye also ready'.

The history of LPMAA in Cumbria goes back almost to the beginning of the Association. A Kendal local preacher attended the Fourth Aggregate Meeting, held at Queen Street Chapel, Huddersfield, in October 1852. On Good Friday 1856 the Workington Branch held a public tea to aid the funds of the Association. LPMAA work in the District developed slowly at first, but by the end of the nineteenth century eight Branches had been formed. These included Workington, Penrith, Barrow, Carlisle, Keswick and Cockermouth, Millom, Wigton and Maryport, and Whitehaven. The Penrith Branch was favoured in December 1887 by a visit from the President, J. W. Laycock (of Keighley), and the immediate past-President, Moses Atkinson.

During the First World War, Walter Taylor, one of the District Conveners, produced a revealing report on the state of LPMAA in the District. Branches had lapsed – or nearly so – at Whitehaven, Kendal and Appleby. A similar state of affairs existed in the Northern Section. Moses Atkinson visited the Whitehaven Circuit in 1916 to restart the Branch. When the General Committee met at Morecambe in May 1920 'well-known brethren' went to Kendal to encourage the Branch there.

There has always been a parallel emphasis on fellowship and mutual aid in the preaching work amongst members in the Cumbria District. As long ago as 1916 an open Conference and Public Meeting was held to consider: a. The Local Preacher and Spiritual Advance, b. The Preacher and His Commission, c. The Local Preacher and Social Questions – all in a single day! In October 1919 an LPMAA Residential Weekend was held at Abbot Hall, Kents Bank, for local preachers to meet 'for prayer and mutual encouragement'. Discussions centred on 'The Fullness of Time', 'The Preacher's Equipment' and 'Prayer'. Thus began the tradition, unbroken except for the 1939-45 war years, of 70 annual Abbot Hall LPMAA weekends.

Early printed programmes, circulated to all Branches, announced that:

This weekend is arranged with the hope that men may return to their circuits inspired by its fellowship to greater evangelistic effort.

In the 1920s and 1930s these weekends attracted attendances of up to 65 Local Preachers plus 20 wives/husbands. Leading speakers included LPMAA personalities – Harold Buss, Winship Storey, Charles Lamb, R. Parkinson Tomlinson and William Noddings. There were also Connexional speakers – Clifford Towlson from Woodhouse Grove School, and Lillian Todd of the Methodist Youth Department. The earliest Conference for which a programme leaflet still exists took place in October 1921. The cost from Saturday afternoon to Monday morning was 14s, plus 1s for staff. Breakfast at 7.00 am on Monday enabled members to catch early trains back home and to work. The speakers that year were Arthur Cowling, Association President, and a past-President J. W. Hampson.

When the weekends were resumed after the war (1946) the Communion Service was for some years conducted by past-President Fred Ogden, of Rochdale. Coming from the United Methodist tradition, he retained his authorisation to preside at the Sacrament of the Lord's Supper. The Abbot Hall fellowship also enjoyed the support and encouragement of successive Chairmen of the Cumbria District. It was only changed to a one-day event in 1993, when changing lifestyle, cost and other commitments reduced the numbers attending. A Day School was held at Penrith instead.

LPMAA in Cumbria has hosted several meetings of the General Committee over the years, most recently at Kendal (1997) which was also the venue in 1965 and 1969. Other locations were Penrith (1988), Workington (1954) and Carlisle (1905). Aggregate has never been held in the District, although its northern circuits received preachers from Aggregate when it assembled in Newcastle-upon-Tyne in 1895. Members who have served LPMAA in the District over many years include 'Ted' Armitage (Convener/Senior Convener), Alex Burton, Secretary/Treasurer of the Kendal Branch, and Richard Hull, Treasurer of the Abbot Hall Conferences, both for 30 years, and William Armistead, Secretary at Sedbergh for 40 years.

Mining areas have traditionally been strong supporters of LPMAA; this has been true of the western industrial belt of the District, where wages were low and unemployment was persistent. The Workington Branch had 70 personal invitations to its anniversary weekends delivered by hand in the 1930s, indicative of the enthusiasm and commitment in many Cumbrian Branches. Benefits were gratefully received, especially by miners and steelworkers if disabled by industrial accidents, and by widows when such accidents left them bereaved. In 1919 the District meeting was urged to send representatives to Aggregate to support proposals for increased allowances for widows.

Across the Pennines, the Thornley Branch in County Durham illustrates the ways that LPMAA responded to needs in another mining area, though mining ceased in that part of north east England many years ago. In the late 1920s the Branch minutes regularly recorded income around £20 per annum, against payments made by the Association to beneficiaries in the Branch which sometimes exceeded £60. In 1928 it was decided to take no action on a request from Head Office to increase sales of *The Local Preachers Magazine* (it was not included in the membership subscription at that time). The reason was '. . . the unfortunate bad conditions prevailing in the District'. Recruitment of Honorary Members was not pursued for the same reason.

A new Secretary was appointed in 1930, his predecessor relinquishing office after serving for 22 years. The Branch continued to consider all applications for benefit most carefully but, in view of the depressed state of the local economy, often recommended applicants to the 'best consideration of the General Committee'. Sometimes a particular amount was suggested adding '. . . or such other sum as the General Committee thinks best.' By 1931 the continuing shortfall of branch income (against benefits paid) stimulated the decision to appeal to the Circuit Quarterly Meeting. The Secretary wrote a carefully worded letter asking that the whole of the collections on LPMAA Sunday be given to the Association. He supported the request by some facts and figures:

> The total number of persons today receiving benefits from the Association are 520 local preachers and 484 local preachers widows making a total of 1,004. The cost to the Association is £25,000 per year or £484 per

week. During the last 20 years the Association has sent into this circuit alone at the rate of £30 a year more than the circuit has sent to the Association.

He added the appreciation of the preachers for the gracious reception of their ministry, and said that they were grateful for the opportunity to serve. The object of the Association was to put a little practical Christianity into operation. The letter also included a request that the various Societies in the Circuit might make this a special week-end effort for LPMAA.

The Branch also made its own efforts. In most years through the 1930s it held what was styled 'A Local Preachers' Convention', partly as a means of drawing together preachers from different Circuits in that part of Durham. In 1936 the minutes particularly noted the attendance for the first time of a lady member. Two years later, a sombre note was struck in the meeting, after a member lost his life in a recent pit disaster. A similarly solemn minute in 1941 records the sympathy of the Branch with a brother and his wife upon the loss of their son in military action. The minutes ceased in 1942, the Branch apparently not resuming activity until 1953.

A fascinating discovery was made in 1998, during the course of office re-organisation at 'Westerley', Grange-over-Sands. An engraved metal plate was found, fixed to a large roll-top desk which had been there longer than anyone can remember. The inscription reads:

Presented to
Mr James Taylor
by the members of the
Darlington (Bondgate) Branch of the LPMAAssocn
as a token of regard
and appreciation of valuable services
rendered as Secretary for several years
July 1900

It must have been a costly and generous gift for that time. The question then arises – how did it come to be at the LPMAA Home at Grange-over-Sands? It is now in the care of a member in the Crook and Willington Branch, Darlington District.

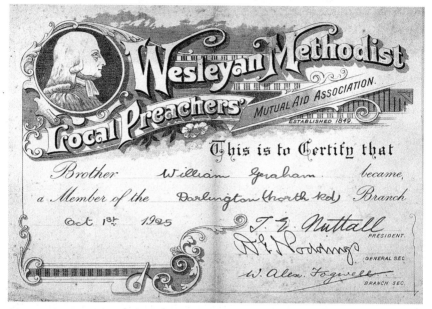

Membership certificate of Wm. Graham

The Darlington Branch (prior to 1964 it was two Branches, North and South) cherishes memories of several notable members, amongst them 'Three Williams' – Wm. Graham, Wm. Lavender, and Wm. Denham. The first two were accountants, though **William Graham** spent the later years of his working life as an industrial welfare officer, for which he received the MBE. In addition to his work as a District and Branch Officer, he was frequently a delegate to Aggregate, was also District Local Preachers' Tutor and a member of the Connexional Local Preachers' Committee. [Further information about William Graham is given in *Workaday Preachers*, p. 102.] **William Lavender** had an untiring interest and love for the work of LPMAA. As well as being an authority on bee-keeping he was a member of the British Astronomical Society. He bore a strong resemblance to King George VI. **William Denham** was originally a Congregational lay preacher. He left coalmining to live and work in the south of England, but returned to the north east after marrying and became a Methodist and a local preacher, serving as LPMAA Branch Secretary for a number of years to 1957.

The Middlesbrough Branch of LPMAA was established in 1884, its second anniversary being fully reported in *The Local Preachers Magazine* of June 1886. The Anniversary Sunday was 2nd May. Services were conducted by the President, G.C.Amphlett (of London), and visiting preachers from Bradford, including a lovefeast at Grange Road Chapel in the afternoon. The Public Meeting on Monday was also held at Grange Road. The Branch Chairman, W. Bulmer (later the first LPMAA Chairman of the Whitby and Darlington District, upon its formation in 1888) presided. The Secretary, H. Smith, presented a report showing the Branch to be in 'a very healthy state'. Addresses were given by the visiting preachers, including the President, and by Rev. J. W. Armstrong. The gathering was described as

> one of the most earnest and intelligent gatherings we have seen in Middlesbrough, and we doubt not but the Middlesbrough Branch has received an impetus which will be lasting.

Emanuel Spence, J.P. was a prominent Methodist, a notable public figure, and a successful business man in Middlesborough for much of the first half of the 20th century. He was elected as a Councillor for the Acklam ward of the Borough in 1910, continuing in that capacity until 1923. In the municipal year 1919-20 he served as Mayor of Middlesbrough. For seven years from 1926 he was a Councillor for the Ayresome Ward, and was elected to the Aldermanic bench in 1933. Amongst other key positions, he was Chairman of the Council's Housing and Parks Committees at various times. His public service was recognised by the award of the OBE in 1939.

In Methodism he was not only a local preacher, but served also in several circuit offices. His name appears in the list of lay members of Connexional Committees in the Minutes of the 1932 Uniting Conference of Methodism. He represented the Middlesbrough and Darlington District as a member of the Connexional Home Mission Committee. The Association attracted his interest during the 1920s. After a two-year term as LPMAA Chairman of the former Whitby and Darlington District (1927-29) he was elected to the General Committee. Re-elected three times for successive five-year periods, he was still a member of the Committee when he died in 1948.

Alderman Spence was a leading contributor to the debate on the relationship between the Association and the Connexional Local Preachers' Committee in 1945 and 1946 (see chapter 17). He emphasised the responsibilities of the Trustees to safeguard the Association's assets, and returned to the same theme in a letter to the Editor of the magazine in November 1945. The debate on relations with the Connexion was gaining momentum. He stressed the importance of adhering to the provisions of the Trust Deed, contending that to interfere with them would lose support for Mutual Aid from Methodist people. At the next year's Aggregate Meeting, at Lincoln, a resolution was moved to suggest that part of LPMAA Sunday collections should be allocated to the Local Preachers' Department. The Alderman moved an amendment, which was carried, to leave the whole matter in abeyance. His last major public contribution to the Association's work was as speaker at one of the five public meetings held at that year's Aggregate.

LPMAA was given an unusual interest in a Trust, set up in Durham in 1895 for 'increasing the efficiency of local preachers'. John Pearson Leybourne recognised the value of their work, especially in the colliery villages, and gave £270 to be used for the provision of facilities to encourage their reading and study. The Trustees included the Superintendent Minister. The Deed stipulated that a committee of ministers and local preachers should be appointed to make rules and appoint officers. All decisions were to be approved by the Circuit Local Preachers' Meeting.

Part of the initial sum was to be used for the purchase of a bookcase and books to form a library for local preachers. The greater part was to be invested to provide income for the purchase of further books – Biblical, Theological, Exegetical and Church History were particularly specified; novels, frivolous and light literature were explicitly excluded. Gifts of books to local preachers on trial, including Wesley's *Fifty-Three Sermons*, and book prizes for success in examinations, set to increase the efficiency of the Circuit's accredited preachers, were also authorised. If the Trust had surplus income, if it disposed of any assets or part of its capital, or if it was wound up, such surplus income or capital proceeds were to be divided equally between LPMAA and the *Wesleyan Foreign Missionary Society* (sic).

20

LPMAA In Yorkshire

Four Yorkshiremen were amongst the twenty-four who attended the meeting in Birmingham on 24th July 1849 to plan the inaugural Aggregate Meeting. Messrs Sharman, Collier and Howarth were from Sheffield and James Uriah Walker came from Halifax. When the Association was formally constituted in October of the same year James Walker was elected to the committee with Messrs Sharman, John Unwin (also of Sheffield, later fifth President), William Nelstrop (Pontefract, later fourth President), Smithson (York), and twenty-six others. Henry Reed from Scarborough and Edward Brooke of Huddersfield became two of the first six trustees. It is not surprising that with such strong initial support in the area, the county was host to four of the first eight Aggregate meetings – Sheffield in 1851, Huddersfield in 1852, Leeds in 1853 and Sheffield again in 1856.

Perhaps because of the diligence of Yorkshire members in seeking out needy brethren in the early years, serious concern was expressed in the York Circuit's Quarterly Meeting. In December 1886 it was recorded that:

> . . . grants from the Local Preachers Mutual Aid Society (a most deserving fund) to aged and poor members in York, amounted last year to £53-4-3d, while the total subscriptions from York amounted to only to £36. This, we venture to think, is not as it should be.

The meeting agreed that a collection for the fund should be made in all chapels.

On the western edge of the industrial West Riding, new local preachers joining the Hebden Bridge Branch had their LPMAA entrance fee paid by the Circuit. This began when the Branch was formed in 1884. The arrangement was not without opponents, causing the Branch to ask in 1907 that either the opposition cease or the question be raised in Circuit Quarterly Meeting for final decision. Opposition ceased! In 1936 the Branch

CONFIDENCE IN MUTUAL AID

itself decided to make members responsible for their own dues.

In 1926 a member gave a 'very descriptive and racy account' of his visit to the Aggregate meeting in Hanley. The brethren listened for 75 minutes(!) 'with great interest to the inspiring address'. At other meetings the Branch gave time to the discussion of such preaching-related topics as the best method of delivering a sermon, and on one occasion, the state of the church.

Relations with the circuit authorities were again under strain in 1953. The Quarterly Meeting unexpectedly decided to allow a University Students' Campaign to use its pulpits on the last Sunday in March, the day traditionally given to LPMAA. The Branch, which had not been consulted and had already made arrangements for preaching supply from other circuits, sent a letter to the Circuit Secretary expressing its:

> . . . bitterness and concern at the manner in which
> this Sunday has been taken away from us.

After the merger with Halifax (1963) the combined Branch of Calderdale was host to General Committee in March 1964. This was the famous 'Fish and Chips Committee', so called because Clifford Lees – described in *The Local Preachers Magazine* in May of that year as 'the indefatigable young Secretary' – decided to use local resources instead of providing the traditional ham salad tea. Thirty years later, an older, but still indefatigable, Clifford Lees recalled that the Branch then had a member who owned a fish and chip shop, which made it possible to provide the indigenous Yorkshire fare to the General Committee, Branch members, hosts, beneficiaries and guests. In those days visits of the Committee were more like Aggregates when it came to numbers, and 175 sat down to the meal. He remembered that the food was served on time, and the problem of keeping the first batch hot had been (almost) solved. Afterwards a panel tackled 'Any Questions?' including one of the burning issues of the time – the place of local preachers and of the Association in a possible united Anglican/Methodist Church.

Nearby Bradford has been visited by Aggregate five times – in 1889, 1906, 1921, 1939, and 1967. When the venue was Elland in 1985 the catering was notable because the luncheon on the Monday was prepared and served entirely on the premises of Southgate Methodist Church, with the Superintendent Minister personally carving the roast beef. One of the Hospitality Secretaries for the 1967 Aggregate was Mrs Emily Burslem, for many years Secretary of the Shipley Branch. She was the third lady to be elected to General Committee, serving on it from 1952 to 1972. When her death was reported in the *The Local Preachers Magazine* of August 1990 the Branch described her as 'something special'. Even after giving up regular preaching in her nineties, she said she always had a sermon ready when she attended worship 'in case the preacher doesn't turn up'.

The Association in Leeds built on a good beginning, despite the aftermath of the Brunswick organ affair (1827) and the exclusions upheaval (see chapter 4). Branches were established and multiplied as interest grew. But inevitably they waxed and waned over the years, often functioning only because of the work of one or two enthusiasts. In December 1938 some keen members called preachers from Armley, Bramley, Stanningley and Pudsey Circuits together to form the Leeds South West Branch. Those present included R. F. Pascoe, later a District Convener.

Like all organisations LPMAA Branches were affected by the outbreak of war, and Leeds South West typifies the situation. The minutes of its 1941 annual meeting relate the problems ['blackout' refers to the suspension of street lighting during war]:

> . . . war conditions affecting in many ways the daily lives of our members of all ages and occupations made it difficult to get a quorum at our meetings, also the blackout for months has added to our difficulties.

Despite those difficulties and the frequent bombing of northern cities, the work was continued and expanded by members not away in the Forces. Branch meetings were held on winter evenings 'during the moonlit period'. Contact with members was maintained, including correspondence with members on active service in the armed forces. Annuitants were visited and new honorary members recruited. Increasing amounts of money were forwarded to Head Office and the Branch showed a slow but steady increase in membership.

Gareth Burn, Leeds North Branch Secretary from 1966 to 1969, recalls one beneficiary, John Smith, a local preacher blind from birth who was very interested in football. The Branch visitor arranged to take John to the Leeds United ground. He described where they were standing in relation to the pitch, and John would then follow the game by its sound. In addition the Association assisted him financially, and contributed to the cost of a holiday.

For some years Leeds Branch, which now covers most of the city's circuits, has arranged a high-profile annual lunch, where beneficiaries can meet Branch members and other guests, including civic leaders. A half-yearly newsletter helps to keep its 250 members informed about LPMAA affairs, and a Branch summer outing is also a valuable means of cementing fellowship.

In 1896 the Easingwold circuit's preachers enquired how to establish a Branch. Where the initiative came from is not clear, but one preacher in the circuit, W. Cussans of Raskelf, whose death is recorded in the minutes of 10th September 1913, had been a member of LPMAA for a number of years when the request was made. Four months after the enquiry the preachers' meeting received a delegation, including Rev. H. T. Brumwell, from the York New Street Branch. The Easingwold Branch was formed, and by 1907 LPMAA Sunday was well-established in the circuit. In 1909 a member attended the Aggregate Meeting and reported enthusiastically about his experience.

In the old East Riding, the Hornsea Branch, formed in the little port many years before, met one January evening in 1943. It seems LPMAA was the only combined gathering for preachers in the two pre-Union circuits centred on the town. From that meeting they launched a broadside by letter at the two Circuit Quarterly Meetings:

> As brethren of both circuits met together . . . we deeply regret that after nine years of Methodist Union, so little has been done to establish union . . . between the circuits. We are persuaded that this is due . . . solely to the persistence of prejudice and apathy which are the unworthy legacy of old-time sectarian differences. In the presence of wide-spread unbelief . . . past differences become the merest trivialities.

The letter concluded by urging the two circuits to welcome every opportunity of uniting in worship and service, thus continuing the

LPMAA tradition of pressing for Union, connexionally before 1932 and afterwards in the circuits. The Branch also followed LPMAA tradition in the matter of social concerns. In 1956 a letter was sent from its annual meeting to the local MP, expressing opposition to the Small Lotteries Bill then before Parliament.

In reporting the District meeting of 26th September 1953, the Branch Minutes noted that Arnold Brown, of Pickering, was the speaker at the evening meeting. Three years later he was appointed LPMAA Homes Officer. A 1955 minute refers to the previous year's Spring District Meeting when Professor T. E. Jessop of Hull (Vice-President of Conference,1955-56) had addressed the evening meeting.

During the 1950s two particular matters arose on which the Hornsea Branch responded. In 1954 the Association offered special help to members in east coast Branches who suffered loss or damage in the storm and floods of 1953. Later, Head Office asked all Branches for information about members who might need residential nursing care because of 'senile decay' or chronic illness. Enquiries were made, but no Hornsea member needed either kind of help.

Methodist Union in 1932 meant changes in Connexional District boundaries, which in turn affected those of LPMAA. Sheffield transferred eight branches into other Districts, and its annual meeting in Rotherham that year minuted 'thankful appreciation and good wishes for the future' to them. Further changes were noted 25 years later. In 1957 Methodism elected 'separated Chairmen' for a reduced number of larger Districts. That year the Sheffield District LPMAA meeting in November welcomed those who gathered for the first time in the 'enlarged District'. Between these dates the Doncaster and Barnsley areas lay outside the Sheffield District. This prevented Sheffield from claiming Barnsley's **Herbert Ibberson**, Vice-President of Conference (1942) and President of the Association (1945), as its own. However, he was the distinguished visitor and speaker at the evening public meeting when the District met at Staveley on 6th March 1943. Immediately after his LPMAA Presidential year he began an eleven-year period as Honorary Secretary of the Association.

A man whose public and Methodist fame did not come until

he moved to Yorkshire was **Richard J. Soper**. Born near Bishop Auckland, County Durham, in June 1878, he received a thorough grounding in the faith and in Methodism. Upon moving to (West) Hartlepool in 1898 he became a very effective Class Leader and leader of a successful boys' class. He moved to Barnsley in 1910, and there became a local preacher and an active member of LPMAA. In 1924 he was elected to the General Committee, and in the same year became a Town Councillor. This led to a year as Mayor of Barnsley in 1930-31, which was followed by his election as M.P. for the borough in 1931. He continued as M.P. until 1935.

After Methodist Union in 1932 Richard Soper was appointed a member of the Stationing Committee and in 1938 was elected (by Conference) as a three-year member of Conference. In the same year the Aggregate Meeting elected him to be President of the Association for 1939-40, not an easy task when war was declared early in September. In the event, having begun the war years as LPMAA President, he concluded them as Vice-President of Conference, for which office he was designated in 1945. He thus became the third man to serve in both positions. He addressed the 1947 Aggregate Meeting just before completing his Vice-Presidential year, evoking the description 'quiet, dignified, earnest' in the Aggregate report. The District LPMAA Chairman of 1937 was Dr L. Ward Kay, who also served as Vice-President of Conference (1953).

The Yorkshire Districts have supplied the Association with ten Presidents in the second half of the 20th century. E. A. Arnold (1954) was manager of a Methodist bookshop. At 76 he was the oldest member ever to serve in the Presidency. He had been an Aggregate journal-writer for many years. Alice Nuttall (see also chapter 18) was the first lady to hold the office (1969). Harold Archer served in 1972. Bridlington provided two Presidents in Cyril Mitchell (1970) and Norman Jones (1980). Donald Nuttall's election as President for 1977 created the first example of a husband and wife both serving in the office. A second example arose in the Derbyshire part of the Sheffield District when Rita and Gerald Sawyer held the office, in 1990 and 1994 respectively. Yorkshire has provided two further Presidents during the 1990s – Allan Dyer (1992) and Doreen Shuttleworth (1996).

One other notable national figure in LPMAA was Eustace Fendick. He was appointed Press and Publicity Officer in 1984 and served in that office for ten years. Eustace had previously fulfilled a similar function for the Sheffield District, and before that for his own Doncaster Branch. He was succeeded as National Publicity Officer by another Doncaster man, Mike Summers.

Reference is made in some other parts of this book to funds, other than those of LPMAA, which were established to help local preachers. There was often a link with the Mutual Aid Association, either directly or through a particular LPMAA person. The latter was the case in 1860 when William Heap, of Halifax, gave £100 to be invested for the benefit of necessitous local preachers in that Circuit. One of the Trustees was a General Committee member, James Uriah Walker, who is mentioned earlier in this chapter and in chapter 9. The Heap Charity still exists, since the late 1960s as part of the Halifax Local Preachers' Benevolent Fund. One of the present Trustees, Mr Walter Beveridge, says it is believed that in the early days the Heap Charity provided boots for preachers who walked long distances to appointments.

21

LPMAA in Lancashire

As chapter 5 shows, the very earliest endeavours to organise mutual aid amongst local preachers were made in Lancashire. This is not surprising. Much of the impetus for Friendly Society development, during the rapid industrial growth in the first half of the 19th century, arose in this part of England. The spirit of sturdy independence that prospered amongst cotton textile workers was fostered in associations of all kinds – trade unions, self-help groups, and by the 1840s in co-operative societies. The idea of associations to secure and promote collective independence began to permeate Wesleyan Methodism in those years. It spilled over into the movement for mutual aid amongst local preachers. The Rochdale Wesleyan Methodist Local Preachers Friendly Society deleted the restrictive adjective 'Wesleyan' from its title at an early stage. However, having retained reformist local preachers (and others expelled from the Wesleyan body) in its membership, it declined to amalgamate with LPMAA until after 1866. Whether it ever did become a branch of the national body, and if so when, is not known.

A number of notable LPMAA personalities have originated in Lancashire, whilst others have settled and served in the Red Rose County. **Charles Heap, J.P.**, of Rochdale, was one of the former group. Born in 1845, his services were nearly denied to the Association, as he entered the Wesleyan ministry when a young man. Upon the death of his father he felt obliged to leave the ministry to return home, where he took charge of the family cotton textiles business. In this he was very successful, and became an influential figure in the town. He held most lay offices in Methodism, and was Rochdale Mission Treasurer for many years. He was elected to the Presidency of LPMAA in 1896, later becoming one of its Trustees, and served as Treasurer from 1908 to 1922, the year before his death. Charles Heap was one of the major financial supporters of the Fillongley Homes for Aged Local Preachers (see chapter 13).

George Royle (later Sir George) was born in Manchester in 1861, and received his early education at Bury Wesleyan Day School. In adult life he left Lancashire and settled in Bedford, playing a prominent part in the public life of the town, including the mayoralty in 1903. He served Wesleyan Methodism at Connexional committee and circuit levels, and LPMAA as President in 1908. His entry in the 1934 *Methodist Local Preachers' Who's Who* states that as a Barrister-at-Law he practised from chambers at Lincolns Inn. It also indicates the unusual distinction of being an Indian Chief of the Tribe of the Iroquois. Shortly after that honour was conferred on him he was able (September 1930) to entertain his General Committee colleagues to tea before their meeting. He revealed to them then that the name he had been given at the decoration ceremony was 'Sunshine'. 'Big Chief Sunshine' lived to enjoy his unusual status until the end of 1949, when he died aged 88.

A President who was a Lancashireman by adoption was **O. O. Noel**, from the Channel Islands. He settled in Southport, and like Charles Heap achieved success in the cotton textiles industry. He was LPMAA president in 1913. Nine years later another 'incomer' to Lancashire occupied the Presidential chair. **Arthur Cowling** was a Yorkshireman, who began his working life in the woollen industry. He started at the age of 9 as a half-timer, and from age 12 to 17 worked full time in the mill. Studying in his spare time he was able to enter the teaching profession and early in the 20th century became Headmaster of Wigan Wesleyan Day School, in which post he continued until retirement at the age of 60 in 1927. He first appeared on the national LPMAA scene as Plan Secretary for the Bolton Aggregate of 1911, and was elected to General Committee the following year. To this was soon added the office of District Convener. He was elected as President for 1922. He fulfilled the Presidential role with such distinction that when the Association needed another Honorary Secretary in 1924 he was appointed. Two years later he became the senior Honorary Secretary. Sadly, his death from a heart attack just after the 1930 Aggregate Meeting denied LPMAA any further years of his outstanding service. Tributes to him (some in verse) occupied more than a dozen pages in the August and September magazines of that year.

In **R. Parkinson Tomlinson, J.P.**, of Poulton-le-Fylde, Lancashire produced one of the great characters of LPMAA. He was one of only three Presidents over the Association's life to be recalled for a second term in that office, and one of only four to have been honoured by the Methodist Conference by election to its Vice-Presidency. He was also one of the distinguished few Mutual Aid men who have been Members of Parliament. Affectionately known by his many friends as 'Parky', it is said that when he became entitled to add the letters M.P. after his name, he asked them to remember that J.P. M.P. meant 'Just Parky, Methodist Preacher'. He so impressed his colleagues by what the senior Honorary Secretary, Harold Buss, called his 'brilliant' Presidency of 1928-29, that in September 1930 the General Committee appointed him Honorary Secretary, following the death of Arthur Cowling.

Thus began a partnership in the secretariat which guided the Association to the middle of the 1939-45 war. It was the special demands of those years which led to Parky's election as President for 1942-43. This was the last service he rendered LPMAA, for he died less than a week before he would have passed the President's Bible to his successor. The memorial tablet in Garstang Methodist Chapel bears the following inscription:

> IN LOVING MEMORY OF
> ## R. PARKINSON TOMLINSON. J.P.
> OF POULTON-LE-FYLDE,
> ENSHRINED IN THE HEARTS OF HOSTS OF FRIENDS
> THROUGHOUT THE GARSTANG CIRCUIT.
> VICE-PRESIDENT
> OF THE METHODIST CONFERENCE 1938.
> PRESIDENT OF THE L.P.M.A. 1928 & 1942.
> BORN MAY 20TH 1881. ASCENDED JUNE 3RD 1943.
> HE PREACHED IN THE PULPITS OF THIS CIRCUIT FOR
> FORTY YEARS AND WAS TRUSTEE OF FOUR CHAPELS.
> HE WAS A WISE COUNSELLOR, A STAUNCH FRIEND,
> A GENEROUS AND ENTHUSIASTIC HELPER.
> HIS CONSTANT PURPOSE WAS
> "O LET ME COMMEND MY SAVIOUR TO YOU."

Rochdale provided the Association with another President in 1936, when **Fred Ogden**, a local preacher of the United Methodist tradition served in that office. In 1947 he attained both his 70th birthday and 50 years as a local preacher. 150 people, including the Mayors of Rochdale and neighbouring Heywood, gathered to share in the celebration. He had a lifelong family connection with the chapel at Spotland where, amongst other commitments, he followed his father, Alderman Thomas Ogden as leader of the men's class. Also like his father, he was prominent in public life, including as a Justice of the Peace from 1931. Fred Ogden's contribution to the annual Abbot Hall week-end conferences, for some years after the 1939-45 war, is referred to in chapter 19. He died in 1966, aged 89.

The Rochdale Branch also remembers with pride the contribution made to its life by a member who did not serve the Association on the national scene. Stanley Crompton held office successively over a number of years as Branch Secretary, Treasurer and Chairman, and also served a term as District Chairman. He used to joke that the District only elected him as a delegate to the Aggregate Meeting whenever this met in a town beginning with 'L' - Leeds 1945, Lincoln 1946, Leicester 1957 and London 1961.

The last Lancashire notable on our list, still with us in retirement, attracted the attention of the *Methodist Recorder* in October 1994, in one of a series of articles about veteran local preachers. The headline, beside a photograph of the beaming smile and white carnation, was:

The one and only Richard Spencer

For more than a dozen years he has headed the list of past Presidents of LPMAA. He took office at the 1958 Aggregate Meeting, almost half his lifetime ago. He was one of the younger Presidents of the Association, though two served while still in their thirties. Dick Spencer's membership in Methodism has always been at Freckleton chapel, where four generations of his family have worshipped. As a member of the General Committee of LPMAA since 1945, and a Convener of North Lancs District for many years, he has preached in every part of the United Kingdom. His other activities have included long service as a County and Local Councillor, and organising the Freckleton Music Festival, of which he was the founder. Those who knew him as a 'regular' at the Annual Aggregate Meeting of the Association – he has attended nearly fifty - recall his vigorous efforts to stimulate debate when (he thought) the assembly had gone to sleep! After nearly 70 years, the last thing Dick wants to relinquish is leading worship and preaching. The *Methodist Recorder* interview concluded with his statement 'If people think I am still worth inviting I will do it for a bit longer.'

The last Aggregate Meeting before the 150th Anniversary was held at Sale in the Manchester and Stockport District, though local arrangements were the responsibility of all four Lancashire Districts. The Aggregate of 1998 assembled in the Avenue Methodist Church. General Committee had met there thirty-three years earlier, in what was described then as 'a brand new church.' The 1965 Committee Meeting was hosted by the recently formed Manchester South West Branch, whose Chairman, Leslie Soper, wrote an optimistic message in the handbook. He emphasised that the new Branch had been formed from the Altrincham Branch and part of Manchester No. 1 Branch because of 'increasing interest within the district in the aims and ideals of the Association.' He felt it necessary, however, to offer a tentative apology if any of the arrangements fell short of the high standard achieved by Branches of longer standing, hoping that allowance would be made for inexperience! Tribute was paid to the previous Branch Chairman, the late Luther Wild, whose enthusiasm for the new Branch, and service as its first treasurer, had contributed much to its success.

This success was not reflected throughout the whole District when, in 1973, the District Chairman wrote in solemn vein to all Branch Secretaries:

> I have been concerned that many Branches are not represented [at District Meetings], not just on one occasion but continually, and I believe we have reached a state of near breakdown in our District organisation, which is a vital link . . . with the people for whom we care.

Was this an experience shared by other Districts of LPMAA? We are glad that Manchester and Stockport maintained its strength to play a major part in entertaining the 1998 Aggregate.

LPMAA members in Lancashire have always taken an active interest in anything affecting the Association nationally. The Conversations between Methodism and the Anglicans in the 1960s, for example, attracted the attention of the Bolton and Rochdale District Meeting in September 1963. Apparently assuming that amalgamation was certain, concern was expressed about the future use of LPMAA funds. A year later the District Meeting Chairman turned to the subject again. He had heard people say they did not want to join the Anglican church. His belief was that the unity of the Church already exists; the question of uniformity was different. The matter did not call for further consideration as the anticipated merger did not take place. This District, like many others, took an equally lively interest twenty years later in the discussions which eventually led to LPMAA being formally recognised as part of the Connexion.

22

LPMAA In Wales

For many years Methodism in North Wales consisted of a narrow, westward extension of the Chester and Stoke District, along the coast. LPMAA followed the same pattern. In organisational terms it was essentially the North Wales Branch. Its Chairmen faithfully signed the Chairman's Bible from 1922 to 1966. After the 1939-45 War the normal term of Chairmanship was two years, although George T. Davies (of Rhos-on-Sea) served four years, 1947-1951. The majority of its Chairmen came from Old Colwyn/Colwyn Bay, Rhos-on-Sea, or Llandudno, although members from Rhyl, Conway and Abergele occasionally held the office. The Branch was sometimes visited by nationally-known LPMAA personalities.

The idea of a separate North Wales District for LPMAA was floated several times in the early 1960s. However, when General Committee met in Wrexham in September 1966 it was still as guests of the Chester and Stoke District. In 1972 the District minute book records the suggestion that 'Welsh people' (i.e. members of LPMAA in Wales) should deal directly with Head Office. By the mid-1970s references were made to Branches in Colwyn Bay and Holyhead, but it appears that no meetings were being held in either place. In the early 1980s, it was reported that the North Wales Coast Branch was active, that there was a new Secretary of Buckley and Deeside Branch, and that the Wrexham Branch would receive 'a visiting team' for its 1985 Anniversary.

The following year the District discussed the implications for LPMAA of the Connexional decision to form a separate North Wales District. In October 1988 a formal proposal was made to establish a N. Wales District for the Association's work, and an invitation was extended to General Committee to meet at Wrexham in April 1989. [This date had fallen vacant because of the inability of another District to entertain the Committee.] A meeting to form the new District was held in March. The General Committee endorsed the arrangements when it met at Wrexham. The Wimborne Aggregate Meeting in June approved the new District, appointing John Rayfield as Senior Convener. The first meeting of the N. Wales District, held in September, expressed its appreciation of the part played by Malcom Lockett (Senior Convener of Chester and Stoke) in bringing the change about.

At that time North Wales had five circuits with over 140 local preachers, only 56 of them members of LPMAA, in three Branches. To try and improve the situation four specific policy objectives were adopted:

1. Better local caring of local preachers and dependants.
2. More involvement in the initial and further training of Local Preachers.
3. Active interest in the developing role of Local Preachers.
4. Improved awareness of, and support for, the work of the Association through District Local Preachers' Days.

There is one very interesting respect in which (so far as we are aware) the North Wales District is unique in LPMAA. It includes the only Branch – Wrexham – ever to have produced its own Circuit magazine. The editor, Emrys Thomas, included in its third issue in June 1994 an item based on an article in *The Local Preachers Magazine* of May 1910, by the Honorary Secretary of the time, Wm. J. Back. That article was entitled 'In the Principality' and was concerned with the condition of LPMAA in Wales. It included a section which had been translated into Welsh by a member who lived in Wrexham. This was presumably intended for particular distribution to Welsh-speaking members. It appears that LPMAA had not been effectively organised in Wales up to that time. The result was that disbursements to Welsh beneficiaries exceeded income from the Welsh Districts in the ratio of 3:1. Figures quoted for the decade to 1910 were:

Income   £1,112   Expenditure   £3,684.

Wm. Back made an observation that is still pertinent today, and is equally applicable to England as to Wales:

If we are able to secure good secretaries we may be able to report good progress during the next year or two.

The Wrexham magazine included reports of Circuit events, notes by local preachers about their work and experiences, anecdotes and quotations, news from the Senior District Convener about the Association's policies and activities, and a *cri de coeur* from the editor for material to be included in future issues. (Bi-annual? The next was announced for December 1994.) He emphasised the point by saying that if there were no contributions he might 'call it a day'. The Circuit LPMAA magazine continued for about eight issues, but then ceased. (Presumably the flow of contributions did dry up!)

The South Wales (formerly Cardiff and Swansea) District is both geographically and numerically larger than North Wales; apart from some concentration in the Cardiff and Swansea circuits, the membership is widely scattered. South Wales hosted Aggregate once in the 19th century (1876) and once in the 20th century (1937). In both years the venue was Cardiff. The General Committee has also paid occasional visits to the District, most recently in April 1993, again in Cardiff. This is remembered particularly for an exceptional public event, over which Lord Tonypandy presided after the Committee Meeting. The size of the gathering, the length of the meeting, the quality of the music, the richness of the atmosphere, and the genial personality of the Chairman all remain in the minds of those who were present. Lord Tonypandy, formerly George Thomas ('Mr Speaker', of the House of Commons), was one of the best known of Welsh local preachers, and was a loyal member of LPMAA.

The last Honorary Editor of *The Local Preachers Magazine*, before the editorial role was added to the duties of Honorary Secretary, was of the South Wales District. J. T. Wells edited the magazine from 1960 to 1970, throughout the 'Decade of Transition' which is the subject of chapter 32.

A former Chairman of another Methodist District has recalled the experiences of his father who was a farm-worker in the Wye Valley during the 1950s, 1960s and 1970s. He served as Branch Secretary and Treasurer for LPMAA in the Wye Valley Mission and then the Ross and Monmouth Circuit, in the Cardiff and Swansea District. In the latter Branch he had no fewer than five members receiving benefit from the Association. As often as his work permitted, he called to deliver their benefits in person, turning the duty into a pastoral visit. Some, it seems, valued this even more than the financial support of LPMAA.

23

LPMAA in the West Midlands

The most significant pieces of visible, tangible LPMAA history are, of course, the buildings in the Matlock area of the Nottingham and Derby District which were important at the time of its origin. They include Marsden's cottage, in which he and Pearson had their conversation in May 1849, and the chapel at Wensley where Pearson was then in membership. A commemorative plaque was installed in Wensley Chapel in 1950.

However the Birmingham District also has places related to the Association's past, in particular the Fillongley Cottage Homes for retired preachers (see chapters 12 and 13) and the Key Hill Cemetery in Birmingham's 'Jewellery Quarter' (mentioned in chapter 7). The graves of three Presidents of the pre-1914 era, of the founder's wife and of one of the original trustees are in that burial ground.

Some District personalities of more recent time must be mentioned here. In the post-Union years Charles Hart (Moseley Road and Sparkhill Circuit) was President in 1934, and **Charles Weatherall** in 1952. The latter was born in Nottingham in 1883, but came to Coventry in the days of the Humber Motor Company. He was active in the National Union of Clerks and Administrative Workers, serving as Chairman of its Midlands Council. Although he came to the District as a result of his employment in the motor industry, he is remembered as one who walked or cycled to his preaching appointments, and who often quoted this well-known jingle as a 'play' on his own name:

> Whether the weather be fine or whether the weather
> be wet,
> Whether the weather be cold or whether the weather
> be hot,
> Whatever the weather we'll weather the weather
> Whether we like it or not!
> Weatherall

He became Treasurer of the Fillongley Cottage Homes Trust for the last few years before the Cottages were sold, and was present at the final meeting when the trust was wound up. His work for LPMAA was recognised by his election as President for 1952-53.

Another leading figure in the Association, nationally as well as in the District, was **John Johnson** of Blackheath, President in 1975, and afterwards Chairman of the Executive Committee of Mutual Aid Homes for several years. John died in 1993, aged 77. As Secretary of the Blackheath Branch he ensured that Presidents in office visited the Branch for its Anniversary week-end at the beginning of February each year.

His close friend, and predecessor as Branch Secretary, was **Ernie Wyle**, known throughout Birmingham and the Black Country as 'Mr LPMAA'. He was elected to the General Committee in the early 1950s. For many years this meant that once a month he would leave home on Friday evening or early Saturday morning, and would return sometime during Sunday night or on Monday morning. He travelled as far afield as Plymouth and North Yorkshire, to attend Committee Meetings and to preach on the Sunday. His business as a roofing contractor brought him many contacts with business people, whom he often persuaded to become Honorary Members of the Association. As District LPMAA Chairman at the time, Ernie Wyle played an important part in planning the Aggregate of 1966, by chairing the Local Arrangements Committee. In the Handbook he pointed out that it would be the last Aggregate to be held in Birmingham Central Hall. At the time of his death in 1972, aged 74, he was still preaching most Sundays.

Birmingham District has produced two of the Association's 'leading ladies'. **Hilda Sendell** became the Association's second female President in 1981. Thirty-seven years earlier (1944) **Lorna Shirley-Smith** had joined the General Committee, only the second woman to do so. Like John Barnsley and David Barr she worshipped at Sandon Road, although her family had originally been members at the Birmingham Central Hall. Born in 1888, she studied at Cambridge before degrees were available to women. She was active in the Temperance Movement and well-known for her strongly-held views on the subject. She was described as 'a good solid preacher' with a commanding presence, a resonant voice and a forthright manner, but was perceived by some as a fierce, autocratic personality. This was, perhaps, reinforced by the fact that she invariably arrived at preaching appointments in her chauffeur-driven car!.

Lorna Shirley-Smith and her brother, who headed the family firm of solicitors and handled much legal business for Midland Methodism, were hospitable people and entertained LPMAA meetings in their Edgbaston home. In 1976, shortly before reaching the age of 90, she gave (with her brother) a large number of books from their library to LPMAA, to be sold to raise money for the expenses of the Coventry Aggregate (1978). This was done at a garden party, at the home of the Branch Secretary nearby, one evening in August of 1976, and produced the sum (substantial for those times) of £150. Soon after this, Miss Shirley-Smith, her brother and their resident servant, who was regarded as a dependant, applied for residence in the Minehead Home, but all three died within a short space of time before vacancies became available. Like Charles Weatherall, she had been a Trustee of the Fillongley Cottage Homes, and was present with him at the final meeting of the Trust. She was nominated for the Presidency, though not elected, in 1950 and 1951, Charles being chosen as President-Elect for 1952.

In earlier years the Birmingham District of the Wesleyan Methodist Church extended as far as Shrewsbury, but for most of the 20th century Shropshire and the urban Black Country circuits have formed the Wolverhampton and Shrewsbury District. LPMAA has been very active in this area, and the District has provided the Association with three Presidents, an Honorary Secretary and two Honorary Treasurers in the last 40 years. It has also entertained the Aggregate Meeting three times in the same period. When Aggregate met at Wolverhampton in 1974 the President, John Kievill (a Somerset man), wrote an amusing account of it in biblical style. These extracts reveal something of the gentle humour of its author, and are included as a tribute to him.

> Upon a summer day, the Mutual Men (many of whom were Women) came from all the coasts of their Island and from in the middle to the City of Wolfrun for their yearly moot . . . And when the Moot was sat down in the Darlington Temple in the chief seat was Granville of Grange, a mighty man in divers affairs which had travelled far and wide over the Island and beyond its coasts to sundry other lands in the world.

And sitting at the right hand of Granville of Grange was Alan the Chief Scribe of all the Mutual Men and which was skilled in all things that pertained to the law of the land, and he it is who sets before the Mutual Men at all times what they should think about and talk about and do about the affairs which pertain to Mutual Men and what they have set their hearts upon. And upon the left hand of Granville of Grange sat Alfred the Second Scribe which was skilled in divers matters which the Queen's Ministers of the Island required to be done for the good ordering of the life of the people, and he it was who propounded to the Mutual Men the commandments by which they should govern their affairs, and furthermore he gathers together all the parchments whereon Mutual Men write about what they think and what they do, and he causes the parchments to be sent out all through the land about every third moon. And also in one of the foremost seats was an ageing and idle fellow John, Up-from-Somerset, which watched over the tents wherein dwelt together the Mutual Men (and remember many of the Men were Women) which no longer desired to dwell in tents of their own. And in another of these seats was Graham which had great understanding in adding up of the mites and pennies and shekels and talents of silver and gold such as merchants gather from their trading and knoweth what taxes they must pay to Caesar and what they need not so pay, and he it is that keepeth all the money bags of all the Mutual Men of the Island. And with these all was Squire which toileth all his days in guarding all the records and registers and parchments that are needed for the proper work which the Mutual Men require to be done.

They looked upon Granville of Grange and spake unto him saying: 'Thou hast done well and we give thee thanks. Nevertheless thou hast been seated in the chief seat these thirteen moons and now thou must go to thy seat behind". And they looked upon the ageing and idle John Up-from-Somerset and spake unto him saying: 'Thou, even thou, shalt be put in the chief seat and thou shalt travel far and wide and shalt tell all men who we are and what we do, and when thirteen moons have gone by, if thou be still alive after all these things thou shalt return to us and another shall take thy place.'

Now on the morrow, it being the Sabbath, the Mutual Men of the Moot (many of them being Women) set forth to all parts of the region of Wolfrun and Shrowsbury (spelt Shrewsbury) and performed the labours appointed to them. And on the morrow the Mutual Men (including those among them who were Women) returned to the Moot and as was their custom they fell to choosing which among them should come into the Chief Seat thirteen moons hence, and each cast their lot among three mighty men of valour which were contending for the place, and it came to pass that when those who could count had counted it was acclaimed that John of Brum should come to the Chief Seat thirteen moons hence. And the Moot then looked upon Bill of the region of Wolfrun and Shrowsbury (spelt Shrewsbury) – that same Bill which had planned the Sabbath labours of the Mutual Men (many of whom were Women) – and they spake unto him saying: 'Behold, thou shalt watch over our special tents, in the stead of the ageing and idle John Up-from-Somerset and he shall henceforth watch no more, but in thirteen moons when he yieldeth the Chief Seat to John of Brum he shall return to the region of his fathers in peace.' And it was so.

[Darlington Temple = Darlington Street Chapel.
Granville of Grange = Granville Berry.
Alan the Chief Scribe = Alan Collen, Senr. Hon. Sec.
Alfred the Second Scribe = Alfred Gilliver, Hon.Sec.
John, Up-from-Somerset = John Kievill, Hon.Sec.(Homes).
Graham = Graham Robinson, Hon.Treas.
Squire = Squire Jones, General Secretary.
John of Brum = John Johnson.
Bill = Bill Simpson (of Cannock Chase Circuit)]

In the years from 1894 to 1941 the Chester and Stoke District, or its predecessors, hosted Aggregate on four occasions, putting it on equal terms in that respect with cities such as London, Birmingham, Sheffield. On the first and last of these occasions, Aggregate met in Burslem; in 1909 and 1926 at Hanley. The huge Bethesda United Methodist Chapel was the venue in 1926 when over 500 delegates assembled, and supplied more than 300 chapels with preachers for nearly 600 services. There were also eight open-air services, and three public meetings each with three speakers! Dr T. E. Nuttall, the outgoing President, had made history earlier in the year, being the first ever LPMAA representative to make a radio broadcast.

Since the 1939-45 war, the District has concentrated its efforts on entertaining the General Committee which it has done on seven occasions: 1957 and 1964 at Crewe; 1960 at Stoke; 1966 at Wrexham; 1971 at Sandbach; 1984 at Alsager; 1996 at Wolstanton. The late Malcolm Lockett, Senior Convener for most of this period, had a leading role in the planning and local arrangements for most of these visits. In 1960 the Committee and guests were entertained by the Lord Mayor for a Civic Tea, whilst in 1964 the Chairman of Cheshire County Council presided over the evening public meeting.

The Potteries author, Arnold Bennett, came from a Methodist family, although he did not embrace Methodism in adult life. In some of his books (for example, *Anna of the Five Towns*) he gives fascinating insights to the Wesleyan Methodism of his youth, such as a Sunday School teachers' prayer meeting, a women's sewing meeting, a revival meeting and a bazaar. For LPMAA it is interesting to know that Arnold Bennett's mother was an Honorary Member.

24

LPMAA in Eastern England

As a group of Districts East Anglia, Lincolnshire, Nottingham and Derby, Oxford and Leicester are more rural than most, with their relatively small number of town circuits and much larger number of country causes. Because their dependence on local preachers has been much greater than the Connexional average, it is not surprising that LPMAA has been strong in these Districts, both in membership and in the vigour of its life. In 1949 the Lincoln and Grimsby District published a special handbook for the Association's Centenary Celebrations. An article in it from the President, Harold Buss, included this tribute to the District:

> The enthusiasm and efficiency of the District and Branch officials in this area have been outstanding, and the District holds a high and honoured place in our records. In 1948, it surpassed all other Districts in income and in the numbers of members.

The Handbook also contained statistics about the District since its formation in 1899, concluding with details of the current position (1948):

Ordinary Members (LP)	628	Annuitants	107
Benefit Members (LP)	48	Income	£1855-7-6d
Honorary Members	489	Expenditure	£2696-10-8d

The most recent District Meeting (April 1949) had been attended by 125 members from the 19 Branches.

The climax of the Centenary Year for the District was a Celebration Day on Saturday 17th September. There was a District meeting in the morning followed by an invitation luncheon in the County Assembly Rooms. A Thanksgiving Service was held in Lincoln Cathedral in the afternoon. The General Committee met afterwards, and in the evening a Great Public Rally was chaired by one of Lincolnshire's past-Presidents of LPMAA, Walter Kirkham.

The speakers were Rt. Hon J. J. (Jack) Lawson, M.P., and F. Harold Buss, President of the Association.

The high point of the day was the Service of Thanksgiving in the Cathedral, at which the Bishop, Rt. Rev. Maurice Harland, preached. The service included presentation of a leather-bound lectern Bible to the Cathedral authorities. This was made on behalf of the LPMAA District by its Chairman, Rusling Savage. He had explained in the Handbook that this was:

> . . . as a token of our appreciation of the splendid thought behind the offer of the facilities afforded for Divine Worship in the Cathedral when the Aggregate meetings of the Association were held in Lincoln in 1946.

The following inscription is engrossed in gold inside the cover of the Bible:

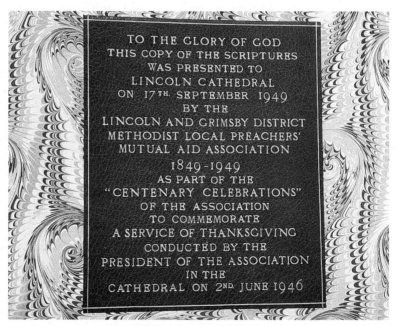

The Bible is still used when a service requiring the Authorised Version is held. The 1946 occasion referred to was the first time that an LPMAA event had taken place in the Cathedral. The presentation of the Bible in 1949 was the second, and there have been two others. The District has hosted the Aggregate

Meeting a total of seven times over the 150 years of the Association's life. In the 19th century the venue was Louth (1857 and 1872), but the 20th century Aggregates were all held in Lincoln (1928; 1946; 1965; 1980; 1995). In 1965 Aggregate began in the Cathedral with a service of worship, at which the preacher was the outgoing President, George Taylor. Business was done in Bailgate Methodist Church, and the concluding public meeting was held at Central. In 1980, Central Methodist Church accommodated the business sessions, and the Public Meeting at the close of Aggregate took place in the Cathedral. Although no part of the 1995 Aggregate was held in the Cathedral, the link with the Diocese was maintained by inviting the Bishop to be the speaker at the public meeting.

It is known that at least six of the Association's past-Presidents were Lincolnshire men. **John Booth Sharpley** had the particular pleasure of presiding when Aggregate first met in his home town of Louth (1857). Like some other LPMAA leaders in its early years, he was identified with the mid-19th century reform movement in Wesleyanism. A memorial tablet in the Free Methodist Chapel, Louth (now demolished), recorded his public work as a 'Guardian of the Poor, Justice of the Peace, Alderman and thrice Mayor of the Borough'. It referred also to his 'sustained efficiency' as a class-leader, local preacher and trustee in Free Methodism in the Louth Circuit. He was secretary of the preachers' meeting for over thirty years. Alderman **Hugh Wyatt** (of Lincoln) was President when Aggregate met on the other side of the River Humber, at Hull in 1893, serving later as first District Chairman in 1899. The President of 1933, **Walter Kirkham**, served twice as District Chairman, in 1929 and 1946.

More Precious Than Rubies, the history of Mutual Aid Homes to 1989, records the roles of **James Fowler** in the development of its work. As President in 1950-51, he formally opened the second 'Westerley' at Grange-over-Sands, and was much involved with the third Home at Woodhall Spa in his own District. He was appointed Chairman of Mutual Aid Homes Ltd in 1958, and was the last holder of that office. When the Company was converted into an Industrial and Provident Society in 1966, he became the first Honorary Secretary (Homes). Jim Fowler named his house after the Association, spelling Mutual Aid backwards – 'Dia Lautum'. ['Dialautum Parl, London', was the Association's telegraphic address for some years between the wars.]

George Taylor, President 1964, came from the deep south of the County. His service in Branch and District office and as a member of the General Committee helped to revitalise some of the weaker rural Branches. He placed his professional expertise as a municipal engineer and surveyor at the disposal of the Association on a number of occasions. Although a Grimsby man, **Dennis Corden** has lived in Market Rasen for the greater part of his active life in LPMAA, for much of that time as Branch Secretary. He travelled as President in 1984-85, succeeding Dr Donald Nuttall as Honorary Secretary (Homes) in 1986. Upon retiring from that office in 1995 he accepted the responsibilities of Senior Convener for the Lincoln District.

The District has also provided the Association with several Trustees, three of them since the Second World War. Councillor **H. J. (Bert) Clayton** was Denis Corden's predecessor as Market Rasen Branch Secretary. **Harold Richardson** was Branch Secretary at Grimsby, and Senior Convener. The third, **Norman Silson**, was precluded from nomination for the Presidency only by ill-health. Norman is known to many folk as a keen astronomer. One of his last engagements before ill-health intervened was a talk at the Willersley Castle Conference in October 1988. Using his own photographic slides, he spoke on 'The Moon and the Stars which You have made' (Psalm 8).

The story of Isaac Green, local preacher of March and Chatteris Circuit, East Anglia, is told by his grand-daughter:

> A grandfather/grand-daughter relationship can be very special – for me it certainly was. Although my grandfather was 67 when I was born we were given 22 years together. In the late 1940s a 10s note was a lot of money to a girl in her early teens, but every other Saturday a kindly gentleman came to see my grandfather and put such a note on his table. Very soon I learned that it was a regular sum granted to him from LPMAA. He had a large family, a poorly paid job and had lost the sight of one eye. The sight of the other eye soon failed, and at 15 I became his eyes and constant companion. I had no idea what LPMAA was, but I remember thinking it must be full of very kind people.

One Saturday afternoon in 1950 he asked me to go with him to buy a new overcoat. We went to Wright's the Outfitters, a shop owned by a Methodist family in March, and the new coat was purchased. On the way home grandfather told me that it was an 'LPMAA overcoat' because without that regular contribution he would never have been able to afford it. Then in his 80s, he still managed to take a few appointments, which sometimes meant long walks together, but he had the 'LPMAA' warmth around him! I proudly read lessons and announced hymns. His 'no sight' meant no notes, but unfortunately he couldn't see the clock either, and a special signal (loud coughs!) was needed. Many years ago, thanks to grandfather's deep faith, I too became a local preacher, and a member of LPMAA.

[Isaac Green had the joy, before he entered the Lord's nearer presence, of knowing that his grand-daughter had become a fully-accredited Local Preacher. His delight would have been even greater when she served the Association as a Branch and District officer, and then as a General Committee member.]

Nottingham and Derby rightly claims its place in LPMAA history as the District in which the Association had its beginnings. For a quarter-century after Methodist Union Nottingham and Derby were each a district in its own right, but in the late 19th century formed a single District as they do today. The Association did not organise work at District level until 1886 when the office of Convener was first established, with District Committees constituted the following year. They were not provided with Rules to govern their activity until 1893. These arrangements were gradually implemented in the Districts; Nottingham and Derby held its first District Annual Meeting in 1894. The Annual Meeting of 1895 was a major event, attracting the following report in the *Rushcliffe Star and Advertiser* on 26th April:

WESLEYAN METHODIST LOCAL PREACHERS

The second annual meeting of the Notts and Derbyshire District Wesleyan Methodist Local Preachers Mutual Aid Association was held at Mansfield on Monday. On the previous day the pulpits in the Wesleyan and Free Church circuits were occupied by delegates, and collections were made in aid of the association. At the business meeting on the Monday morning the Mayor of Mansfield (Ald. Alcock) was elected president for the ensuing year, and gave an interesting address on the claims of the 'aged brethren'. Derby was selected for the next annual meeting. About 130 delegates and local preachers of the Mansfield circuit were entertained to luncheon by the Mayor, who was heartily thanked. The afternoon session was devoted to the reading and discussion of papers by Mr J. H. Buckley, F.R.A.S., of Leicester, on 'Modes of Preaching'. Mr S. Pickering, of Mansfield, on 'The Preacher and the Sermon', and Mr T. Parker of Grantham, on 'Can anything be done to make our preaching successful?' Tea was provided in the schoolroom, and largely attended. A public meeting was held in the chapel, presided over by the Mayor of Mansfield, and addressed by Messrs R. Parker, of Grantham, V. Smith, J.P., of Langley Mill, J. Wardle, of Nottingham, and W. Dixon, District Secretary. As a result of the conference £52 has been forwarded to the general secretary.

Several members of the Alcock family were prominent in Mansfield Methodism in those days, amongst them **John Simpson Alcock, J.P.**, a local hosiery manufacturer, President of LPMAA, 1926-27. An Alderman of Nottinghamshire County Council, he served on several Connexional Committees and for a number of years was District Home Missions Treasurer.

LPMAA was vigorous in the Nottingham area in the early 1950s. Leaflets and handbooks from that period give this picture. The Nottingham Branch, embraced then (as now) all the Circuits of the city and adjacent areas – North, South, East, West, Central, Mission. A twelve-page booklet publicised the arrangements for the Branch Anniversary on Sunday 25th October 1953. One hundred and six preachers conducted 140 appointments in 79 chapels, including one of the Wesleyan Reform Union. The booklet gave some details from the Branch Annual Report. There were 209 members, including life and honorary members. The list of Officers included the names of those described as 'Group Secretaries' for the several Circuits. The Branch Local Preachers' Fellowship, to be led by the Chairman, was announced for the following day. A full page advertised a series of Training Classes being conducted by the Connexional Tutor, Miss Elsie Camplin, at the Albert Hall Mission during the Autumn. Support in the preaching work was an important part of Mutual Aid in Nottingham in those years.

The Branch Annual Meeting on 13th February 1954 approved arrangements for the General Committee visit to the Branch in October that year. On that occasion the meetings were held at Parliament Street Chapel. The evening public meeting was chaired by the LPMAA President (E. A. Arnold, of Sheffield). He was 'supported' by both the Nottingham District Chairman and the Branch Chairman; the principal speaker was the President-Elect, Albert Shaw, later to be Honorary Secretary of the Association. The Branch statistics again appeared in the handbook, showing a membership increase of 12 on the year. The Sunday was observed as LPMAA Sunday, and the General Committee members were joined by over forty of the Branch's own preachers to fill 130 appointments in 77 chapels.

In March the following year the District Annual Meeting was held at Long Eaton Central. It had something of the character of a modern-day Aggregate. Over 90 delegates from eight Branches (including the large Nottingham Branch) assembled on Saturday 19th March at 10.00 am. Adjournment for luncheon in the local Co-operative Hall was at 1.00 pm. The printed menu (four courses and coffee) included a toast list – HM the Queen, LPMAA, the Town of Long Eaton, and Our Hosts – with the Superintendent Minister and two local Councillors among the speakers. The business was resumed at 2.30 pm, the afternoon session being followed by tea. A major public meeting at 6.30 pm completed the day's proceedings. Sunday 20th March was LPMAA Sunday in most of the chapels of the Long Eaton, Ilkeston and Kimberley Circuits; about half of the delegates filled the appointments in them.

Nottinghamshire also provides an incident illustrating the hazards of motor-car travel in the early days. John White, the 1930 District President, was travelling by car from his Newark home to address a meeting in Long Eaton (west of Nottingham). On the way his car broke down and he hailed a passing motorist to enquire if he was going in that direction, but received a negative reply. A few moments later the motorist returned and said, 'Jump in, I'll take you to Nottingham. I think you are the President of LPMAA. I recognise you from your photograph in the *Methodist Times*.' The identity of the man who gave the lift is unknown (as a reader of the *Methodist Times* probably a Methodist) but his recollection of the photograph enabled John White to fulfill his engagement.

25

LPMAA in the Home Counties

South East England, or the Home Counties, by whatever name it may be known, is inevitably dominated by the Greater London conurbation. Historically the location of the Sovereign's principal residence and the Houses of Parliament, the hub of the nation's financial life, the focus of its major transport routes, the largest concentration of population – and therefore the largest consumer market – in the United Kingdom, all contribute, with other factors, to the creation of its distinctive character. In Methodist terms, the outer areas of its London Districts include many Circuits of more rural nature, but which are still affected by the socio-economic influence of the London region.

The Mutual Aid Association has not been exempt from this influence, including the effects of population mobility. The Home Counties have raised a number of its leaders, though not all were natives of the South-East. Because of their national standing some of these are mentioned in other chapters where their particular contributions are most relevant. Tribute is paid to others here. Similarly, the London area is referred to in connection with its hosting of Aggregate Meetings (chapter 27) and some of its activities are noted under the heading 'Intellectual and Spiritual Aid' (chapter 29). Brief further mention of these things is made in this chapter. Two of the five LPMAA 'Westerley' Homes are located in London Districts. The first of the five, at Westcliff-on-Sea, is in the North East District. The last one to be opened is at Rickmansworth (close to Head Office) in the North West District. Although the Association's Head Office has had many addresses over 150 years, it has always been located in the London area.

A genuine Home Counties man and LPMAA's outstanding personality for three decades, was **F. Harold Buss**. His formal service to the Association began with his election to the General Committee in 1912 when he was 35, young by the standards of the time. It did not end until 1956 when he stepped down after 30 years as Honorary Secretary. During four of these years he held the position alone, and for the last 22 years had been the senior partner.

These paragraphs from the resolution of the Aggregate meeting in the year of his retirement show the esteem in which he was held:

> As a member of the General Committee since 1912, as Joint Honorary Editor from 1917 to 1921, as sole Honorary Editor from 1921 to 1926, as President of the Association in 1932 and again in the Centenary Year of 1949, and as Honorary Secretary to the Association from 1926 to 1956, Brother Buss has established a record of service without parallel in the long history of the Association.

> In all his varied leadership during this lengthy period Brother Buss has worthily maintained the high ideals and traditions of his predecessors and under his wise and able leadership the Association has widely extended its activities in benevolence and in fellowship.

> His grace, courtesy and charm have at all times exercised a powerful influence for good: his sincerity and fairmindedness have commended him to all. His modesty, his dignity, his eloquence, his statesmanship, and above all his unfailing kindness have won for him a deep and warm affection in the hearts of all officers and members of the Association.

London contributed to the making of history in 1964, the year that Harold Buss died. In that year his son Geoffrey was elected to the General Committee. In due course he became Honorary Secretary, later Senior Honorary Secretary, thus creating the only example in the life of LPMAA when members from two generations of one family have held these offices. Again, the Aggregate meeting expressed its appreciation of the service of Senior Honorary Secretary **Geoffrey Buss** when he retired from that position in 1994:

> The Aggregate Meeting places on record deep gratitude to Geoffrey Buss for his sixteen years' service to the Association as an Honorary Secretary. He was elected to the General Committee in 1964. In 1978 he was elected Honorary Secretary and served as President in 1979-80.

The resolution went on to record that he:

succeeded Alfred Gilliver as Senior Honorary
Secretary in 1987. His detailed knowledge of the
work of LPMAA has been acquired over many years
in the London North West and South East Districts.
All this enabled him to give positive leadership in
the Association's discussions with the Connexional
Local Preachers Committee representatives in the
Standing Joint Committee, on the 'Becoming One'
document of 1992. [See chapter 34].

Thomas Chamberlain (1819-1889) was elected to the
General Committee in 1851, served as Honorary Secretary in 1854-
55, as President in 1856, and was appointed a Trustee in 1860.
Becoming Honorary Secretary again in 1861 he held that office until
1885, when he emigrated to New Zealand for health reasons. From
1864 to 1885 he combined the role of Chief Editor with the duties of
Honorary Secretary.

He had gone to live in London while still a youth, moving
after three years to a position in Windsor, where in due course he
became proprietor of the business. Gradually acquiring the
confidence of his fellow-citizens, he was elected to the Windsor
Borough Council, later being elevated to the aldermanic bench and
serving a term as mayor. In Wesleyan Methodism, Thomas
Chamberlain began to preach when in his early 20s, siding with the
Reformers during the upheavals of the 1850s. This resulted in his
expulsion from Wesleyanism, after which he was prominent in the
Wesleyan Reform Union, including five years – 1859, 1862, 1863
(jointly with Edwin Benson), 1864, 1869 – as its President. The
Borough of Windsor and LPMAA both made generous
presentations to him when he left England.

Charles Samuel Madder (born 29th May 1827, died 20th
November 1909), President in 1880-81, was a member of General
Committee for many years and became a Trustee a few years before
his death. *The Bucks Herald* of 27th November 1909 devoted 18
column inches to a memorial tribute and report of his funeral; *The
Bucks Advertiser and Aylesbury News* extended its coverage to twice
that length!

He was born in Norfolk. His family moved to London
when he was seven and to Windsor the following year, where he
began work in a draper's shop in 1839. After eight years in the

same trade in Kent he went to Aylesbury in 1850 as a traveller for a drapery firm there. In 1857 he set up his own drapery business in the town, remaining there for the rest of his life. Twice married, both his wives pre-deceased him. He had joined the Wesleyan Methodist Church in 1852, becoming a local preacher in 1858 and a member of LPMAA in 1864. Charles Madder's Presidency was two years after laymen were admitted to the Wesleyan Conference. It is not surprising, therefore, that he was a representative to Conference on several occasions. He played a leading part in the former Bedford and Northampton District, on its Synod, as member of its Home Mission and Chapel Committees and as treasurer of the Worn-Out Ministers' Fund. Locally he served as class-leader for 46 years.

He was prominent in the public life of his adopted home-town, holding office at various times as an Overseer and Guardian of the Poor, member of the Board of Health, and later served as a Councillor of the Urban District. He was also a keen supporter of the temperance movement. All these bodies, LPMAA and the Wesleyan Church were represented at his funeral. What was then the 'new' Buckingham Street Chapel owed a great deal to the initiative, enthusiasm and generosity of Charles Madder.

A quaint story about him was told in *The Local Preachers Magazine* of February 1907 by one of his Aylesbury colleagues who owned a pony called 'Gospel Charlie'. The pony had been on the Circuit Plan for 23 years, appointed to take preachers to the chapels where they were planned. When challenged about making the animal work on Sundays, the owner replied, ' He's a Jew, and has his day of rest on a Saturday.' Shortly after the Buckingham Street Chapel was built, Charles Madder was photographed in the trap, 'Gospel Charlie' in the shafts, in front of the porch of the new chapel. His colleague offered the photograph through the magazine, at one shilling per copy, all profits going to LPMAA. It is not known how many copies were sold!

An example of an early Branch Anniversary weekend was found recorded in *The Local Preachers Magazine* of June 1886. On Sunday 9th May sermons were preached at Maidstone by the President of that year, G. C. Amphlett, and others. The following evening the Superintendent Minister presided over a public meeting at which singing was 'led by the various choirs of the Circuit'. The Superintendent Minister took 'the opportunity of eulogising the work done by local preachers'. He was pleased that a library for them had recently been started in the Circuit. A later speaker picked up this point, saying he was glad that attention was being paid to their intellectual attainments. The President expressed his pleasure at finding a minister in the chair, and in hearty sympathy with the work of local preachers.

In the years before 1957, when there were six London Districts, the London South District was a pioneer in the development of an annual conference for study and fellowship. An announcement in the November 1947 issue of *The Local Preachers Magazine* gave details of the third such weekend. It was arranged for 29th November to 1st December, at 'Elfinsward', a conference centre in Haywards Heath. The subject chosen was 'Methodism', and in three sessions the programme covered

1) Its Doctrines, Sacraments and Fellowship
2) Its Place in the World and its Message for Today
3) Its Overseas Mission: A Review and a Forecast

The speakers were the President of that year, Percy Timperley, Richard Burnett (editor of the magazine), and W. H. Kneen, both future Presidents. A fourth session took the form of a conversation on 'Books that have Helped Me'. Sunday worship was at Perrymount Road.

By 1961 – after District reorganisation – the conference had moved to a location in Eastbourne, and had become a joint enterprise of the new London South West and South East Districts. The 1961 week-end was reported in the November magazine. Its theme had been 'An Eternal Gospel to Proclaim'. The three sessions were all led by Rev. N. Allen Birtwhistle, then the Connexional Secretary for Ministerial Training, who spoke on the 'Truth of the Gospel', 'The Furtherance of the Gospel', and 'The Fullness of the Gospel'. The Elfinsward Conference and its successors have been a valuable source of fellowship and preacher development for many years.

26

LPMAA in the South and West

One of the earliest recorded LPMAA events in Cornwall was a meeting of the General Committee at St. Austell in July 1924. The promise of 'something special' elicited a paragraph from the Honorary Secretary in the magazine for August of that year. Writing before the Committee met, he said:

> Our congregations in Cornwall are 'sermon tasters'. Tradition says that a Cornishman likes 'a new pasty every day and a new preacher every Sunday'. To the land of 'crame' we must take the cream of our sermons.

In the following month's magazine he described the visit as 'highly successful' and went on to say:

> A satisfactory number of the Committee attended, especially considering the great distance. We were marshalled by Bro. Worthington, of St. Austell, and valuable assistance was rendered by Bros. Howell Mabbott, S. Mitchell, Pascoe, and others. The effort was a big one, for 300 pulpits were supplied on the Sunday by the Committee, as well as by visiting brethren from London, Exeter, Barnstaple, Plymouth and the Cornwall Circuits It seems to me that it is impossible to tabulate results: when we remember that practically every pulpit, from the largest to the smallest, was occupied by laymen, it gives some idea of the immense reserve power that Methodism possesses, capable, voluntary, and devoted in its loyalty to the Christ, who is Head of his sanctified followers. It was a real joy that Wesleyans and United Methodists combined in this great effort; for Local Preachers' Sunday at least there was a glorious bit of Methodist Union. Why cannot it always be so?

So another opportunity was taken to underline the enthusiastic support that LPMAA always gave for the Union in wider Methodism that it had consistently shown in its own ranks. It was reported that 51 applications for benefit had been considered at the St. Austell meeting, the total granted representing a weekly sum of £27-7-0d, an annual expenditure of £1,425 [equivalent to about £100,000 at late 20th century prices.] No wonder the Honorary Secretary concluded by saying that legacies and donations as well as collections were needed to meet the increasing outlay.

General Committee visits to Cornwall in more recent time are recalled by Dick Hale. In both 1973 and 1994 the venue was Truro; for the latter he had substantial responsibility. In 1973, the arrangements had been master-minded by another Richard – **Richard L. Frank**, a Yorkshireman who had made Cornwall his county by adoption and was one of its LPMAA stalwarts. First elected to General Committee in 1951, he served as a member through the 1950s and much of the 1960s. He was District Chairman in 1962. A lawyer by profession, it was reported that he left the 1964 Aggregate breathless by the facility and ease with which he expounded the intricacies of the Charities Act, during a debate on the Anglican-Methodist Conversations. He was subsequently called upon to contribute two substantial articles to *The Local Preachers Magazine*, on Episcopacy (September-October 1964) and on Anglican-Methodist Union *and* the LPMAA (November-December 1964).

In common with many other Branches of the Association at this time, the Newquay Branch devoted part of its meeting in November 1964 to discussing the likely effect upon LPMAA of any future amalgamation of Methodism and the Church of England. These discussions may well have been illuminated by Richard Frank's articles, mentioned above. The Branch minutes record the outcome of the discussions very clearly:

> . . . whatever results from the Anglican/Methodist conversations, it was our duty to see that our great organisation was in no way weakened in its work of benevolence among our aged and needy brethren.

Perhaps the minute should have said 'and sisters', especially as in 1967 it was noted that the weekly allowance to a local preacher's widow, who had been a beneficiary for some years, was being continued.

The first signature in the District Chairman's Bible, which was introduced in 1929, is that of Howell Mabbott (he had been LPMAA President in 1920). The list shows that five were women, the first being elected in 1972.

The year 1968, again in common with Branches in other parts of the country, found the Newquay members expressing their concern over the loss of financial support for LPMAA. It appeared that some congregations were dividing their allocations between the Local Preachers ' Department and the Association, now that the day had become 'Local Preachers' Sunday'. It was resolved to send copies of the recently published joint leaflet to every Society and to all Circuit ministers.

A great strength of LPMAA in the Cornwall District, for almost half a century, has been its emphasis on study and further development for preachers, what the Association's founders called 'Intellectual and Spiritual Aid' (see chapter 29). The annual residential weekend, held at Treloyhan Manor, has been the focus of this, and past programmes reveal the range and depth of its subjects. Some have been related directly to the preachers work (specific Biblical Study; Theology in Preaching), some to the devotional life (Prayer; Spirituality), some to the Christian witness in society (Christian Use of Money; Christians at Work). The Conference leader has frequently been a past-President of LPMAA, who has also been the preacher at Sunday morning worship in a local chapel. Up to 50 members have gathered for these weekends, which were held for many years in March, but since Treloyhan Manor changed to 'summer only' opening they have been held in May.

Brief reference has been made in other parts of this book to aspects of LPMAA activity on some of the islands surrounding mainland Britain, such as the Channel Islands (chapter 16) and the Isle of Man (chapter 31). The Isle of Wight claims mention here. The leaflet detailing arrangements for a visit of General Committee to the Isle on 1st and 2nd October 1938 announces the Committee Meeting at Pyle Street, Newport at 3.30 pm on the Saturday, followed by tea at 5.00 pm, provided by the President of the Isle of Wight Branch, Mr F. T. Phillips, County Councillor. He also presided at the public meeting at Quay Street chapel in the evening, when the speakers were James Morgan (President) and Councillor R. J.Soper, J.P. (President-Elect), of Barnsley. The leaflet bemoaned the fact that benefits paid on the Isle of Wight had exceeded the income for many years, in 1937 by £98-19-0d against £24-16-0d. On the Sunday, 15 members of General Committee, 39 Isle of Wight local preachers and three ministers conducted 107 services in 54 chapels in the two Wight Circuits (East and West).

In the Association's Centenary Year, 1949, the Exeter District was taking very seriously its commitment to entertain the General Committee the following May. A committee of 12, with power to co-opt, was appointed, which met in October. It enlarged itself by co-opting four people, and set up three sub-committees – for Plan-making, for Transport and for Hospitality. It was decided to arrange *three* public meetings, with General Committee speakers, at Exeter, Taunton and Barnstaple. The following autumn the District Meeting received a report on the Committee's visit and passed a resolution of thanks to its Secretary for his efforts in organising it. The District minute book of this period contains an interesting list of 22 names, including one woman, under the heading 'Now Demobilised'. These must be members who had served in the armed forces during the 1939-45 war.

The Association's District structure has usually corresponded with that of the Methodist Church. Before 1957 Exeter and Plymouth were two separate Districts. The Conference of 1957 approved a scheme for a 'separated' Chairman for most Methodist Districts. At the same time the number of Districts was reduced by amalgamating smaller ones and redrawing boundaries. Plymouth and Exeter became a single District. LPMAA in Devon decided this would be impracticable for its work there and evolved a plan to function in sections corresponding to the former boundaries. By 1961 this had been found unsatisfactory, and a decision was made to operate in two Districts as before. The first meeting of the reconstituted Exeter District was held in February 1962, and this structure has been continued.

Throughout this period there was also ongoing concern about the effectiveness of Branch organisation in the District. One Branch Secretary was asked to resign, recurrent efforts were made to find officers for Branches that were not functioning, and there were periodical expressions of concern that 'the co-operation of some Branch Secretaries left much to be desired'. Exeter cannot be the only District to have experienced these problems.

During the 1950s two names began to appear in the District minutes that later became well-known in LPMAA nationally – J. W. N. Kievill and W. R. Shapland. In due time both served as President of the Association, John Kievill in 1974-75 and Will Shapland in 1982-83. John Kievill was Honorary Secretary (Homes) from 1968 to 1974, and Will Shapland was Chairman of the Case Committee from 1983 until it was discontinued in September 1996.

Section V

CONTINUITY AND CHANGE

The first three sections of this book looked at major periods in the history of LPMAA - the circumstances and events that led to its formation, the difficulties that it faced in establishing its work during the later 19th century, the ways in which it adapted to the evolving social, political, economic and ecclesiastical context in the 20th century. There are, however, a number of important themes running right through the story, which demonstrate the continuity as well as the change in the Association's life. The annual Aggregate Meeting and *The Local Preachers Magazine* are the most obvious examples of these, but there are others, and this section deals briefly with some of them.

Not everything can be said, not every possible theme mentioned, but in their various ways those included here illustrate the full breadth of Mutual Aid amongst Local Preachers. It is, and from the beginning always has been, much more than raising money and meeting material needs. Caring personally for those to whom they are bound by faith and calling is a particular privilege and responsibility of local preachers. Mutual help, encouragement and support in the preaching work, keeping members informed about the significance of changes in church and society, promoting and strengthening the fellowship of local preachers cannot be measured in money terms. That is why they have been important, and are even more important now, in the ongoing work of LPMAA.

27

The Aggregate Meeting (Some Places, People and Programmes)

Its Name • Its Size • Its Venues • Its Form
Its Characteristics • A Centenary and a Bi-Centenary
Preaching on Aggregate Sunday • Aggregate in the Future

ITS NAME

A recurrent topic of discussion over the generations, both within LPMAA and amongst Methodists more widely, has been the continued use of the rather quaint-sounding word 'Aggregate' to describe the Association's annual assembly. Its broad meaning is 'to gather together', or (when used as a noun) 'a gathering together'. In this sense it is an entirely appropriate term, for the annual meeting of LPMAA is indeed a gathering together of Methodist local preachers, in fact the largest gathering together held in any year. Jokes about its other meanings are part of the folk-lore of LPMAA – aggregate is the raw material of concrete, some preachers are just as solid and soulless, or perhaps their faith stands on foundations as firm as concrete – aggregates are types of geological formation composed of a mixture of elements, just like Methodist preachers – aggregate means to gather a flock into a fold, as a metaphor perhaps more meaningful than the others.

The unhelpfulness of the word to modern ears was raised in debate on the Annual Report at the Aggregate Meeting of 1996, evoking cries of 'No, no!' as well as 'Hear, hear!' from members of the assembly. In replying to the debate, the Senior Honorary Secretary was able to draw on his considerable knowledge of LPMAA history. He pointed out that the Association was formed at a time when Wesleyan Methodism was divided by issues surrounding the authoritarian actions of the all-ministerial Conference. These included expulsion from the Wesleyan church of several ministers believed to be involved in reformist activity. The same fate befell many local preachers. These actions gave the name 'Conference' entirely unacceptable overtones.

There was therefore strong resistance in the inaugural Aggregate Meeting to the adoption of the word 'Conference' to describe itself. More positively, the Aggregate Meeting was not seen solely as an official meeting to transact business, but rather as a gathering together of local preachers for fellowship, mutual encouragement and support. To the present time any member of LPMAA may attend the Aggregate Meeting, though hospitality and preaching appointments are only available for delegates elected by the Districts and for members of General Committee. District delegates and General Committee members are entitled to vote in the election of President, other officers, members of General Committee and on other resolutions.

ITS SIZE

The Aggregate Meeting has varied greatly in size. In the early years or in wartime it sometimes consisted of only a few dozen members, whilst at other times, such as the Centenary Year (1949), it has exceeded 600, as did the inaugural Aggregate in 1849. The election of delegates by Districts was introduced in 1899. The minutes of the Local Arrangements Committee for the 1904 Aggregate give details of the work involved in arranging such large Aggregate Meetings. The Nottingham and Derby District Meeting on 20th April 1903 unanimously confirmed its invitation for the Aggregate to meet in Nottingham the following year (11th-14th June 1904). It resolved to nominate one of its own men, William Smith, to be designated President-Elect for that year. Plans were made to advise the Wesleyan District Synod, and the Quarterly Meetings of the United Methodist Free Churches and the New Connexion, that the LPMAA Aggregate would be assembling in their District in June 1904. Each Branch was called upon to nominate two members for the Arrangements Committee. (In those years the District included Leicester and extended as far south as Peterborough.) Amongst its routine business, the Meeting appointed 28 delegates to the 1903 Aggregate.

About 80 attended the first meeting of the Arrangements Committee. Seven sub-committees were appointed:

Plan Committee	27 members
Chapel Committee	10 members
Hospitality (homes)	42 members
Railway Committee	10 members

Dining (catering)	10 members
Finance Committee	20 members
Services/meetings	14 members

It was decided that the main sessions would take place in Wesley (Broad St.) Nottingham, and that public meetings should be arranged in Nottingham's Albert Hall, and at Leicester, Burton, Derby and Mansfield. Preliminary consideration was given to the organisation of open-air services.

Four hundred delegates would be provided for, initial targets being set for Branches as follows:

Leicester	80	Newark	25
Derby	40	Grantham	20
Ilkeston	40	Melton Mowbray	20
Mansfield	30	Castle Donington	15
Loughborough	15	Southwell	10
Bingham	10		

After the Aggregate the Committee met once more, on 27th July 1904, under the chairmanship of the Association's new President, William Smith. Only 18 members attended! Reports from sub-committees revealed that 625 homes had been secured, that all three open-air services had been successful, and that catering (at five different locations) had been very satifactory. It was regretted that 30 per cent of ticket-holders had not attended; if they had returned their tickets a considerable saving might have been effected. Catering costs were £114-5-9d. Sadly there were many failures by delegates, for inadequate and unworthy reasons, to fulfil preaching appointments. Substitutes had to be found, and in the end only one appointment out of 590 was left without a preacher. Accounts totalling nearly £150 were approved for payment, and £850 was sent to the General Secretary at Head Office.

At the Nottingham and Derby District Meeting in April of the following year (1905), a resolution was passed requesting General Committee to limit Aggregate to 400 members, in order to reduce the strain on hospitality and finance. This doubtless reflected the District's experiences in 1904.

In more recent times the number of District delegates has been 150, allocated in proportion to District membership; with General Committee members, including past-Presidents, this has produced Aggregate Meetings of approximately 200. As Methodism has contracted, a District hosting Aggregate cannot reasonably be expected to find hospitality and preaching appointments for more than that number. The fellowship dimension has often extended beyond the membership; many enduring friendships have arisen from hospitality given and received during Aggregate, and local preachers have sometimes been invited to lead worship again in congregations where they first went on an Aggregate Sunday.

ITS VENUES

Venues for Aggregate Meetings have been numerous through the 150 years of LPMAA. Not surprisingly, London has entertained the Aggregate more times than any other town or city. It has been able to do so as a group of Districts – sometimes as many as six, sometimes four, latterly two at a time, either north or south of the River Thames. On 14 occasions the venue has been in the Greater London conurbation; on two others the Districts have favoured an out-of-town location. Sheffield takes second place having hosted Aggregate eleven times, twice using a venue other than the city itself. Birmingham comes a close third with ten Aggregates, one of these being in Coventry. Clearly a major consideration in choice of venue has been the securing of sufficient hospitality to accommodate large numbers of delegates, and the availability and accessibility of enough preaching appointments on the Sunday. [A list of venues and dates is included as Appendix 1 to this chapter.]

The largest Aggregate Meeting since the Centenary assembled in Westminster Central Hall in 1961. All four London Districts were involved, and 500 delegates, plus hundreds of London area preachers, were planned to conduct over 1,600 services. The Aggregate was honoured that year by a past Vice-President of Conference, Professor Cecil Pawson, who as a delegate himself addressed the meeting on Monday afternoon about preaching. The current Vice-President, George Thomas M.P., was one of the speakers at the principal public meeting. This was chaired by the Chancellor of the Exchequer, Rt Hon. Selwyn Lloyd.

The President of the Association, Albert Bailey J.P., served in the Vice-Presidency of Conference a few years later, the last LPMAA President to do so.

Aggregate concluded on the Tuesday morning with a service of Holy Communion in Wesley's Chapel for which over 200 delegates had stayed on. The magazine report, written that year by a youthful David Walmsley, contained some interesting observations. He commented that it had been a delight to see a predominantly male Aggregate bow to the commands of a lady, Miss Ruth Wren, the Joint Secretary of the Arrangements Committee. He concluded by noting that more younger preachers seemed to be taking an active part in the Association. Certainly with a membership that had risen to exceed 19,000 in total, nearly 1,000 new members having joined during the year, 1961 must be seen as a high point in the second half of the 20th century.

In the years prior to and during the 1939-45 war the majority of delegates attending would travel by train. Mainline railway routes, therefore, were also significant in the choice of venue, and resolutions were regularly passed by Aggregate Meetings expressing gratitude to the railway companies for granting concessionary fares to delegates. In the later decades of 20th century adequate parking facilities and proximity to the motorway network, particularly to a main interchange, have become progressively more important. The switch to car travel called for different appreciation of the railways' role. In 1996, the Aggregate Handbook listed many people and organisations to whom thanks were extended, including 'Railtrack, for free use of the station car-park'!

Civic authorities have often been gracious and generous in welcoming this great assembly of local preachers into their areas, sometimes with amusing consequences if local briefing has been incomplete, ignored or misunderstood. At Sheffield in 1969 the Lord Mayor entertained the Aggregate for luncheon on the Monday, but the caterers had not been warned that the majority of guests were likely to be total abstainers. There was some embarrassment at the large quantity of wine left unconsumed and the inadequacy of the supply of fruit juice! On some occasions the civic representative at the luncheon had apparently not grasped the nature of the company, and made reference, in responding to the toast of the 'County Borough of . . .', to 'this large gathering of clergy'! Aggregate luncheons have become almost notorious for over-running the time allocated for them, a problem that first occurred at the Inaugural Aggregate in 1849, as was noted in chapter 9. The gentle procession to and from the dining hall invariably occupies twice the time that one person would need, as members pause for a few words with a friend or to allow slower-moving colleagues to catch up.

ITS FORM

The changing nature of Aggregate Meetings can be illustrated by a comparison of the programmes for three that were held in West Yorkshire – 1921, just after the first World War, 1939, just before the second, and 1985, well into the modern period.

In 1921, members enjoyed a reception hosted by the Lord Mayor of Bradford, Lt. Col. Anthony Gadie, J.P., in the Cartwright Hall, Manningham Park. The celebrated evangelist Gipsy Smith, M.B.E., was the preacher at a rally in Eastbrook Hall on Sunday evening. He was also the main speaker – there were three others – at the principal public meeting in the same hall on Monday. Halifax, Huddersfield and Keighley also had public meetings at the same time. The Aggregate business that year included receiving greetings from the Transvaal and Swaziland Local Preachers Association, brought by its President Elect. A report was presented by Richard Lindley (co-editor of *The Local Preachers Magazine*), who had represented LPMAA at the American Methodist Local Preachers Assembly.

By 1939 there had been substantial changes to the Aggregate programme: there was only one public meeting, though with four speakers including the Vice-President of the Conference (R. P. Tomlinson, also an Honorary Secretary of the Association). A session was devoted to Local Preachers' Work, under the titles *'Local Preachers in Public Life'* and *'Our Fellowship in the Gospel'*. Over 500 pulpits were supplied with preachers, many of them for two services; there were still five open-air meetings. A leading member of the Arrangements Committee for the Aggregate was Eric Foster, joint Secretary and Plan Secretary, who was also General Secretary for the next Bradford Aggregate (1967).

The Aggregate of 1985, held at Elland, was overshadowed by the death a few months earlier of the President Elect, Rowland Purton. The note of explanation which replaced his photograph in the Handbook that year included this brief tribute:

> The passing of Brother Rowland is a great loss to the Association. He was well-known as an author of children's books. He had taken early retirement as a Headmaster and was hoping to devote his time to many interests, notably the LPMAA. This was not to be.

The Aggregate had therefore to elect two Presidents – one to serve immediately and one to be President Elect for 1986. So it was that Ross Adkins became the first President since 1902 to take office at the Aggregate which elected him, and the President's Address was given on the Monday. At an earlier period in the Association's history this had been its usual place. The 1985 Aggregate also gave time to the preaching work, hearing an address by the retiring Connexional Local Preachers Secretary, Rev. John Stacey, and then considering Local Preachers' Studies under the leadership of Rev. Michael Townsend.

Another unusual problem arose in 1986 when the Aggregate was jointly hosted at Chester-le-Street by the Darlington and Newcastle-upon-Tyne Districts. There were only two nominees for the 1987 Presidency, and for the first (and so far the only) time in the Association's history there was a tied vote. The newly-inducted President had therefore to give a casting vote to decide her successor. The precedent thus created was that the candidate who had been longer in LPMAA membership should be elected.

Its Characteristics

Many members attending Aggregate are conscious first of that undefinable quality, its 'atmosphere'. A number of elements combine to create this, some obvious, others less so. There is the renewal of old acquaintance, the building up of new friendships, the ease with which conversation develops between folk who have never met before. Above everything else, there is the consciousness that all are there because of a shared conviction about the importance of proclaiming the Christian faith in words and actions. Worship is the supreme means by which all this is collectively

Some of the LPMAA china brought to the Aggregate by various members in 1995.
Most pieces date from very early in the Association's history

Close up of one piece showing the picture from the original
Membership Certificate (see p. 107)

expressed, whether the simple devotions at the opening of each session or the major public service on the Saturday evening. With the exception of that central worship event, Aggregate maintains the Methodist tradition of unaccompanied singing. It is a never-to-be-forgotten experience to sing in a large gathering, at the beginning of Aggregate, the customary hymn 'And are we yet alive'.

The Association is indebted to those who have led this singing as precentors. Some who have fulfilled this function in the last half-century are still remembered by older folk, e.g. C. Ernest Snowdon, of Hull (1943-63), and Bill Simpson, of Cannock (1964-80). Since 1980 Norman Carless, of Stourbridge, has served as Aggregate precentor. He recalls occasions when, having struck up a particular tune, members with strong wills and voices have insisted on singing an alternative, so that the whole of the first verse of a hymn has been sung to two different tunes at the same time! On other occasions the singing has become slower and slower during a hymn, despite the efforts of the precentor to 'keep it going'. Aggregate fell strangely silent one year, when the President asked for *both* verses of the National Anthem to be sung. An integral part of the precentor's role is to act as toastmaster at the Aggregate luncheon on Monday. Apart from leading the singing of Grace, this involves announcing the toasts and the speakers. Achieving the right degree of formality without becoming pompous has not always been easy, especially when (as is often the case) some of the speakers are locally well-known public figures.

For many years a central feature of the second day's programme was the Service of Remembrance for those members of the Association who had departed this life since the last meeting of Aggregate. They usually number several hundreds, and names are not normally read out or mentioned. Many are included in the page set aside for the purpose in each issue of *The Local Preachers Magazine*. It has always been regarded as a great privilege to be called upon to preach the Memorial Sermon.

An important change was introduced in 1990 when, as a result of pressure to make more time available for debates on the business agenda, it was decided to incorporate the Act of Remembrance into the Saturday evening Communion Service. The appropriateness of this was recognised, but it has placed extra responsibility upon the preacher. The congregation now includes many people who are not members of LPMAA, and who hope for preaching appropriate to a Communion Service, rather than a sermon tailored to a specific Mutual Aid purpose. It is, of course, sometimes a deeply moving occasion, when opportunity is offered to give thanks for the lives of friends and fellow-preachers who have entered the Lord's nearer presence during the year. It is also a time to remember joyfully the assurance we have of the greater life beyond this world. The gathering has sung gladly and vigorously of

> . . . the saints who before us have found their reward;
> When the shadow of death fell upon them we sorrowed,
> But now we rejoice that they rest in the Lord.

as well as affirming confidently that we are all indeed 'Marching to Zion'.

A CENTENARY AND A BI-CENTENARY

Two meetings of Aggregate call for particular mention. One is the Association's own Centenary Year Aggregate, the other is the Aggregate of 1996, the year when Methodism commemorated the bi-centenary of the first Conference minute on local preachers. The 1949 Aggregate was probably the outstanding event in the history of LPMAA. It was held in Westminster Central Hall, and a short summary in the Handbook gave this information:

> 600 delegates and nearly 100 officers and General Committee members will be attending. Almost 500 Methodist homes in the six London Districts have been opened to guests for the week-end. On Sunday 12th June [Trinity Sunday, with which Aggregate coincides from time to time] 2,250 services will be conducted in 1,287 London Districts' chapels by members of Aggregate and 727 non-delegate local preachers.

F. Harold Buss, the senior of the two Honorary Secretaries, who had served as President in the year of Methodist Union (1932), was recalled to serve a second term in that office for the Centenary Year. He wrote a special hymn for the Association's Centenary (Appendix 2 to this chapter). The Handbook included a letter of greeting to LPMAA on this notable anniversary from Rev. E. Benson Perkins, President of the Methodist Conference. It contained this perceptive paragraph:

> The completion of this hundred years of service finds the Association still rendering great service along the lines of fellowship, but facing altered conditions respecting the economic position of local preachers who have reached the days of retirement. In that respect considerable changes will be needed, and doubtless the LPMAA, maintaining its spirit of fellowship and service, will adapt itself under these new conditions.

In 1996 the Aggregate Meeting again included Trinity Sunday, but only because the Association had decided to amend its rules to allow Aggregate to meet on the first week-end of June in that year. This was so that it would be in session on the day chosen by Conference to mark the bi-centenary of the formal establishment of Circuit Local Preachers' Meetings. It was also the year when Aggregate approved the arrangements for LPMAA to become part of the Connexional structures. There was the strongest ever Connexional presence at the Bromley Aggregate – the President of Conference preached at the Saturday evening Communion Service, the Connexional Local Preachers' Secretary addressed Aggregate on Monday afternoon, and the Secretary of Conference was the speaker at the final public meeting.

PREACHING ON AGGREGATE SUNDAY

A small number of delegates from the Districts are usually Honorary Members, but there is a general understanding that local preachers attending Aggregate place themselves at the disposal of the Local Committee for appointments on the Sunday. This is one way in which the Association can make some return for the hospitality received from the host District. Aggregate preachers are invariably received most graciously by the congregations. It is an additional responsibility to represent LPMAA in a Methodist pulpit – if their worship is not well-led folk can be pardoned if they form a poor opinion of the Association.

A popular topic of conversation in Aggregate on Monday morning is the previous day's experiences. In the past this would have included comparing notes not only on the size of congregations but also on the size of the collections, which were traditionally given in their entirety to LPMAA on that Sunday. Preachers were normally handed the day's collection money after evening service, to pay in to the Treasurer first thing on Monday morning. This practice has given place in later years to remission by cheque from local stewards to LPMAA, via Branch Treasurers or directly to Head Office. In the years preceding the 1914-18 war, however, the Aggregate Handbook regularly contained an exhortation to preachers to arrive early on Monday to pay in the collections before the day's business commenced, coupled with the statement:

> It will greatly facilitate the work of the Treasurer(s)
> if the brethren will, as far as possible, pay in the
> Collections by cheque or in gold.

This reminder that the gold sovereign was still in general use then raises a puzzling thought – how did preachers change a pocketful of silver and copper coins into gold between Sunday evening and early Monday morning?

Another unusual and interesting reminder of things as they once were, and of how they have changed, appeared in the notes to the Plan for Aggregate Sunday 1902. There were 760 services, at 334 chapels in the three London Wesleyan Districts and 26 chapels of the United Methodist Free Churches and Methodist New Connexion. Of these appointments, 57 were marked with an asterisk (*). The note explained that at these Chapels

> . . . the Morning Service is Liturgical. In all cases,
> however, arrangements have been made for an
> Officer of the Chapel to take the liturgy if necessary,
> but it will be better if the appointed preacher can
> take the whole Service.

Many Wesleyan congregations in cities continued to use the Order of Morning Prayer well into the 20th century, but it may have been a surprise to any preacher from the country who found himself planned for such a service. It seems that worship leaders who were not accredited preachers were sometimes used in those days.

Aggregate in the Future

The year 1987 was a time for a change of Senior Honorary Secretary. Alfred Gilliver had served for a total of twenty years in that and other LPMAA national offices. His last article as Senior Honorary Secretary appeared in *The Local Preachers Magawine* of May 1987. In it he cast his thoughts about the future in the form of 'An Impossible Dream', portraying Aggregate as a central feature of the Annual Local Preachers' Convention. Daily Bible studies, a market-place for books, information and modern communications equipment, working parties preparing reports for the Connexion on matters pertaining to local preaching, and, of course, major acts of worship, were all part of the Convention. Alfred's dream was set in the summer of 1999, and included the statement:

> Nowadays, of course, local preachers who are not members of their own benevolent Association are rare birds indeed.

All the business, he said,

> . . . was dealt with expeditiously but in the true sense of fellowship for which this gathering has been famous for 150 years.

He concluded his article by saying:

> I do not mind if my 'impossible dream' never comes true provided something equally fruitful actually happens!

APPENDIX 1 TO CHAPTER 27

The Venues of the Aggregate Meeting

(Venues after 1932 are included under appropriate Methodist Districts)

London

1849	1875	1935
1854	1885	1938
1860	1902	1949
1864	1917	1961
1869		
Letchworth		1975
Tunbridge Wells		1982
Bromley		1996

Sheffield

1851	1881	1932
1856	1900	1953
1866	1914	1969
Chesterfield		1981
Staveley		1994

Birmingham

1850	1899	1948
1858	1912	1966
1890	1927	
Coventry		1978
Selly Oak		1993

Leeds

1853	1918	1945
1886	1934	1960
1903		
Wakefield		1976
Morley		1991

Manchester

1863	1898	1930
1874	1913	1944
1884		
Sale		1998

Newcastle upon Tyne

1883	1910	1955
1895	1925	1968
Chester-le-St		1986

Bradford

1889	1921	1967
1906	1939	
Elland	1985	

Hull

1878	1908	1958
1893	1923	1987

Liverpool

1887	1916	1952
1901	1933	1973

Norwich

1859	1973	1977
1865	1962	1992

Nottingham

1888	1919	1943
1904	1936	1959

York

1867	1891	1947
1880	1905	1970

Bristol

1855	1907	1954
1892	1922	

Lincoln

1928	1965	1995
1946	1980	

Northampton

1870	1972	
L'cester	1882	1957
Rugby	1988	

Plymouth

1897	1931	1983
1915	1956	

Southampton

1971		
B'mouth	1929	1950
Reading		1942
Wimborne		1989

Bolton

1896	1924	1940
1911		

Stoke-on-Trent

Burslem	1894	1941
Hanley	1909	1926

Wolverhampton

1963	1974
Walsall	1990

Blackpool

1951	1964
Preston	1984

Cardiff

1876	1937

Derby

1862	1979

Louth

1857	1872

Ashton-under-Lyne

1868

Bath

1861

Darlington

1920

Huddersfield

1852

Keighley

1871

Kings Lynn

1877

Oldham

1879

Tiverton

1997

APPENDIX 2 TO CHAPTER 27

THE CENTENARY HYMN (D.C.M.)

1. O gracious God, whose love was near
   Our fathers' steps to lead,
   Whose grace, through all their toil and fear,
   Supplied their utmost need;
   Thy presence was their refuge, Lord,
   Thy servants' strength and stay,
   And for Thy love, with one accord
   We grateful tribute pay.

2. They sought to prove their love to Thee
   By love to others shown,
   And with Thy blessing rich and free
   Thou didst their labours own;
   For others' sakes the cross they bore,
   Fulfilling Thy behest,
   Assured who serve the weak and poor
   Please their loved Master best.

3. With thankful hearts we celebrate
   The valiant men and true,
   Who strove with faith and courage great
   Thy work of love to do;
   The noble band of pioneers,
   Inspired by Christlike care,
   Who toiled through long and weary years
   Their brothers' load to share.

4. As now with reverence we recall
   Our leaders past and gone,
   Upon us may their mantle fall
   Who in their steps go on;
   May we who labour in their place
   Thy power and presence know,
   That this glad ministry of grace
   To greater things may grow.

5. We praise Thee, Lord, whose favour crowned
   The former years with good,
   For all the joy our hearts have found
   In this blest brotherhood;
   Grant us Thy grace to labour on,
   Thy smile our great reward,
   Happy to serve, till life is done,
   Our brethren and our Lord.

28

The Local Preachers Magazine

Beginnings • Controversy and New Editors
Less Frequent, and 'Free'?
A Larger Magazine, A Wider Circulation

BEGINNINGS

The Local Preachers Magazine is one of the principal sources of information about the history of LPMAA. The fact that it has been quoted extensively in many chapters of this book is evidence for that. It is also the oldest source, indeed the only one for the early decades of the Association's existence. Having been established in January 1851 it is very nearly as old as LPMAA itself. It was then published every month, so that an annual volume commonly exceeded 400 pages. A section of each issue was devoted to news and information about Association meetings, events and activities, under the heading 'The Mutual Aid Association Reporter'.

From 1853 to 1894 the magazine's full title was *The Local Preachers Magazine and Christian Family Record*. The hope and intention was that it would serve the purpose of a Christian household magazine as well as meeting the needs of local preachers and Association members. This accounts for the great diversity of material in the early volumes, ranging from devotional articles and poems, general Methodist news and cultural contributions, to items specifically concerned with preaching and the work of LPMAA. The importance attached to the magazine in those years, and the controversies that surrounded it, are fully described in chapter 11. However, to mark 40 years of LPMAA, the January 1890 issue included what was entitled 'A Brief Sketch' of the Association, written by A. Russell Johnson, Honorary Secretary 1881-1902, President 1884. He recounted its origin and slow growth, its gradual acceptance by the Wesleyan Connexion, and the steady expansion of its beneficence. His article also made reference to the magazine, and these few sentences indicate clearly how it was perceived towards the end of the 19th century.

For years it was carried on at a heavy pecuniary loss, but it was maintained principally as an advertising medium. At the end of 1864, seeing that there had been a loss of upwards of £1,500 during the fourteen years of its existence, the paid editor was dispensed with, and since 1865 it has been edited gratuitously by certain members of the Committee. Since that time the circulation has increased, and for years it has been self-supporting. Originally published with forty pages at 4d, it was reduced in 1857 to thirty-two pages at 2d, which is still its price. It has been sent gratuitously to every honorary member since the Annual Meeting of 1860.

The magazine has frequently occupied time in the Aggregate Meeting, for example, at Louth in 1872. The attendance at that Aggregate numbered only about 70, but they must have been very pleased to learn that over 27,000 copies had been sold during the previous year. This represented a monthly average exceeding 2,200, at a time when membership of LPMAA had still not reached 2,000. The financial surplus was £18. In 1891 particular thanks were expressed to the editors, with a request that the magazine should be illustrated.

CONTROVERSY AND NEW EDITORS

There was nevertheless some discontent with it, which surfaced forcefully in the Aggregate of 1894. Russell Johnson proposed that publication should cease at the end of the year, only 'The Mutual-Aid Reporter' section being printed after that date. This would save at least £100 a year. There was lively debate, in the course of which one of the editors, G. C. Amphlett, disavowing any personal feelings in the matter, advocated continuing the magazine. His co-editor, J. Wesley Walker, supported a suggestion that it might be amalgamated with another periodical. Aggregate decided to continue publication, but desired General Committee to consider a possible amalgamation. The General Committee appointed a sub-committee to do this, and in October received and adopted the sub-committee's report. At the Aggregate Meeting in 1895 this was presented. The sub-committee had rejected the idea of amalgamation with another publication, preferring to recommend acceptance of an offer made by

> a literary gentleman of great experience to undertake under the guidance of our present Editors the management of the contents, of course gratuitously.

It transpired that this was Rev. Isaac E. Page, formerly Editor of *The Kings Highway* (magazine of the Holiness Movement). He was keen to see the Association and its magazine prosper, and had provided a scheme of contents to foster this. Mr Page's plan had been accepted by the General Committee and was read out in Aggregate. G. C. Amphlett explained his position, saying that only one person should be responsible for conducting the magazine. The meeting then moved to re-appoint the editors, and a small sub-committee, with instructions to arrange with Mr Page for the adoption of his ideas. Amphlett declined re-appointment, and so Rev. Isaac Page became the first, and so far the only, minister to hold national office in LPMAA. J. W. Walker was re-appointed co-Editor. (At the August meeting of General Committee G. C. Amphlett made a further statement, and the matter was then dropped).

The July issue of 1895 included an article by the new editorial team headed 'A New Beginning'. It contained a generous tribute to Amphlett, and also this significant observation:

> We are not sure how all the brethren will take to the new order of things, and enjoy the lighter diet which may be provided as they have done the more substantial fare of the past.

Although the heading 'The Mutual Aid Association Reporter' was now discontinued, it was recognised that news of LPMAA affairs and activities appealed to older, retired members. It kept them in touch with their brethren in the active work. However, the character of the magazine had changed irrevocably, symbolised by the omission of *Christian Family Record* from its title. Page continued as joint editor until 1909, in the later part of the period as consulting editor. When he finally retired, at the age of seventy, his service and influence were recognised by the presentation of an illuminated address and a gift of £108 from the Association. The year 1923 saw a small but significant development. At the beginning of that year it was decided to send a free copy of the magazine to each annuitant for one year. There were objections on commercial grounds (was the cost justified?), but also letters of appreciation to the Honorary Secretary. In November General Committee decided to continue sending the magazine to annuitants without charge.

In 1949 Richard Burnett, then editor of *The Local Preachers Magazine*, wrote the second part of *A Goodly Fellowship*. He included two chapters, totalling 30 pages, about the magazine. In the first chapter, 'Local Preachers Magazine in the Making', he described its beginnings and early difficulties, with pen portraits of some of the men who helped to ensure its survival. The second chapter, 'The Magazine and Its Editors', traced its development to the time of the 1939-45 war, at the beginning of which Burnett himself was appointed editor. He had therefore to guide it through difficult times, and with regret, saw it reduced to six issues annually, rather than twelve. He could, however, modestly claim that circulation was higher than at any other time in the magazine's history. Richard Burnett was elected President of LPMAA for the year 1953-54, and died in 1960, aged 62, whilst still editor of the *Methodist Recorder*.

LESS FREQUENT, AND 'FREE'?

There was always the hope that it would be possible to return to monthly publication, and an announcement was made in the July/August issue of 1946 that this would happen from the beginning of 1947. However, it did not, the General Committee being informed in December 1946 that alternate monthly issues would continue for a further year. The editor's predicament was aggravated by an embargo on printing during the fuel crisis in the early part of 1947. When change eventually came, in 1970, it was to reduce the numbers of issues to four per year, and quarterly publication has continued to the present time. This has emphasised the importance of the magazine as a 'house journal' for the Association, and the principal channel of communication with the membership. A large proportion of the available space is taken up by reports of the annual Aggregate Meeting, of General Committee, of District and Branch meetings. There is information from Head Office, the LPMAA Homes, the Association's national officers, and a selection of 'Letters to the Editor'. Nevertheless, room is usually found for some book reviews, and articles on preaching, biblical and theological topics and worship, as well as for Connexional communications.

For more than a hundred years the magazine was sold, at a modest price, to those members who chose to purchase it and to anyone who found it interesting. Honorary members, whose subscriptions then were much greater than local preachers' subscriptions, received a copy gratuitously as noted above. In an endeavour to ensure that all members received it, Aggregate resolved in 1959 to include the magazine (still published then six times a year) in the membership subscription. This was raised from four shillings to five shillings to cover the cost and postage. Ten years later attention was drawn to the fact that these items had increased to the point where the subscription no longer covered them. The General Committee referred the matter for the consideration of the Finance and General Purposes Committee. In October 1970 its recommendations to reduce the magazine to 16 pages and publish only quarterly were accepted. The Honorary Secretary took on the editorial responsibility. Rule changes were submitted to and approved by the Aggregate Meeting in 1971 (the year when decimal currency was introduced) to delete the office of Honorary Editor, and to raise the subscription to 50p, the equivalent of ten shillings. The magazine was priced for purchase at 5p, including postage, so that four issues absorbed 40 per cent of a member's subscription.

Concern about escalating printing and postage costs continued into 1974, and before the end of the year a doubling of the ordinary members subscription to £1 had to be proposed. Before this had even reached the Aggregate Meeting a resolution was put to the General Committee for the re-introduction of a charge for the magazine. This was referred to the Finance and General Purposes Committee which recommended, at the beginning of 1976, that this should not be done. The magazine was then taking 36p out of each member's £1 annual subscription.

A LARGER MAGAZINE, A WIDER CIRCULATION

Following the incorporation of editorial responsibilities into the duties of the Honorary Secretary, three further holders of that office have nurtured their charge through two decades of change. New printing technology, new styles of graphic design, and new circulation opportunities all in turn required attention. The latter arose because of the developing relationships with the Methodist Connexion, and are mentioned in chapter 34. To ensure that all preachers, both local and ministerial, receive the Connexional Secretary's Annual circular, it has been included in the August issue of *The Local Preachers Magazine* which, since 1992, has been distributed to *all* preachers, not only to LPMAA members. The Connexional Local Preachers' Office has contributed to the cost of doing this. Some other issues have been expanded to incorporate additional, more broadly-based, material.

The enlarged magazine and wider circulation has proved an effective way of reaching all ministers and local preachers. LPMAA Head Office maintains a database of all local preachers, widows/widowers of former members, and honorary members to make this circulation possible. It has enabled other wider circulations of the magazine, for example, a special issue in 1996 when Methodism marked 200 years of Circuit Local Preachers' Meetings. The latest development in the history of the magazine has been the move into desk-top publishing. This has produced significant cost savings. Another effect has been to shorten the time between editing and publication, so that news, reports of General Committee proceedings, and other important information can reach readers more quickly.

For many years there was no mention of *The Local Preachers Magazine* in the Association's Rules, other than the inclusion of the 'Honorary Editor' in the rule listing the officers. However, by 1963 a rule had been made stipulating the purposes of the magazine and that it 'shall be published and distributed as directed by the Aggregate Meeting'. When the editorial role was taken over by the Honorary Secretary, the office of Honorary Editor disappeared from the rules (1972); at the same time, responsibility for directing the publication of the magazine passed to the General Committee. Notwithstanding the controversy that has surrounded it in several periods of its life, *The Local Preachers Magazine* now has a secure place in the affections of LPMAA members, as well as in the Association's Rules, where its purposes are defined thus:

> *The Local Preachers Magazine* shall be the official organ of the Association and shall be directed towards making known the work of the Association and assisting local preachers in their calling. The Magazine shall be published and distributed as

directed by the General Committee subject to any specific directions given by the Aggregate Meeting, and the management and distribution shall be the responsibility of the General Secretary.

29

Intellectual and Spiritual Aid

*From the Beginning • The Interest Is Sustained
The Work Becomes Established
Intellectual and Spiritual Aid Since the 1939-45 War*

From the Beginning

At an early point in the inaugural Aggregate Meeting, in fact during the debate on the first resolution giving the Association its name, there was some discussion of the meaning to be attached to the words 'mutual aid'. The concern was widely shared; the amendment to clarify the intended meaning was actually proposed and seconded by members from East Anglia. The official report of the proceedings records that

> Brother B. Hardy from the Swaffham Circuit . . . asked a question in reference to the name of the Association. He was encouraged to put it from some remarks which had been dropped. If it were intended in their meeting to converse upon subjects calculated to increase their personal piety, he would look upon that as mutual aid. Or if upon subjects calculated to promote the interests of Methodism throughout the world, that would be mutual aid. He therefore wished to ask what was the extent of the mutual aid spoken of in the designation of the Association? He was decidedly of the opinion that the meeting should not be tied down, because there were men of mind, and men of piety there. Were the words 'mutual aid' to be applied solely to pecuniary aid, or to embrace spiritual aid as well?

The Chairman concurred with the general tenor of Hardy's remarks, but pointed out that they would need a very long time to explore the full extent of mutual aid. They could not do everything at once. He urged that they should do what was clearly before them, to create an organisation for the relief of members in sickness, in distressed old age, and at the time of death. Hardy nevertheless moved that the words of the resolution should be, '. . . mutual, pecuniary, and spiritual aid'. Keed, of Lynn, seconded the amendment, which (in the words of the report) 'was negatived by a large majority'. This does not appear to signify disagreement with the intention of the amendment, but rather that the name of the Association should contain the all-embracing phrase 'Mutual Aid', without this being defined too precisely. The idea of mutual help and encouragement in the Christian life and in the preacher's calling was not forgotten. Shortly before the close of the Aggregate on the following day, Keed moved:

> That in order to sustain and increase the deep affection and spiritual union reciprocated here these two days between the brethren, it is desirable that we hold an aggregate meeting of Local Preachers annually, and that our main object then be the spiritual elevation and improvement of the brethren, in order to secure which, arrangements be made for special religious services;

His seconder was Summersides, of Belper, and the resolution was agreed. So, right from the beginning, it was recognised that mutual aid in the preaching work, as well as in times of material need, was properly part of the Association's role.

THE INTEREST IS SUSTAINED

There were probably two reasons why relatively little was done to fulfil this dimension of mutual aid in the early decades. One was almost certainly that the need for 'pecuniary aid' was very pressing, and maximum effort had to be devoted to raising the funds needed to meet it. The slow growth in membership did not make the task any easier. The other reason was that positive steps to formalise study and training for local preachers in Wesleyan Methodism were not taken until the 1870s, and the 'spiritual elevation and improvement of the brethren' (referred to in the resolution) would have been understood very much in terms of the 'special religious services' for which the resolution called.

The Local Preachers Magazine (and *Mutual Aid Reporter*) made a substantial and sustained contribution from its first publication in 1851. It carried regular series on biblical and theological themes, as well as occasional articles on aspects of the preaching work. Some of these are quite intriguing, raising questions about the needs they were written to meet. Others had quaint-sounding titles, doubtless fashioned to attract the attention of readers in the mid- and later 19th century years. In 1872 the magazine provided a series of articles on 'The Principles and Rules of English Grammar', which was followed in 1873 by a series on 'Local Preachers and Their Work'. Further contributions included 'The Lord's Supper – Its Nature, Design and Observance' (by a former Anglican vicar), an essay on 'Prayer', and a regular feature called 'Choice Selections'. One of these was an article on 'Lay Preaching', reprinted from the *Methodist Recorder* in anticipation of the admission of laymen to the Wesleyan Conference. Most issues of this period contained one or more sample sermons.

The Aggregate Meeting of 1874 was held in Manchester, and elected a Manchester man, Abraham Andrew, as President. In his letter in the September magazine of that year he referred to the special pleasure of taking office in his home city, and then raised the possibility of intellectual and spiritual aid being discussed at the following year's Aggregate.

> The better fitting of local preachers for their work, by improved education, has lately been brought to our notice; and this, we must all admit, is a matter of too great moment to be quietly put aside . . . with our organisation and magazine, we have at command some of the means necessary for affording each other 'mutual aid' in training and discipline for our work. The subject, I think, may be properly brought up at our next annual meeting.

Shortly before that next Aggregate the magazine carried an article on the subject by B. Hardy supporting the President's proposal. He recalled that nearly 26 years ago, at the inaugural Aggregate, he had secured support from a number of influential brethren for a motion urging that mutual aid in the preaching work should be included in the Association's activities. As already noted, 'in the infant stage of the Association [Hardy's own phrase] the motion was not adopted, . . . nothing else appeared then to be either prudent or practicable.' Referring to the proceedings of the last Wesleyan Conference, Hardy quoted from its minutes:

> It is desirable and necessary, considering the experiences of our work, and the fact that our supply of ministers is drawn from our local preachers, that steps should be taken to secure in every circuit an ample and efficient supply of this most useful class of labourers; and that superintendents should direct their special attention to eligible and promising young men in their respective circuits, with the view to their becoming local preachers, and, as far as is practicable, should direct their reading and studies to that end.

Hardy's view, for which he affirmed there was considerable support, was

> . . . that the improvement of local preachers in education, intellectual attainments, theological knowledge, preaching qualifications, piety, and general fitness for their important work, should not be lost sight of.

He believed this was a dimension of mutual aid in which the Association was well-equiped to engage, as had been stressed by President Andrew a few months earlier. The role of the magazine in this was underlined by a letter to the Editor in the December issue 1875, in which the writer said:

> I would make it much more a local *Preachers'* magazine than it is. I should like to see a Theological Editor appointed, to whom should be entrusted about ten pages in each number. Part of this space should be occupied by a series of lessons in elementary theology suited for young and unlearned local preachers.

The magazine did not only promote the intellectual and spiritual development of its readers by means of biblical or theological articles and sermons. Literary and artistic criticism also found a place. A notable example appeared in the issue of August 1874; an un-named contributor analysed the famous Holman Hunt painting *The Shadow of Death*, which had aroused considerable interest at exhibitions during the previous year. Hunt had become an eminent religious artist by this time, though his earlier picture *The Light of the World* (1854) is still his best-known work (the original is at Keble College, Oxford, a later version in St Paul's

Cathedral). The magazine article pointed out that, true to his Pre-Raphaelite roots (see chapter 6), Hunt had visited Bethlehem, Nazareth and Jerusalem in pursuit of realism for this portrayal of the adult Christ in his workshop. As he stands up from his work, stretching his arms, he casts a shadow in the shape of a cross on the wall behind. The writer quoted from Holman Hunt's own commentary to make the point that the painting exemplifies the dignity of labour and the duty of work. Preachers of the time may well have found stimulation of thought in both the picture and the article about it.

THE WORK BECOMES ESTABLISHED

As has been noted in earlier chapters, the 20th century brought social and economic changes that affected LPMAA significantly. Developments in Methodism as the century progressed also had consequences for the Association. Gradually intellectual and spiritual mutual aid became a more explicit element in its life and work. *The Local Preachers Magazine* continued to play its part, but more by reporting local preachers' conferences and study days held in the Districts and by publication of book reviews. Some material directly related to the preaching work was still included.

In the mid-1940s the Connexional Local Preachers' Secretary sought financial help from the Association for the Department's training work. There was a certain irony in the situation that then arose. LPMAA had recognised that study and preacher-development were an important form of mutual aid. The organisation of conferences and study sessions was undertaken by voluntary officers, and costs were met by members participating. However, the Association's charitable income could not be used to support this kind of educational work undertaken by *another body*, without an appropriate rule-change to authorise it. The full story has been told in chapter 17, but the outcome was that LPMAA day and residential conferences formed a substantial part of the in-service training programme in many parts of the country.

The Association supported and stimulated this development. In December 1946 the senior Honorary Secretary suggested to the General Purposes Committee that weekend fellowships or retreats should be encouraged by financial help. The

Office Sub-Committee was authorised to consider applications up to £20 towards incidental expenses, such as printing costs. Amongst the Districts to benefit from this policy in the first few years were Carlisle (£10), London South (£7-5-0d) and Lincoln (£3-5-6d). A wide range of themes and subjects was pursued; leadership was often provided by members of the Association, some of whom were Connexional tutors for Local Preachers' Studies, some having other experience or expertise for the task. Help was readily given by local ministers or by outside lecturers invited because of their specialist knowledge in particular fields. In a number of places a tradition developed, over many years, of annual residential study week-ends, which were sometimes fully booked as much as a year in advance.

Detailed programmes of some of these events have been preserved, which, with reports of other conferences printed in the magazine, give a good impression of the varied subject-matter covered. Often the topics were related to the ongoing week-by-week work of leading worship, and preaching in that context. Sometimes topics reflected the importance of keeping members well-informed about changes taking place in Methodism or in wider society. Also a fellowship and conference weekend for General Committee members and invited guests has been part of the Association's annual programme of events for half a century. Interesting initiatives have been taken in some Districts to incorporate the intellectual and spiritual dimension into regular half-yearly District meetings. Sometimes the traditional 'after-tea' meeting has been adapted towards enlightenment rather than entertainment. In other situations the opportunity afforded by a Presidential visit has been used to encourage thought and discussion about worship and preaching.

There is a major difference between this element of Mutual Aid and what the founders knew as 'eleemosynary' aid, that is, alms or charitable giving. Whereas the latter is measurable in terms of money received and members assisted (of which the Association's records give year-by-year details), intellectual and spiritual aid is not measurable in that way, and is not fully recorded. It would not be meaningful to know that in a given year a certain number of members shared in conferences, study sessions, refresher courses, for a precise total of hours. The benefit gained cannot be measured. What is important is that many have found mutual help and encouragement in the Christian life and the preacher's calling through the fellowship and activity of LPMAA.

In this context they have met fellow-preachers from many parts of the country, and have been able to interact with those from very different social and cultural backgrounds. Preachers from rural, agricultural areas have met with colleagues from urban, industrial circuits. Those from relatively affluent areas have been able to share experiences with others from areas of economic depression. This in itself has been enriching, giving new and deeper insights into the Gospel. The remainder of this chapter, therefore, looks briefly at some examples of this kind of mutual aid, drawn from programme leaflets and District or Branch records.

INTELLECTUAL AND SPIRITUAL AID SINCE THE 1939-45 WAR

In reporting the proceedings of the 1947 Aggregate Meeting, Richard Burnett, editor of *The Local Preachers Magazine*, commented on certain speeches:

> These are not days in which mere rhetoric has any considerable influence. . . . we need to re-examine these facile phrases, ask ourselves what we mean by them, and whether they really mean anything at all. . . . As preachers we should be conscious of the intellectual climate of our day.

This was a signpost for intellectual and spiritual aid within LPMAA in the post-war years.

What was known in the 1950s and 1960s as the 'Rosehill Conference' was organised by the London South West District of LPMAA. The programme and booking form for 1959 stated that the fee for the weekend would be 34s (£1-14-0d, or £1.70 in modern decimal currency). This covered residential costs for High Tea on Saturday to High Tea on Sunday. Travelling directions by bus were given, and there was no reference to the adequacy of car-parking space! After the District boundary changes of 1957, 'Rosehill' was also supported by the Southampton District and some Branches of the former Oxford and Gloucester District. It took its name from the Salvation Army conference centre near Reading where it was held annually until the early 1960s, when it moved to 'The Hallams' at Chilworth, in Surrey.

The 1959 Conference theme was 'The Living Church'. The first and last of the four sessions were led by the Social Responsibility Secretary of the British Council of Churches, on 'The Universal Church' and 'The Future Church'. The third session, on 'The Overseas Church', was led by a minister from the Methodist Missionary Society. The second session, which from the programme looks possibly the most stimulating of all, was on 'The Local Church'. Three members of the Conference contributed in turn on 'The Village Church', 'The Town Church', and 'The City Mission'. Conference members chaired the sessions and led closing devotions at the end of each day. The guest of honour was the President of LPMAA for that year, William E. Davies, who conducted morning worship on the Sunday. The Rosehill programme of 1959 is fairly representative of the kind of study event that was promoted in many LPMAA Districts in the 1950s and early 1960s.

Even during the 1939-45 war there had been some imaginative approaches to intellectual mutual aid. A very successful radio programme of the war years was 'The Brains Trust', in which leading figures from science, education, the arts, and world travel were invited to answer questions sent in by listeners. The idea was adopted by London North East District for its meeting in March 1942, held at Wanstead. The after-tea event took the form of a Local Preachers' Brains Trust. The Superintendent Minister took the chair, his junior colleague supervising the local arrangements. The panel included Sister Grace Dent, who, according to the District Minute Book, set a precedent the following year upon being appointed the District's first woman Chairman. Other panellists in the 1942 Brains Trust included H. W. Carpenter and Owen Rattenbury, District Conveners. There is no record of the questions asked, although the leaflet publicising the event asked for questions in advance in writing on LPMAA, lay preaching, or conduct of services. The minutes do, however, state that the event was very successful in all ways, adding that the collection nearly covered the cost of 1,000 handbills printed. Encouraged by this success, a Brains Trust evening was held again after the District Meeting on 3rd April the following year (1943) at East Ham Central Hall, the incoming Chairman's home congregation.

The idea of a team to answer previously-submitted questions, or those asked by members of the audience in the meeting, has appeared in various guises in many places over the years. This has not been only as an event in itself but also as an element, often the concluding session, of full-day or residential study conferences. A Preachers' Forum was organised by Darlington District LPMAA in conjunction with a meeting of its District Committee in 1992/93. There was great interest at that time in two particular topics. One was *Faith and Worship*, then still the 'new' Connexional training programme for local preachers On Trial. The other was the plans being made by the Local Preachers' Committee for a scheme of Continuing Development for fully-accredited Local Preachers. Similar events were held by other Districts to raise awareness and stimulate informed thought about these very significant developments for the preaching work.

There are references in some of the chapters in Section IV of this book, 'Our Roots Are Our Branches', to intellectual and spiritual aid initiatives in various Districts. These include Cornwall (Treloyhan Manor), Cumbria (Abbot Hall) and London (Elfinsward). Often they began through the enterprise and enthusiasm of one or two members, but once established they acquired a momentum which has maintained them for many years.

30

The Wider View

Overseas Relationships – the USA, the Antipodes,
Southern Africa
The Sierra Leone Mutual Aid Association
Social and Political Concerns • COPEC 1924

From the very beginning Methodism has always had a
'wider view'. It is most clearly embodied in John Wesley's famous
and often mis-quoted statement, 'I look upon all the world as my
parish.' Most Methodist groups and organisations have, in one
form or another, developed this wider, outward-looking view.

- Women's Work began in 1858 as a Committee for
  the Amelioration of the Condition of Women in
  Heathen Countries.
- The Guild Movement supported medical work in
  West Africa from 1912, including the Ilesha
  Hospital since the 1920s.
- MAYC encouraged its members to 'live on a large
  map'.
- NCH has ensured that the church maintains an
  active concern for less fortunate folk in our own
  country.

It has also been true of LPMAA, both in the worldwide
dimension and in the more immediate setting of this nation. This
often reflected the convictions and influence of leading laymen in
Methodism, but through the annual Aggregate Meeting it has also
commanded the support of the Association's membership. Local
preachers were confident that, acting collectively through the
Association, their opinions and actions would be heeded in both
church and state.

Overseas Relationships – the USA, the Antipodes, Southern Africa

The second half of the 19th century saw considerable expansion of overseas trade and travel. Sailing ships gave way to steamships, ships of wood to ships of iron (later steel), paddle-wheels to the screw propellor; ocean travel became speedier, safer and more comfortable, whether for business or pleasure. Methodist local preachers were amongst the travellers, some of them joining the flow of migrants going to begin a new life in other parts of the world. One of the Association's early leaders, Thomas Chamberlain, relinquished his offices in 1885 in order to settle in New Zealand (see chapter 25).

It appears that LPMAA first made official relationships with a local preacher association overseas in 1880. *The Local Preachers Magazine* of June 1886 included a memoir of William Jameson, who was born in Sicily in 1810. Coming to England in his youth, he left a Catholic background to become a Wesleyan and a local preacher. He joined LPMAA soon after its formation. The memoir states:

> In the year 1880 he visited the United States, as the first delegate from the Local Preachers Mutual Aid Association, to the National Convention of Local Preachers in America.

Whilst there he contracted an illness from which he never fully recovered, and he died in February 1886, aged 76. Another early instance was in October 1890, when a delegation from the Association attended the Conference of the National Association of Local Preachers of the Methodist Episcopal Church of America, at Fort Wayne, Indiana. The following February *The Local Preachers Magazine* carried the text of the address given by one of the delegates, Charles Boot (of Cornwall). He began his remarks 'Mr President, Ladies, Honoured Fathers and Brethren'. This American Association was some years ahead of LPMAA in having women in membership and present at its Annual Conference. After lengthy expressions of pride, unworthiness and gratitude, he came to the main purpose:

> We are honoured in conveying to you the fraternal greetings of the Local Preachers Mutual Aid Association of England – an Association established in the year 1849, now numbering more than 6,000

members and having an income of nearly £8,900. During the last year it paid to 357 aged brethren and widows the sum of £4,246.

Two other members of the delegation, Barr and Teale, gave a 'very interesting and instructive account of their reception and the impressions formed by the visit', to the Aggregate Meeting in June 1891. William Kilner and William Stephenson (see chapter 12) were elected as delegates to the American Local Preachers' Conference at Harrisburg, USA, the following October. Next year the representative was Charles Heap, who later became LPMAA President (1896), and Treasurer (1908 to 1922).

Representation was not just one way. In 1900 Aggregate was addressed by Hercules Atkinson of Philadelphia who 'expressed the sentiments of the brethren of the church from which he had come', saying that the National Association of Local Preachers in USA represented 35,000 preachers. At the meeting of the General Committee in August the same year J. E. Virgo, former Secretary of of the Australian Preachers' Association, brought greetings from 'down under'. Three months later the General Committee received from America a letter which referred effusively to the 'union now happily formed between local preachers in England and America', and suggesting the formation of a worldwide union of local preachers.

Not all these exchanges were official. Members travelling abroad sometimes found opportunity to attend local preacher assemblies in other countries. In January 1906, D. G. Engleburtt provided a very full account for *The Local Preachers Magazine* of his visit to the Natal Wesleyan Methodist Local Preachers' Association Convention in June the previous year. He had taken with him a letter of introduction from the Honorary Secretaries of the Home Association (W. E. Skinner and W. J. Back), and wrote of the hearty welcome members of the Convention gave their 'unexpected English visitor'.

Being invited to address the gathering, he spoke about the work of local preachers and of Mutual Aid, and conveyed 'what, I presume, I was authorised to do' – the good wishes of the Home Association to the Natal brethren in their work. The Natal Association had 110 members, about 40 being present at the Convention. It had been in existence since 1880. Bro. Engleburtt advised them to follow the LPMAA custom and send their own representatives to circuits when collections were to be taken for their Association, rather than have grants from Quarterly Meetings. Another visitor to the Natal Convention represented the 45 local preachers of Cape Province, where an Association had recently been formed.

THE SIERRA LEONE MUTUAL AID ASSOCIATION

At about this time the first steps were being taken amongst local preachers in Sierra Leone to form their own Mutual Aid Association. The magazine of May 1906 contained a request on behalf of local preachers overseas, including Sierra Leone, for readers to send their past copies of it for despatch to these destinations. Three years later, James Magnus King Davies wrote to the Editor reporting the formation of a LPMAA in Sierra Leonne. 'Better to be late than never,' he said, adding that the organisation is in 'full working order'. The inaugural meeting, held on 11th July 1908 in Wesley Methodist Church, Freetown, was attended by 32 preachers in addition to the founder, J. M. K. as he was popularly known.

The text of a lecture on 'The Growth and Development of the Sierra Leone Association up to its 21st Anniversary (1929)' enables some impressions of the body to be formed. [The text was lent for consultation by a lady from Sierra Leone, now resident in this country, who was elected to General Committee in 1997]. The London Office of the Home Association gave help and information. J. M. K. Davies was President from the beginning until December 1911. Regular correspondence was being held with the London office during this period. The District Synod granted permission for Local Preachers' Sunday to be held in October every year. Forty-five pounds was handed on to the new President at the beginning of 1912, and J. M. K. was appointed Honorary President for life. In 1913 'sick and death aidance', as it was called, was extended to the wives and children of members.

Early in 1915 J. M. K. 'exchanged time for eternity' and a memorial service took place in April. At the end of 1920 the balance in the accounts exceeded £240. Throughout these years the Sierra Leone Association pursued intellectual and spiritual development by regular monthly meetings. The 1929 lecture included information about the range and breadth of the topics. A small library was also provided. Much more recently (July 1980) J. R. Clarkson, the new secretary of the Sierra Leone MLPMAA, wrote to the General Secretary of LPMAA at Rickmansworth for information to benefit his 110 members. Copies of current literature were sent, with a letter of good wishes and an offer of further help if requested.

Relationships between LPMAA and similar Associations in other countries continued during the 1914-18 war and were maintained after it. The Bolton Aggregate of 1924, for example, received letters of greeting from the Transvaal and Swaziland Local Preachers' Association and from the Local Preachers' Association in Victoria (Australia). Replies were sent, along with letters to other Associations, including that in the USA. One of the members of Aggregate had just returned from Australia and conveyed a cordial message from the Victoria Association. Others, including J. Simpson Alcock and Harry Dawson (both future Presidents), were commissioned to take the greetings of LPMAA to the Local Preachers in New Zealand, Australia and the USA, during forthcoming visits to those countries.

Alcock reported on his visit to New Zealand at the following year's Aggregate. George Orchard, the delegate to the USA, wrote about his experiences there in *The Local Preachers Magazine* in October 1924. He commented particularly on the very different way that American Methodism used local preachers. They conducted services in prisons, hospitals and other institutions, but not in churches, where the majority of services were taken by ministers. He found much interest in and high regard for the work of LPMAA and great appreciation of the visits of representatives in past years. In the same issue the Honorary Secretary referred to letters received from Local Preacher Associations in North America, several parts of Africa, and the Antipodes.

Contacts became less frequent after the 1939-45 war, although cordial relations continued with local preacher organisations in some places (for example, Sierra Leone, as mentioned above).

SOCIAL AND POLITICAL CONCERNS

The 'wider view' of LPMAA, its leaders and its members, has not been solely in terms of relationships with local preachers and their associations in other parts of the world. There has been a real awareness that the Christian Gospel is concerned with the physical and material dimensions of human life, and that preaching faith is undermined unless that concern is actively demonstrated. The earliest example was at the end of the very first Aggregate Meeting in 1849. Attention was called to orders recently issued for opening the General Post Office seven days a week, thus requiring employees to work on Sundays. The brethren were urged to 'stir up' the people to protest against Government desecration of the day. A wider expression of this active concern was shown by the identification of many members of LPMAA with the 19th century temperance movement.

The larger question came to the fore in the autumn issues of *The Local Preachers Magazine*, 1909. Discussion was initiated in September by Harry Dawson, who was elected President twenty years later. His article dealt with the implications of 'the great Social Movement' (later simply 'Socialism') for Methodism and its local preachers. He observed the emphasis on the humanitarian side of the Gospel, and pointed out the parallel decline in the observance of Sunday, attendance at worship and church membership. Developing his argument about policy, message and spirit, over three pages, Harry Dawson urged open-air preaching, stressing that:

> . . . we must not preach the Church . . . When Methodism seeks only to save its own life it will lose it.

The ensuing correspondence (in October and November) appeared under the heading 'Local Preachers and the Great "Socialist" Problem'. One letter was described as 'A Rejoinder to Bro. H. Dawson', the writer stating that as a Christian he was out to fight Socialism, which, he said, aimed to make people good by Act of Parliament. Richard Lindley, co-editor of *The Local Preachers Magazine* from 1909 to 1921, President in 1915, expressed far more concern about indifference than about opposition. He recognised that many men had begun to realise the power they had through the right to vote, and the strength that expanding trade unionism gave them. Nevertheless, he was convinced that increasing wealth, stemming from business and industrial success amongst Methodists posed a greater problem. His conclusion was the need for Christian laymen 'to consecrate wealth and brain to Christ's service'. Another contributor wrote, 'You are going to urge people to reform, whilst witholding reformed conditions.'

The Association continued, through resolutions of the Aggregate Meeting, to express emphatic views on matters of public concern. Some of these resolutions were sent to leading politicians, including Prime Ministers. It is not surprising that in the later 19th century the licensed liquor trade attracted attention. In 1889 a resolution urged Government to allow people a direct veto over the issue and renewal of such licences in their own localities. The following year Aggregate affirmed its judgement that traffic in intoxicating liquor is seriously harmful to the social, moral and religious welfare of the community. It recognised the intention to diminish that traffic, but implored the Government not to make public money available for the compensation of public house licencees whose licences were withdrawn. Government policy was supported when it reflected the convictions of LPMAA members; e.g. the 1893 Aggregate approved unanimously a resolution in favour of the Liquor Traffic (Local Control) Bill.

Similar concern arose during the 1914-18 war. In 1915 the Aggregate Meeting resolved to send a letter of thanks to the King for his splendid example to the nation in abolishing alcoholic drinks from all royal residences during the war. Two years later, in a very different tone, the meeting supported a resolution imploring the Government:

> ... in view of the shortage of grain for the making of bread and to assist in the ending of this war . . . to at once prohibit totally the use of any grain for the manufacture of alcoholic liquor.

Another aspect of the matter was dealt with at the first post-war Aggregate Meeting through a resolution in which 'this meeting begs the Government' to deal with the danger to the interests of children by them being taken into public houses.

Members of the Association also registered their concern on social questions through their local Branches. The Salisbury Branch, for example, called attention to the high levels of unemployment prevailing in 1921. This was affecting many local preachers and General Committee was urged to prepare a special scheme of mutual aid amongst members.

COPEC 1924

A major conference on Christian Politics, Economics and Citizenship (abbreviated to COPEC) was held at Birmingham Central Hall in April 1924. It was attended by 1,500 delegates from all major branches of the Church, from the Student Christian Movement, YMCA and YWCA, universities and theological colleges. Twelve ecumenical commissions had prepared papers for the Conference, each report being prefaced with this statement:

> The basis of this Conference is the conviction that the Christian faith, rightly interpreted and consistently followed, gives the vision and the power essential for solving the problems of today.

The editor of *The Local Preachers Magazine* judged the conference sufficiently important to devote eight pages of the August issue to a summary of its proceedings. The membership of the Association was certainly encouraged to take 'The Wider View'. Referring to the twelve reports, the writer of the article stated: 'The gospels live again in these volumes.' Under the title 'The Nature of God and His Purpose for the World', the first volume laid the theological foundation for all the rest. It was followed by reports on Education, The Home, The Relation of the Sexes, Leisure, The Treatment of Crime, International Relations, Christianity and War, Industry and Property, Politics and Citizenship, and the Social Function of the Church. The twelfth volume put these themes into historical perspective. More than half of the article was occupied by reference to specific issues from some of the reports. From 'Leisure', on the matter of Gambling, came this quotation:

> ... no countenance should be given to it in Christian organisations, as in holding of lotteries, raffles, and similar appeals to the gambling spirit.

'The Relation of the Sexes' dealt with marriage, and such highly-sensitive questions as divorce, prostitution and contraception, upon which the writer said that the Conference showed itself anything but squeamish before a frank and reasonable discussion. The 'Industry and Property' report yielded these statements:

> The evils of unemployment are intolerable to the moral sense. The causes must be sought and removed . . . Extremes of wealth and poverty are likewise intolerable.

To summarise the approach of COPEC to these and other important political, economic and social concerns, the article included this affirmation from the theological foundation volume:

> The attempt to create an individualistic Christianity, and to represent religion as a love-affair between a lonely soul and its God is false to Christ's whole method.

LPMAA harmonised with this COPEC emphasis, and continued to express its social concerns between the two World Wars. In both 1923 and 1924 the Aggregate Meeting passed a strongly-worded resolution on the harmful effects of gambling. The first one expressed:

> . . . determined opposition to the legalisation of betting, the establishment of betting houses, the creation of new vested interest by licensing bookmakers. The widespread practice of betting and gambling is an evil which disastrously affects the economic, social and moral life of the community. This Association is opposed to the imposition of a duty on betting, which by legalising betting and licensing bookmakers and betting houses would involve support by the state of this evil.

The next year's resolution:

> . . . views with alarm the widespread adoption of lottery in raising money for charitable purposes, in the form of Sweepstakes, Raffles and Lottery competitions, believing that when these are not illegal, they are contrary to the spirit of the law. They make a direct appeal to the possibility of gain by chance.

The resolution urged members of the Association to dissociate themselves from all these things. In 1926 opposition to a betting tax was reiterated. A further resolution (1932) registered deep concern over the growth and spread of gambling, and urged all local preachers and the Methodist Press to warn of its dreadful effect and moral degradation.

From time to time other issues evoked response. In 1934 a resolution was passed on the subject of Sunday boxing competitions. The London County Council had recently prohibited these, and the Aggregate Meeting urged other local authorities to follow its example. Extension of the Sunday opening of cinemas was also opposed.

After the 1939-45 war, changes in public policy and in the social witness of Methodism through the reorganised Christian Citizenship Department, created a new context for social concern and action. Members of LPMAA, like many other Christians, gave their support more and more to other voluntary associations addressing the wider issues about which they felt strongly. These convictions were still expressed through Association Channels; as recently as May 1998 *The Local Preachers Magazine* contained an article by a member urging the Association as a body to give active support to international relief agencies.

31

The Impact of Technology

Early Days – Simpler Ways • The Aggregate Meeting Journal
Publicity and Public Relations
Administrative and Communication Systems;
Systems to Strengthen Service

EARLY DAYS – SIMPLER WAYS

The General Secretary, William Noddings, presided over the staff at Head Office in the years between the wars

Twentieth century history has been greatly influenced by developments in mechanical, electrical and electronic technology. This chapter traces the effects of some of these changes on the way LPMAA has done its work, both internally and in the presentation of itself to Methodist people. Two decisions made by the General

Committee before 1900 deserve mention. In 1891 the purchase of gummed and perforated labels for use in distributing the magazine was authorised; in 1899 it was decided to acquire a typewriter for use in Head Office. At meetings in October 1914, the Office Sub-Committee agreed the purchase of an oak filing cabinet for correspondence, at a price of £7-12s, and a nest of drawers for a card index of members, Branches and Districts, at £2-6s. The Committee then inspected and approved these items! Head Office was to have everything necessary to give efficient service to the Association and its members. By 1924 duplicating facilities were needed, and on 5th April that year the General Committee approved the purchase of a rotary duplicator. Its price was not minuted, but thirty-two years later (27th April 1956) the Finance and General Purposes Committee recommended that nearly £167 should be spent on a power operated duplicator, after allowing for the trade-in value of the earlier machine.

Understandably, the major impact of modern technology on the Association's activity has been during the last forty years of the 20th century. It can be identified in three main areas:

• The Aggregate Meeting journal
• Publicity and public relations
• Administrative and communication systems (Head Office; the LPMAA Homes)

A fourth area – the adoption of new data transmission techniques in connection with the preparation of *The Local Preachers Magazine* – is mentioned in chapter 28.

THE AGGREGATE MEETING JOURNAL

From the beginning, the official record of the proceedings of the Aggregate Meeting has been kept in the form of a journal, faithfully handwritten by duly appointed scribes, usually working in pairs. The variety of handwriting, frequently showing signs of haste, makes interesting – if difficult – reading for later researchers. The only typed material included is chiefly lists of names (such as scrutineers of the ballot), the text of rule-changes, and the scripts of some Presidential addresses. Such were the demands of the task that appointment as a Journal Writer was often regarded as punishment for some unknown sin!

In 1992 this fate befell a member who was professionally involved with modern information technology, and brought the appropriate equipment to Aggregate for producing the Journal. The lap-top computer and portable printer aroused reactions ranging from disbelief to disapproval ('It can't be a proper record if it's not handwritten!'), from amazement to excitement and enthusiasm. There were even expressions of pity for the journal-writer who, being enslaved to the machine, would no longer be able to speak in debates. This, of course, has been entirely untrue, and Aggregate seems to take the new method of producing its record as quite normal.

PUBLICITY AND PUBLIC RELATIONS

Chapter 18 (Social Change and LPMAA) includes reference to increasing prosperity, leisure and personal mobility. The means, the time and the opportunity to do other things led to the gradual demise of public meetings as a social activity and as a major channel of public communication. That chapter noted also the use by the Association of broadcast media for publicising itself and its activities. When the cinema became established as a major means of enlightenment and entertainment, people soon got used to receiving information visually rather than by hearing alone. It is not surprising that the Association eventually considered the use of film to inform people about its work, and to seek support for it. Neither is it surprising that the title adopted for its first venture was the title of the Centenary history, *A Goodly Fellowship*. The easy availability of portable 16mm sound film projectors encouraged hopes that much larger audiences might be exposed to attractive up-to-date presentation of Mutual Aid activity. The General Committee, meeting in Douglas, Isle of Man, on 12th September 1964, heard details of the arrangements for the film's first showings during the autumn of that year:

> Premiere – London, 20th October – invited audience
> First provincial screening – Birmingham,
>   24th October (General Committee weekend)
> Willersley Castle Conference – 6th/8th November

The November-December issue of *The Local Preachers Magazine* carried a full-page advertisement for the film (reproduced overleaf), which shows how its use was envisaged.

A
GOODLY
FELLOWSHIP

The first colour film of the work of the LPMAA has been released and is available for use by Branches and Districts to assist in their advocacy.

It is probably the most expensive item so far produced for this purpose and it is desirable that it is used to the best advantage. Every effort should be made to bring together a large company of people to see it, not 10 or 20 at the annual meeting, but perhaps after an evening service in a church on LPMAA Sunday, or to a gathering of Circuit Youth Groups, or at a District Public Meeting. If arrangements can be made for a number of Branches in a District to use it in a given period – say a week or a fortnight – that would be useful.

A good 16mm sound projector will be required and instructions about use and packing, etc. will accompany the film. Running time, 28 minutes. Commentary by Robert Dougal, Chief Newsreader of B.B.C. Television. Bookings to: The General Secretary, Methodist Local Preachers Mutual Aid Association, 25 Marylebone Road, London, NW1.

Within five years consideration was being given to a second film. At meetings of the Finance and General Purposes Committee during 1969 acceptance of a quotation between £2,500 and £2,900 for a half-hour colour film was recommended, which the General Committee agreed. After some delay, caused partly by. disagreements over the script, the new 23 minute film – *A Ministry of Caring* – was eventually premiered in London on 11th October 1974.

The release of a third film, *Shared Burdens – Mutual Aid in Action*, was announced in *The Local Preachers Magazine* in November 1982, to be ready for distribution the following month. Within a year, however, the Association had to respond to new technology again; this latest film was made available on videotape, for use in house groups and similar meetings. When a fourth film was decided upon, it was produced only on video-tape, with the title *A New Family*. In 1996 the General Committee authorised the purchase of computer equipment specially for publicity purposes both nationally and in the Districts. Computer presentations have been produced on living and working in LPMAA Homes, and about the Association as a whole. Being portable, these are used to publicise the work of LPMAA at a variety of Methodist events, at career conventions, and on other suitable occasions. Visually attractive material for the portable display boards used in these settings is also created by the use of information technology.

The widespread use of audio-cassette players opened up the possibility of another avenue of communication, particularly with blind or partially-sighted people. During the 1980s occasional enquiries were received about producing a 'talking magazine'. The number of potential users was initially quite small, but by 1994 it had risen to seven. A member of General Committee offered to record each quarterly issue of *The Local Preachers Magazine* so that this could be supplied to them. Depending on the number of pages, between three and five hours of recording time are needed for each issue, plus the time for making the required number of copy tapes. Advice was taken from The Royal National Institute for the Blind, and the first 'talking magazine' was mailed out early in 1995. By 1997 twenty-three people were receiving it, and a tape is sent to each LPMAA Home where there are residents who wish to benefit from the scheme. Costs have so far been met by specific donations and gifts of audio-cassettes.

ADMINISTRATIVE AND COMMUNICATION SYSTEMS

The memories of someone who was a junior clerk at Head Office in the early 1950s indicate how things have changed. All records were handwritten then, which kept four staff busy for most of the year. There were three other members: a book-keeper, a secretary and the General Secretary with overall responsibility. Cash handling was an important part of the work, both receiving it from Branches and withdrawing it from the Bank for disbursement, for example, for the distribution of Christmas gifts to beneficiaries. Operating the 'Addressograph' machine to prepare the thousands of wrappers needed for the despatch of each issue of the magazine occupied one clerk for a fortnight. In those days the General Committee met six times a year. The December meeting was held at the Mission House, Marylebone Road, where Head Office was located. It was customary for the President to entertain the Committee members to tea, and Head Office staff did the catering. In return they were treated by the President to seats at a theatre!

In 1966, when 'Park View' at Rickmansworth was acquired for another residential home, Head Office moved to an adjacent property, 'The Grange'. New equipment, including an electric typewriter and a photocopier, was installed. Meanwhile Branches were affected by changes in record-keeping systems. The Kalamazoo system for recording receipts and payments by Branches was adopted in the late 1970s. It was still handwritten, but enabled cash book, receipts and advice of payment notes to be produced with a single entry. This had two particular advantages. First, it captured, in common format, the information required for the statutory audit of accounts. Secondly, it helped to ensure responsible central control of expenditure.

By 1979 plans were made to move Head Office into basement accommodation in the 'Park View' extension, and to sell 'The Grange'. A new General Secretary was appointed in the same year. Soon afterwards the computerisation of records, procedures and systems at Head Office was put in hand. By the mid-1980s these systems were operational. They were used initially for membership records, to replace typewriters for word processing purposes, to produce accounts and balance sheets, and to maintain records of investments. It was not difficult to add local preachers who were not members of LPMAA to the database. This made possible the direct mailing of the Annual Connexional Letter to all preachers (including ministers) with the August issue of *The Local Preachers Magazine* each year from 1992 (see chapters 28 and 34). The database now includes:

> Local Preachers (Ordinary and Life Members)
> Honorary Members and Honorary Life Members
> Beneficiaries
> Widowed Spouses of Former Local Preachers
> Local Preacher non-members.

By 1993 computers, using a specialist information system to keep records of residents and their care needs, had been installed in all five LPMAA Homes. With appropriate training, management staff were able to take full advantage of the benefits this offered.

SYSTEMS TO STRENGTHEN SERVICE

A further change of General Secretary took place in 1996. This came at a time when there was urgent need for more detailed information to enable better monitoring of the financial performance of Mutual Aid Homes, which had been causing concern. Systems which had served the Association well in the 1980s had been overtaken by the pace of change. The equipment mentioned earlier, in connection with Publicity and Public Relations, used the Microsoft 'Windows' operating system. This was used almost universally in business by that time. The new General Secretary was therefore authorised to invest £20,000 in high-powered Personal Computers for Head Office, also using 'Windows'-based systems. Every member of staff was provided with a computer and, with the benefit of appropriate training, use them to good effect. The computers in the LPMAA Homes have been upgraded to communicate with the new Head Office equipment.

This network of machines and systems makes it possible for the Association to have access to the Internet for electronic mail, and a presence on the World Wide Web. Information about LPMAA can thus be made available across the world. It also facilitates rapid communication between the various operating units of LPMAA, with suppliers, and with the growing number of Branch and District Officers who find computers a more effective aid to book-keeping than the old Kalamazoo system.

The most recent use of modern technology in the work of LPMAA has been in the production of this book. The story of Mutual Aid does remind us, however, that technology is a servant not a master. It helps the Association to function effectively, but cannot replace the personal caring and sharing that are the essential qualities of its life.

Section Six

LIVING MEMORY AND PRESENT HOPE

The final section of the story of LPMAA deals with its more recent history. Much of this is within the lifetime and memory of those who read it. Not everything that has happened in the later decades of the 20th century has yet fallen into proper perspective. Many of the changes whose effects are described are ongoing; in a real sense change is the only permanent feature of the scene. Economic, social and political factors are still important elements of the context in which the Association functions. Methodism continues to adapt to its numerical contraction, and through the last half-century LPMAA has consistently sought a meaningful identity and role in the contemporary situation.

One year after the 150th Anniversary celebrations of the Association, the 21st century begins. Questions are being asked about the life, organisation and worship of the church, about the place of preaching in its worship, and about the future role of local preachers. These questions will only be answered sometime after the year 2000. One thing is certain: whilst Methodist Local Preachers exist, so will the Association through which they express mutual care, concern and support.

32

The 1960s – a Decade of Transition

The Time • The Man • The President of 1961
Onward Through the Decade • Is LPMAA a Charity?
The Connexional Context

THE TIME

The 1960s was a period of great change in most spheres of life. The constraints of the post-war years had been gradually overcome during the 1950s. Much post-war reconstruction had been accomplished or was in progress. A generation that had no remembered experience of wartime was leaving full-time education to enter employment. Standards of living were rising, car ownership was growing rapidly, hours of work were reducing and holidays increasing. As a result of this people had the means and the time to enjoy a widening range of leisure activities. The Beatles dominated the popular music culture, mini-skirts dominated female fashion, and the flight from organised religion accelerated. The description 'the swinging sixties' was widely-used to describe these years, commonly to denote the questioning of all forms of authority, sometimes its outright rejection.

Methodism did not escape the effects of all this. The numbers of members, ministers, local preachers and chapels shrank. Traditional emphases were weakened, for example, total abstinence, attendance at worship, the use of Sunday. There was a steady shift from evening to morning service, and activities after lunch began to include things that would not have been contemplated thirty years earlier. In this context, Methodism spent a large part of the decade in formal discussion with the Church of England about a possible merger between the two denominations. LPMAA engaged in talks about closer relations with the Connexional Local Preachers' Office, reassessed its role in the light of all these changes, and embarked on significant organisational restructuring. It is to some of these matters that we now turn, with the senior Honorary Secretary of the period as our guide.

The Man

Albert E. Shaw was born in Yorkshire in 1902. In the course of his career as a journalist he came to live in London, where he settled in the Harrow Circuit, worshipping in the Pinner congregation. He was not at that time a member of the Association, but in 1944 was encouraged to join by the young and enthusiastic secretary of Harrow Branch, Squire Jones, whose early experience of LPMAA had been in Lancashire. The two became personal friends, and shortly afterwards served together as Society Stewards at Pinner. Albert Shaw was soon appointed a Convener of London North West District, and was elected to the General Committee in 1947. By 1953 he had become Editor of *The Local Preachers Magazine*, and served as President in 1955-56. On completion of the Presidential Year, he was elected an Honorary Secretary of the Association, following the retirement of Harold Buss. He served in this office until 1968, with the designation Senior Honorary Secretary when that was formally adopted in 1967. Following his death in August 1977, his colleague and successor, Alan Collen, wrote in a memorial tribute:

> He was a shrewd judge of character and quickly found those who could help him in his task. He was a fine orator, persuasive and powerful in debate, and a firm leader, organiser and administrator, yet supremely modest in his personal demeanour and ambition . . . His term as Honorary Secretary was busy . . . mainly in defining and advancing the Association's policies, and in re-aligning the structures and administration to fit its activities and organisation with the changing times.

Albert Shaw's contributions to *The Local Preachers Magazine* as Honorary Secretary were substantial and penetrating comments on matters affecting the work of LPMAA. He gave strong indications of the ways he intended the Association should go, and of the consequences of not doing so. In his article of September 1961 he stated his views thus:

> If any organisation is to maintain its position it must keep close watch on all that is happening in its own particular field and adjust its own thought and amend its own contribution to ride the changes. The

alternative is slow stagnation and eventual disappearance.

This warning might have been thought superfluous in a year when nearly 1,000 new members had joined the Association, and total membership had exceeded 19,000. The most significant piece of business at the 1961 Aggregate Meeting had been the first step towards bringing local preachers who had not joined LPMAA within the scope of its beneficence. Albert Shaw's September article referred to it in this way:

> Let us not disguise the fact that from the moment I became an officer of the Association I was convinced that sooner or later the Association would have to widen its field until it was able to say with sincerity and truth that it was prepared to give assistance to any local preacher or his dependants. I began to write about it in the Magazine, I emphasised it during my Presidential Year, and since becoming your Honorary Secretary I have used every opportunity to make the idea widely known. It was gratifying at the Aggregate Meeting to see that so many delegates were prepared to support a full exploration of the possibility.

It was not, however, quite so uncontroversial as his note made it seem, for there had been an attempt to amend the resolution put before the Aggregate. The resolution asked the Rules Revision Sub-Committee to consider the matter and make recommendations. An amendment was moved to refer the matter to Districts and Branches before the Rules were changed. The mover of the amendment was not out of sympathy with the principle involved, but with the method being proposed to pursue it. There was support for the amendment, one speaker saying that the whole principle of mutual aid was involved. Another suggested that enquiry should be made into the role of the Connexional Necessitous Local Preachers' Fund. The amendment was lost, after the Honorary Secretary had made it clear that draft rule changes would be available for discussion in Districts before the next Aggregate Meeting. In his notes in the September magazine he added:

> I should be failing in my duty if I did not utter a warning that this will not be the end, that it may

well have to be the beginning of a series of changes which will be far-reaching in their effect.

He concluded by sharing a vision of the Association in which every member pledged to speak with every other member in his or her own Branch at least once a quarter, and that in small groups within each Branch, members would undertake to speak with each other every week. This would ensure that none was ever out of touch, and that need of any kind would be detected and met at an early stage. This is how the mutuality of mutual aid is truly expressed.

THE PRESIDENT OF 1961

In **Albert Bailey**, the Association had a man who was prominent in Methodism and who was honoured in 1966 by election as Vice-President of Conference. He was a member of the British delegation to the World Methodist Conference in Oslo during August of his LPMAA Presidential Year, and reported on this in the autumn edition of *The Local Preachers Magazine*. He had returned from Oslo rather disturbed by the divisions which he saw between the many different Methodist traditions. There were Congregational Methodists, Episcopal Methodists, Reformed and United Methodists, and many others. He stressed that they were all there to learn from each other. The Oslo experience illuminated for him the conversations with the Anglican Church that dominated British Methodism throughout the decade.

He wrote also about the work of the British Methodist Conference, emphasising the issues of surplus chapels and shrinking membership, on both of which he felt good work had been done. As a member of the Connexional General Purposes Committee and the Central Finance Board he would have been well-informed on these matters.

Albert Bailey held a number of offices in the Cannock Chase Circuit and the Wolverhampton and Shrewsbury Methodist District. This did not preclude him from fulfilling a wide range of public duties, including service as a local government councillor for more than twenty years, three of them as Council Chairman. He was a magistrate, a school governor, a member of a hospital management committee and Chairman of Cannock Area Health

Committee. Because of his Methodist commitments, his public offices and business responsibilities, it was frequently the case when Albert Bailey was not at home, that he was attending a meeting. The writer of the biographical notes in *The Local Preachers Magazine*, at the time of his induction to the LPMAA Presidency, revealed a neat sense of humour. He intimated that the epitaph 'Gone to another meeting' had been chosen by Mrs Bailey in readiness for her husband's demise!

On returning from the World Conference, President Bailey used the phrase 'Back at the Grindstone' in his magazine notes, to describe his involvement in LPMAA affairs. In particular he referred to a meeting (over two days) of the committee set up to revise the rules. He borrowed words from the Prime Minister of the day who had used the term 'Wind of Change' to describe the far-reaching political developments then taking place in Africa. The 'Wind of Change' was certainly beginning to blow through the organisation and activities of LPMAA. The Rules at that time permitted amendment only every third year. 1962 was such a year, and the Secretariat was determined that the Aggregate, due to meet at Norwich, should be recommended to adopt the extensive changes being prepared.

'The Changing Situation' had been the theme of the Willersley Castle Conference in November, 1961. Members of General Committee spoke on aspects of change – in the world and in Methodism. Some of the issues stimulated lively discussion. The annual pilgrimage service at Wensley Chapel on the Sunday afternoon had a special flavour in 1961. The chapel had just been re-opened after redecoration and the installation of new electrical and heating systems. This had been made possible by contributions from General Committee members to supplement what the local congregation had been able to raise. Amidst its wider current concerns the Association has always remembered its origins and early history.

The year came to its end for LPMAA with one of the most important General Committee meetings for many years. It received, amended and approved the work of the sub-committee appointed to revise in their entirety the Rules of the Association, the appendices governing Mutual Aid Homes Ltd, and the Standing Orders of the Aggregate Meeting. The General Committee worked for nearly six hours to make the result intelligible and, it was hoped, acceptable to the following year's Aggregate. This must surely have been the longest General Committee meeting of all time!

ONWARD THROUGH THE DECADE

We leave 1961, as we began it, with senior Honorary Secretary Shaw. In his magazine notes of January 1962, written just before the General Committee met, he referred to the revision of the Rules:

> An organisation begins with a few rules and regulations. The organisation grows and times change, growth and change both bringing the necessity for new or altered Rules. Periodically a complete revision becomes necessary; it is the same house, the same room, but the colour scheme is changed and the furniture is moved round or modernised. That, in effect, is what is happening now.

He made some interesting comparisons with the Rules as they existed in 1918. The redrafted rules sought to rectify inadequacies, irrelevancies and inconsistencies. Every effort had been made to be as clear as possible, but he pointed out that simplicity can be a snare, quoting the chemist who displayed a notice 'I dispense with accuracy.' The concluding summary began and ended with these words:

> The new Rules, after months of careful study and preparation by the sub-committee, after thorough examination by the General Committee, and later after the wider scrutiny of the Aggregate Meeting, will not satisfy everyone nor will they cater for every possibility ... What matter if at the end of it all we can have a clearer picture of what we all have in mind to say and do; what matter if at the end of it all we can submerge our differences and agree to go on as a united whole, loyally accepting the regulations which a clear majority of our brethren have agreed to be the best obtainable.

In that spirit LPMAA moved through the 1960s to deal with important matters affecting its internal affairs and its external relationships. 1961 set the stage for all this.

In readiness for the Aggregate Meeting of 1962, the Honorary Secretary and the President both returned to the subject of Rules Revision in the May magazine. The President stressed that although LPMAA was originally a benevolent organisation, it had grown into a Fellowship of Preachers, and had gained the confidence of the Methodist Church. There was a risk of losing that confidence, but he was certain that what they were now doing would:

> . . . enlarge the sphere of our operation, preserve the will and the genius of our founders, secure the status of the local preacher and the place of the Association in the Church for all time.

The Senior Honorary Secretary dealt concisely yet comprehensively with the substance of the changes that Aggregate would be asked to approve. They were:

- a restatement of the objects of the Association
- extension of its assistance to all local preachers
- changes to election procedure (abolition of nomination speeches)
- discontinuation of entrance fees
- elimination of a rule that allowed former LP to continue as ordinary members
- changes in the working relationship of Branches and District with Head Office
- some financial changes
- an interesting new rule to reflect the provision in the Trust Deed for dissolution.

He emphasised again that the revised rules would provide the foundation for future progress. The 1962 Aggregate duly accepted them.

When Aggregate met the following year, in Wolverhampton, it received the General Committee's Annual Report for the year ended December 1962 and found the Norwich decision described as 'the most significant event of the year'. It was advised that application had been made under the 1960 Charities Act for inclusion of the Association in the Register of Charities. This would grant automatic relief in tax and rates [referred to again below].   Advantage had also been taken of the 1961 Trustee Investments Act to make better use of the Association's investments. The Report said:

> Wise trusteeship does involve securing a proper and an adequate return for money held in this way.

The effects were to increase the Equity content of the funds in relation to fixed interest stock, in order to secure rising income and capital appreciation, and help offset the growing expenditure. This anticipated guidance given by the Charity Commissioners two years later:

> . . . a charity, which is not receiving more than 4.5 per cent on the market value of its capital, is receiving less than ordinary reasonable management could be expected to provide, and an immediate duty lies upon the trustees to consider re-investment.

The Report urged members to take every opportunity for expressing gratitude to Methodist congregations for their continuing generous support. 1962 income was the highest ever recorded, with collections and donations both reaching record figures; legacies again exceeded, £21,000, as they had in the two preceding years. The income, including members' subscriptions (nearly £10,000), was used to maintain the benevolent work. The word 'beneficiary' had now replaced 'annuitant', and during 1962 weekly payments totalling almost £32,000 were made to 875 beneficiaries. Lump sum grants had doubled to nearly £900, and funeral allowances continued at about £3,500 in the year. The cost of printing and distributing *The Local Preachers Magazine* to all members increased to nearly £3,400. Athough the subsidy to Mutual Aid Homes fell to £6,000 (less than half the previous year's figure) there was a warning that this deficiency was expected to rise in future years. The report paid tribute to 588 members who had died during the year, and to many who continued to serve in various ways, singling out for special mention the General Secretary and Head Office staff.   The new Rules, changes in investment policy, new legislation, and the administration of Mutual Aid Homes were all making big demands on them.

Is LPMAA a Charity?

The pursuit of registered charity status, mentioned above, was a more lengthy process than might have been expected. Further amendment of the recently-revised rules was needed. The decision to seek registration under the 1960 Charities Act was taken by the General Committee in April 1962. This had been preceded during February and March by legal consultations to establish whether or not the Association was already recognised as a charity and, if not, whether it could be. As the Honorary Officers began to consider the matter, the Association's solicitors received an enquiry about its legal recognition as a charity. LPMAA was certainly treated as a charity for fiscal purposes by the Inland Revenue authorities; Mutual Aid Homes Ltd was similarly entitled to relief from Income Tax. It was unclear whether registration under the 1960 Act would be granted, or if it were not, whether tax relief would be lost. Then, as at most times in the Association's history, there were several lawyers on General Committee; in one of his letters the Honorary Secretary recorded that they had no doubt LPMAA would be able to secure registration. The Association's solicitors agreed that application should be made, to resolve any doubt about its charitable status.

A memorandum therefore went to all General Committee members, setting out the situation, in preparation for a resolution to be presented at the April meeting. It began with the question 'Is LPMAA a charity?', but whilst recognising that most members would unhesitatingly say it was, went on to explain why there was legal doubt. Inland Revenue authorities had by this time notified the need for all charities to register. Even though there had been some feeling against formal links with State recognition and regulation arrangements, the matter had to go forward. The resolution also recommended the Mutual Aid Homes Executive to make application on behalf of Mutual Aid Homes Ltd. The Association's application was made to the Charity Commission in September 1962, with the request that it should include Mutual Aid Homes. A delay of nearly nine months was attributed to pressure of work, presumably arising from the very large number of applications for registration submitted by charities. The Commission then confirmed that the application was being considered, but requested a copy of the Memorandum and Articles of Association of Mutual Aid Homes Ltd, so that its position also could be reviewed.

After a further five months, the Charity Commissioners replied in November 1963. Several past legal decisions were quoted to establish that an association such as LPMAA 'can be a charity only if *poverty* is an essential qualification for the receipt of relief.' This was not the case under the rules as they stood, so the application could not be accepted. The Commission did not leave the matter there, but had consulted the Inspector of Taxes. He had drawn attention to a letter of 27th February 1925 from the Honorary Secretary of that time (W. J. Back) stating that the Association's funds were applied for the relief of poverty. On the assumption that this was still the case, the Charity Commission suggested possible amendments to the rules to overcome the difficulty. In particular, 'consolidating the fellowship of those called to be local preachers' could not be an object charitable in law. If this could be expressed as 'a motive actuating those concerned', it would be free from objection. Specific suggestions were made for the re-wording of rules to ensure that *need* was an explicit condition for receiving any benefits offered by LPMAA. Further action would await provision of draft amendments to the rules.

By 16th December the Honorary Secretary was able to inform the Charity Commission that the General Committee had agreed to recommend appropriate changes to the next Aggregate Meeting. These included deletion of the rule relating to Funeral and Death Benefits, making these dependent solely upon need. The only other obstacle was the small and rapidly-declining number of Benefit Members, local preachers who had joined LPMAA before 9th March 1912. There were fewer than 150 still alive. A special plea was made for the retention of this small group, who were entitled to sickness benefit by right, not by proving need. The payments amounted only to some £300 in that year, and he asked that this should not invalidate the application for charitable status.

On 7th March General Committee endorsed the wording of rule amendments for presentation to the 1964 Aggregate Meeting, and the Commission was notified. Further correspondence established that the proposed changes would be acceptable, and that Mutual Aid Homes would be registered as a subsidiary of LPMAA. The Aggregate Meeting, at Blackpool that year, approved the amendments unanimously, the Charity Commission was advised, and on 21st July 1964 the certificates of registration were received.

This was not quite the end of the charity registration saga. As Alfred Gilliver records in some detail in *More Precious Than Rubies* (pages 29 and 30), steps were taken in 1965 and 1966 to dissolve Mutual Aid Homes Ltd and re-establish it as a society registered under the Industrial and Provident Societies Acts. As such it would still be legally able to own property. The society was to be composed of all General Committee members, meeting as the Mutual Aid Homes Society. The work of Mutual Aid Homes would therefore no longer be a separate activity, but would be a major responsibility of the whole of the General Committee. The Society was registered on 1st September 1966, at which time the office of Honorary Secretary (Homes) was created.

A small but important consequence was the need to ensure that the status of the Society as a subsidiary charity of LPMAA would not be impaired by the change from limited company to industrial and provident society. This was done, in preparation for the 1966 Aggregate Meeting at Birmingham, by correspondence with the Charity Commission earlier in the year. By late summer the legal status of LPMAA, including Mutual Aid Homes, had been clarified and ensured. It could now adapt and develop its work to meet the changing needs of the later 20th century.

THE CONNEXIONAL CONTEXT

One other major issue demanded substantial attention during the 1960s. This was the relationships of LPMAA with the Methodist Connexion. Earlier chapters have shown how these have varied over the years. The sometimes acrimonious correspondence in the *Methodist Recorder* and *The Local Preachers Magazine*, which followed the 1945 Aggregate Meeting, is reviewed in chapter 17. It resulted from the equivocal response of the Aggregate to a recommendation allowing LPMAA to give financial support to the Connexional Local Preachers' Office. This soured the atmosphere for nearly a generation.

The matter came back into consideration, in what proved to be much more congenial circumstances, in 1963. The Association had just completed a drastic overhaul of its rules, and had embarked on the process of establishing its own legal position. Under strong leadership, it was gradually coming to terms with the implications of heavy investment in the provision of residential care for members and their dependants. A new ecumenical climate was developing, and Methodism engaged in conversations with the Church of England about a possible merger between the two denominations. The likely impact of that on local preachers and their Mutual Aid Association was a frequent subject of discussion in LPMAA meetings during this period. Changes in Methodism itself, chiefly of a contractional nature, also helped to create a situation in which people were more ready to discuss how future change might be handled.

At Preston in 1963 the Methodist Conference passed this Resolution:

> The Conference requests that in every Circuit some opportunity be given annually for all congregations to learn about the work of the Local Preachers' Department.

As Secretary of the Connexional Local Preachers' Department, Rev. David Francis had the task of stimulating response to this request. Amongst other steps, he made an approach to LPMAA seeking collaboration on a number of points. He put these into a memorandum dated 21st November 1963, first summarising the background to the Conference resolution. This was partly financial; the Department's income had fallen short of its expenditure on expanding services to Local Preachers by more than £1,000 in each of the last two years. There was, however, a more important dimension – the need to promote intelligent understanding and wider appreciation amongst Methodist people of the work of local preachers and the Department. This would lead both to improved financial support and the recruitment of more new preachers.

In proposing a joint approach, Mr Francis recognised that there would be misunderstandings to dispel. Many people supposed that 'LPMAA Sunday' was a Conference direction, that when they gave to a collection on that day they were supporting local preacher recruitment and training. Others saw LPMAA Sunday collections as belonging to the Association by right, and would resist change. He therefore identified three specific points on which he felt progress could and should be made:

> 1. Official and public mutual recognition of both the vital work and the financial needs of each organisation.

2. Local congregations should be free to modify or enlarge the scope of their 'LPMAA' or 'Local Preachers' Sunday'.
3. The production of joint appeals literature to stress the different aspects of the needs of local preachers.

Attitudes to LPMAA/Local Preachers' Sunday were changing, and Mr Francis felt that his office and LPMAA should jointly guide the changes. A linked approach to what were inevitably linked tasks must surely be the best way.

In December 1963 the General Committee, acting on the recommendation of the Finance and General Purposes Committee, authorised the officers to meet Mr Francis and report their discussions to a future meeting. This resulted in the setting up of a Standing Joint Committee, for which eight representatives were appointed by General Committee in March 1964. The Joint Committee met for the first time on 23rd June. A number of points from its discussions were reported to the General Committee in July:

- the need for closer relations
- the ignorance of Methodists about the two organisations
- the value of personal representation in the Circuits
- the dangers of a percentage division of collections on Local Preachers' Sunday
- legal and constitutional problems
- joint statements on matters concerning the 'calling' of local preachers

In the last *Local Preachers Magazine* of 1964, the Honorary Secretary reminded readers that LPMAA is an association of Local Preachers who are accredited through a process administered by the Local Preachers' Department. The Standing Joint Committee had already met twice. It had agreed that if Methodist people really knew what both organisations were doing they would give whole-hearted support. He hoped they would be able to move forward in the true spirit of mutual aid.

The next issue (January 1965) contained an article by the Connexional Secretary, written at the Editor's request. He identified some issues of concern to local preachers, including their training, change and development in their role and work, corporateness in worship, and the conversations with the Church of England. He was warmly received by the Aggregate meeting of 1966, when he spoke about the way ahead for joint action by LPMAA and his Department. Meanwhile the Standing Joint Committee continued its meetings.

The first visible and tangible result of its deliberations was a combined leaflet about local preachers and the two organisations concerned with them. Its publication followed agreement between LPMAA and the Local Preachers' Department to act together, from 1967 onwards, in the production of publicity material for an annual 'Local Preachers' Sunday'. The Connexion's need for new preachers and LPMAA's caring ministry amongst local preachers would both be advocated.

The leaflet's text, reproduced opposite, summarised the main features of each body, with a clear statement that it had the support of both. [The nursing home (at Barleythorpe) was closed soon afterwards. A fifth residential care home was opened at Rickmansworth.]

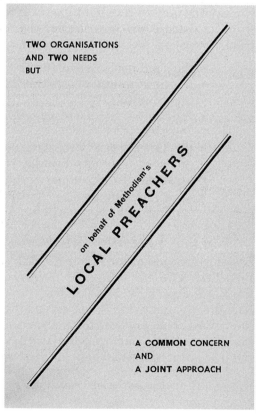

TWO ORGANISATIONS
AND TWO NEEDS
BUT

on behalf of Methodism's

LOCAL PREACHERS

A COMMON CONCERN
AND
A JOINT APPROACH

Cover of the first Local Preachers' Department and LPMAA joint leaflet

LOCAL PREACHERS CONDUCT MORE THAN 16,000 SERVICES EVERY SUNDAY

The Local Preachers' Department

is responsible to the Methodist Conference for the recruiting, training and general welfare of Local Preachers

it arranges correspondence courses, examinations, continuation studies, preachers' schools, and assists study groups and individual students

it prepares special textbooks and handbooks for preachers and maintains a comprehensive Lending Library

it guides and assists Circuits in all matters affecting Local Preachers

it maintains the accepted discipline of the Methodist Church, and honours those who have given long service as Local Preachers

it receives its income mainly from Society, Trust and Circuit grants, and from subscriptions and donations

it is administered by a Connexional Committee, half the members of which are laymen.

LPMAA

is a voluntary organisation which assists all Local Preachers, their widows and dependants when in distress

it distributes weekly allowances to more than 800 needy Local Preachers and dependants; it makes lump sum grants when circumstances indicate such a need

it has established four Eventide Homes for elderly Local Preachers and their wives, their widows and dependants

it maintains a fifth Home for those elderly brethren who need nursing care and special attention

it organises week-end Fellowships for Local Preachers and their wives

it publishes *The Local Preachers Magazine* six times a year

it receives its income from the Church collections and from grants, subscriptions, dividends and donations

it is administered entirely by Local Preachers and is not controlled by the Methodist Conference.

THERE ARE MORE THAN 21,000 FULLY ACCREDITED LOCAL PREACHERS

So, by the end of the 'Decade of Transition' the Association had brought its organisation up-to-date, established its position in law, and entered into a working relationship with the Methodist Connexion. These were separate yet linked achievements – with them LPMAA entered the modern period.

33

Residential Homes in the 1990s

A Centenary Event • Forty Years On;
Causes and Consequences • Further New Initiatives.

A CENTENARY EVENT

The first Mutual Aid Home, 'Westerley,' at Westcliff-Sea was formally opened on 12th October 1949. Forty years later, on 14th October 1989, the President of the Methodist Conference, Dr John Vincent, preached at a special service held in Wesley's Chapel to celebrate the Ruby Anniversary of Mutual Aid Homes. The theme of the sermon was *'Local Preaching as an Order within the Church'*, but the President also contributed a short note to the printed Order of Service for the occasion:

> Today, we are celebrating 40 years of residential care provided by LPMA. Preaching in our churches has its own rewards but they are not financial, and for 140 years LPMA has provided assistance to preachers in need. The homes are an extension of that assistance, giving the care, support and company that many people need in old age.

> On this 40th Anniversary I commend this work, and send warmest greetings to all who have pioneered it, and who now make this caring possible. Our churches owe much to the dedicated service of preachers. Our support for LPMA is just one way we can express our gratitude for that service. We give thanks for LPMA and pray God's blessing on this continuing and expanding work.

From the inception of LPMAA in 1849 the need for appropriate forms of living accommodation for frail elderly members has been recognised. The idea of almshouses (the mid-19th century alternative to a workhouse) was referred to by the Honorary Secretary, William Harris, at a public meeting during the

Aggregate of 1851. At that early stage in the Association's life it was not possible from a small membership with limited resources to do more than alleviate the worst extremes of poverty by money assistance. In the last years of the 19th century, something was done by the private initiative of a group of affluent LPMAA members to provide a few cottages for retired local preachers (chapter 13). Developments in public policy (chapter 15), and changing social attitudes and expectations, called for a different approach from non-statutory philanthropic bodies by the time of the Second World War.

FORTY YEARS ON

The story of the Mutual Aid Association's response to the new situation, from the mid-1940s to 1989, is told in detail in *More Precious Than Rubies* [by Alfred Gilliver, published to mark the 40th Anniversary of the opening of the first Mutual Aid Home in the Association's Centenary year. It is still available from Head Office of LPMAA, Chorleywood Close, Rickmansworth, Herts.]

It is important to recognise the immense impact that involvement in the provision of residential care had on the Association and its work during this period. An increasing proportion of its resources was devoted to expanding the number of residents who could be accommodated, by acquiring and opening additional homes. More of the annual revenue was taken up in maintaining and operating them. At the same time less was required to meet members' needs for weekly benefit or lump sum grants. Applications for financial help were steadily declining. The Report presented to the Aggregate in 1989 showed that 97 members and dependants were being cared for in the five Mutual Aid Homes at an annual cost to LPMAA of £147,310, and that 176 beneficiaries had received a total of £43,299 during the year in weekly allowances or single grants.

Even more significantly, the Homes began to dominate the thinking of many members. The residential care dimension took central place in the Association's publicity material, and fewer Branches had their own beneficiaries to care for. Many people began to think of Mutual Aid as something that happened mainly in a handful of locations; to benefit from it members had to leave their home areas, families and friends. There has, of course, never been any doubt about the quality of care provided in the LPMAA Homes. The fact that they provide a Christian environment made it much easier for residents to overcome any sense of strangeness or isolation. Increasingly, groups of members from Branches within easy travelling distance of a Home made visits to share a little of the life there and to see Mutual Aid at work in that setting. They were usually enheartened and encouraged by the experience.

However, the Annual Report quoted above contained in its concluding paragraphs a very important warning sentence:

Many of the avenues for meeting present needs involve very substantial capital expenditure.

At a time when current outgoings were broadly in line with current income it was necessary to remind the Association that changing patterns of need would call for flexible thinking about how they should be met. Over forty years there had been very considerable investment in purchasing, equipping and upgrading the five 'Westerleys'. It could not be assumed that capital resources would be available for outlay on the same scale in the future. Indeed it soon became apparent that a key issue in the not-too-distant future would be maintaining a sufficient level of occupancy to reduce the heavy demands on revenue for subsidising Mutual Aid Homes. In 1995, the Homes were accommodating 77 residents and receiving £269,455 from LPMAA. During the same year 114 beneficiaries received £51,506. [Figures as reported to the 1996 Aggregate Meeting.]

CAUSES AND CONSEQUENCES

The changes revealed in the statistics for 1989 and 1995 reflect the influence of several factors in Methodism and in modern society. Both the numbers of fully accredited Local Preachers *and* the number in membership of LPMAA had fallen by about 300 over this period. This indicated a gradually shrinking constituency from amongst whom beneficiaries and residents might arise. Secondly, public attitudes to residential care for elderly people had changed. There is a much stronger preference to continue living at home until absolute frailty or lack of resources make it impossible, rather than transfer to residential care whilst still fit and moderately active. This view was given statutory support by the all-party National Health Service and Community Care Act of 1990, which came into operation in 1993. Thirdly, a much wider range of choice had become available to older people when they eventually decided to seek residential care. As this decision tended to be delayed until beyond the age of 80, it is not surprising that the choice was more often to stay in the home area near family and friends, rather than move a long distance to an unfamiliar setting. When a Mutual Aid Home was the favoured option, the older age of moving in meant fewer years' residence, which also increased the number of vacant rooms.

One further consideration influenced the Association's policy-formers as they prepared proposals to guide the General Committee and the Aggregate Meeting in making decisions to deal with the evolving situation. This echoed the warning of the Annual Report of 1989 about the capital-intensive nature of modern-day Mutual Aid. Fixed capital, that is, the buildings and equipment of five Homes, is neither flexible in its use nor mobile in its location. There was no easy way to reduce the residential capacity to match the lower level of demand. Closure of a Home would seriously impair provision in one area and might cause demand to decline further. It would also be harder to meet increased demand if it should arise in the future.

The only practical alternative was to look for other ways of using vacant capacity. On one hand this would make the Homes more viable; on the other it would help to maintain residential care for members in all five Homes. This strategy was re-inforced by a splendid paper, presented to the Aggregate Meeting of 1994 at Staveley, by David Wigley, Chief Executive of Methodist Homes for the Aged. The Association had enjoyed consultative contacts with MHA for many years and had collaborated in the provision of a sheltered housing development in Psalter Lane, Sheffield. David Wigley underlined, first, the high percentage occupancy needed for an efficient and effective residential care operation. Secondly, he emphasised the need for organisations caring for the elderly to identify with the current philosophy of domiciliary and community-based services. This enables older people to continue living in their own homes when that is their preference.

The second of these two thrusts was only taken slowly into the Association's collective thinking, but the first received immediate attention. There was a frustrating delay when the Charity Commission was unable to deal with requests for guidance because of Health and Safety problems in its own premises. The Commission eventually advised that charitable status would not be invalidated by the creation of a category of Additional Eligible Beneficiaries. This would include Methodist ministers, members of the Diaconal Order, local preachers on trial, and accredited lay preachers of other denominations, their dependants in each case also being eligible. The necessary amendment to the rules of LPMAA was brought to and approved by the Aggregate Meeting held at Lincoln in 1995.

There was, of course, no certainty that this change would result quickly, or indeed at all, in greatly increased occupancy. Enquiries were therefore made of the Charity Commission about the possibility under charity law of accepting as residents people who were not local preachers or additional eligible beneficiaries, or dependants of someone in either of those categories. It was ruled that this was permissible, so long as such people were charged the full economic cost. They could not be subsidised from funds contributed for the support of local preachers or their dependants.

It was also necessary to ensure that this did not restrict accommodation for elegible applicants; a limited number of rooms would therefore have to be kept vacant. It was decided following this further widening of the basis for admission that vacancies would initially be offered to honorary members of the Association. This was first advertised in the autumn of 1995. Simultaneously, more attention was given to developing the temporary or short-stay element in the work of Mutual Aid Homes, whereby members or dependants could take a holiday break or could be cared for at a 'Westerley' whilst family carers had a respite holiday. By 1996 this had grown to the equivalent of two permanent residents.

Reference has already been made to the National Health Service and Community Care Act, and to the recognition of growing preference to live independently, with appropriate support, as long as possible. LPMAA had been anticipating that some prospective residents might have been discouraged from seeking a place in one of its Homes. This would have been the effect if assessing officers of local authority Social Service Departments, judging that residential care was unnecessary, withheld financial assistance. However, experience of the first three years of the Act's operation indicated that this had not occurred to any significant extent, in view of the age, state of health, and inability to cope alone of Mutual Aid applicants. The essential dimensions of the situation for the Association and its residential care provision in the 1990s thus became clear, albeit gradually. Meanwhile the work continued.

FURTHER NEW INITIATIVES

On the Ruby Anniversary of Mutual Aid Homes, and of 'Westerley' at Westcliff-on-Sea in particular, a commemorative plaque (beneath the one marking the opening in 1949) was formally unveiled by the President of 1989, John Lawley, on 12th October that year. 40th Anniversary celebrations followed at Grange-over-Sands in 1991, and at Woodhall Spa in 1995. By this time the occupancy of the five Homes had fallen to the low level (77) and the subsidy had risen to the high level (over a quarter of a million pounds) mentioned earlier in this chapter, and the action described above had been taken.

Another important element of policy for utilising the LPMAA Homes more effectively was the recognition of the need to improve residents' accommodation, as far as possible, to include *en suite* facilities. This was more practicable in some rooms than others, because of size, shape or position, or because of the structure or layout of the buildings. Once the decision had been made to proceed, a number of practical matters required attention. During the process of conversion there would be unavoidable disturbance for residents, extra work for the staff, and some rooms would have to be vacant for periods of time while the adaptations were being made. It was inevitable that substantial invested funds would have to be released in order to meet the cost, and special meetings of the appropriate committees were convened to authorise this.

Work was put in hand at Westcliff-on-Sea soon after Easter 1996. In the course of the work in one room, a copy of *The Local Preachers Magazine* for July-August 1951 was discovered tucked behind the skirting board. It was handed to the Home Manager, who surmised that it may have been pushed in by one of the earliest residents who thought there was a draught blowing through! The alterations were completed by the end of September at a total cost of £140,000, and a re-dedication event, with Rev. Peter Barber, Connexional Local Preachers' Secretary, as special guest, was held on 13th November 1996. Minehead was second in the programme. Work began in July 1996 and was completed the following April. The cost at Minehead was £130,000. The rededication on 7th June 1997, combining the 40th Anniversary of the Home, had Rev. Frank Topping as special guest. The third Home to be upgraded was Grange-over-Sands, where work commenced in September 1996 and was completed, at a cost of £165,000, in May 1997. Susan Howdle, a former Vice-President of Methodist Conference and Chairman of Methodist Homes, was the special guest at the re-dedication on 9th July 1997.

At the present time (April 1998) the programme remains to be extended to Woodhall Spa and Rickmansworth. The net effect of work to date has been to provide 13 *en suite* rooms at Westcliff, where a total of 17 residents can enjoy private facilities, and 21 *en suite* rooms at Minehead in which 22 residents can be accommodated. At both of these homes one room remains without *en suite* facilities, and is considered suitable only for short-stay residents. At Grange-over-Sands 17 rooms out of 20 have *en suite* facilities. If double occupation were to be maximised these rooms could accommodate 24 residents, but this is unlikely to be achieved in practice. There is currently a total of 100 residents in the five homes, an occupancy level of almost 99 per cent.

The senior member of staff at each Home, now styled 'Home Manager', has full responsibility for the Home's budget, and for the training and development of the staff. This required a substantial training programme for senior staff themselves, in management of staff, finance, buildings and plant. A notable feature of this training was the extent to which tutors could be found from amongst members of the Association acting in their professional capacity as management consultants. Local Preachers come from all walks of life, and LPMAA has benefited over the years from advice given by lawyers, doctors and other professional people in its membership. Now it was the turn of high calibre business people to make their expertise available for the benefit of the Association. The professionalism of its senior staff has become highly regarded by its friends and competitors alike.

34

The Association and Methodism in the late 20th Century

Closer and Closer • A Direct Approach • Step by Step
The Next Stage • The Last Lap.

CLOSER AND CLOSER

'Relationships with the Connexion', as identified in chapter 32, was one of the important matters to occupy the attention of LPMAA and its officers during the 1960s. Meetings of the Standing Joint Committee continued through the 1970s and Local Preachers' Sunday gradually became more widely recognised as an opportunity to put the need for new preachers before the congregations, as well as to commend the work of Mutual Aid. By 1977 the Standing Joint Committee had begun to discuss ways of bringing LPMAA and the Local Preachers' Office and Committee closer together. It appeared that the best way forward would be to see whether in Circuits and Districts co-operation and merging of structures might be possible. Rev. John Stacey, then Connexional Local Preachers' Secretary, wrote to a number of people in different parts of the country asking for their views on how they thought this might work in their areas. He specifically affirmed that this was not the kind of judgement that could be reached in the 'isolation' of Westminster (his own wording). In asking for replies by 1st February of 1978 he hoped to be able to prepare a document for the Standing Joint Committee in that year.

A DIRECT APPROACH

In fact, the next step was more dramatic than that. Being invited to address the Aggregate Meeting at Derby in 1979, John Stacey made the main thrust of his speech an appeal to the Association to 'take Conference into its system', echoing Archbishop Fisher's appeal to the Free Churches some years earlier to 'take episcopacy into their system'. The February 1980 issue of the *The Local Preachers Magazine* carried an article by John Stacey, summarising for the wider readership what he had said to the Aggregate. His paragraph on the past, written with a barely-concealed smile, could almost serve as a summary of parts of this book:

> Methodist ministers tended to regard LPMAA as a kind of fractious trade union, always ganging up against the management, always bent on seeing that the laymen got their rights. What made it worse was that LPMAA was always regarded, rightly or wrongly, as exceedingly rich. Doubtless the Connexional Secretaries at Westminster lay awake at night and thought how satisfactory it would be if only the Conference and the Local Preachers' Department could get its hands on all that money. On the other side, it was not unknown for members of LPMAA, feeling that the Wesleyan Conference had treated local preachers with a cool disdain, to take up an anti-establishment and anti-ministerial stance, and find psychological compensation for their rejection in a fierce assertion of the independence of LPMAA.

He then pointed out that these old suspicions had been replaced in more recent time by a process of reconciliation, of which the Standing Joint Committee was one result, and went on to urge the need for reconciliation between the organisation structures of LPMAA and the Conference:

> I invite you to consider taking the Methodist Conference into your system. Not, you will notice, the other way round. For the Conference to take over LPMAA . . . is legally impossible. But it is otherwise if the initiative is with you. Any such consideration in your working parties, in your committees, in your Aggregate, would take time. You might find some disadvantages. Your greatly prized independence would in some way, however academic, be limited, though I think your independence of action would be little affected. There are helpful precedents to follow. And the advantages? You would be visibly and organically within the Connexional family, secure in the

goodwill of ministers and people alike, and you would have shown the rest of us what we greatly need to know, how to transcend our own history without betraying it in the interests of our oneness in Christ.

John Stacey concluded his article by affirming a theological basis for his approach. A religion having 'the Word made flesh' at its centre cannot rest in what is referred to as 'spiritual unity!' The Christian faith does not divorce spiritual from physical, personal from structural. Unity must be indivisible. The Incarnation compels it. Likening himself to a lion in a den of Daniels, he concluded by saying that if, in a Christian context, we are to talk about unity, then there must be a unity of body as well as spirit.

A few pages further on, the magazine included the customary report of the General Committee proceedings (13th October 1979), which contained this statement:

> An ad hoc committee consisting of G. J. H. Buss, N. Carless, J. Allan Dyer, A. J. Gilliver and the General Secretary was appointed to examine the suggestion of Rev. John Stacey that the Association should consider coming within the orbit of the Methodist Conference.

In the same and subsequent issues during 1980, members' letters were published reflecting different views of the matter, from an unequivocal 'No', through various shades of 'wait and see', to 'let's get on with it'. The ad hoc committee report was presented to the General Committee on 25th April 1981; its proposals were agreed unanimously for submission to the Aggregate Meeting at Chesterfield in June of that year, where they received overwhelming majorities. They were:

- to undertake discussions through the Standing Joint Committee leading to cross-representation between General Committee and the Board of the Division of Ministries
- to initiate discussion with the Division of Ministries about matters of deep concern to local preachers and to report to the next Aggregate
- to approach the Wesleyan Reform Union about a similar arrangement.

There were, of course, those who wanted more and wanted it more quickly, but the Association had deemed it wise to follow the old adage 'Make haste slowly'. Writing on the subject in *The Local Preachers Magazine* of August 1981, the Senior Honorary Secretary put it this way: 'Let us be content that we are moving – and in the right direction.'

STEP BY STEP

The following year's Aggregate Meeting approved the rule change necessary to permit two representatives of the Board of the Division of Ministries to be appointed to the General Committee. This would not become effective until the Methodist Conference had amended its Standing Orders to provide for corresponding representation of LPMAA on the Divisional Board. That was safely accomplished at the 1982 Conference, without the delay that treating it as provisional legislation would have caused. The Senior Honorary Secretary was therefore able in *The Local Preachers Magazine* of November 1982 to indicate the probable timetable for implementation:

October 1982   LPMAA General Committee will nominate two representatives to serve on the Divisional Board for the Connexional Year 1983-84 (subject to confirmation by 1983 Aggregate).

March 1983   The Board of the Division will appoint two representatives to serve on the LPMAA General Committee.

April 1983   The General Committee will approve the text of a brief report on LPMAA affairs to be incorporated into the Local Preachers' section of the Division of Ministries report to Conference.

The representatives of the Board would then attend the meeting of the General Committee and the Aggregate Meeting in June, and a representative of the Association would speak briefly to Conference about the LPMAA report. The following March (1984) the LPMAA representatives would attend the annual meeting of the Divisional Board.

This timetable was duly fulfilled, and the new relationship became visible when Rev. John Stacey (Connexional Local

Preachers' Secretary) and Mrs Judy Jarvis (Chairman of the Connexional Local Preachers' Committee) attended the General Committee and Aggregate at Plymouth on 11th June 1983 as the first appointed representatives of the Division of Ministries. John Stacey paid tribute in the General Committee to those who had prepared the ground for this historic occasion, naming particularly Albert Shaw, Alan Collen and his own predecessor, Rev. David Francis. Addressing Aggregate, Mrs Jarvis said that the Conference, meeting in Middlesbrough at the end of the month, would be asked to approve additional items in the agenda of Circuit Local Preachers Meetings. These would bring certain matters of concern to LPMAA into that meeting, including Local Preachers' Sunday arrangements and support in the Circuit for the Association.

So it was that, four years after John Stacey's speech at Derby, Alfred Gilliver (Senior Honorary Secretary) formally presented the first report on the work of LPMAA 'for information only' to the Middlesbrough Conference. The brief report recorded benevolent grants of nearly £40,000 in 1982, and £87,000 for the support of Mutual Aid Homes, expressing gratitude for collections, grants, legacies and donations from Methodists and Methodist congregations exceeding £150,000 in total. It also emphasised the importance attached by the Association to consolidating fellowship amongst local preachers.

In his speech, Alfred Gilliver reminded Conference that it had elected four former Presidents of LPMAA to be its Vice-President in the fifty years since Union. He assured the President of Conference, Rev. Amos Cresswell, of the prayerful support of LPMAA during his year of office. The Association was grateful for the memorable Holy Communion Service that, as Chairman of District, he had conducted during the Plymouth Aggregate a fortnight earlier. After referring to the fact that the five Mutual Aid Homes were fully occupied, Alfred Gilliver concluded by saying:

> The process of growing together is far from complete and I hope that in years to come we shall be able to report new and exciting ventures in fellowship.

Both Conference and the Association gradually warmed to the new situation.

The Next Stage

Cross-representational arrangements were now extended to District level, where District Local Preachers' Secretaries became ex-officio members of their District LPMAA Committees. The Association was given reciprocal representation on District Local Preachers Committees. In both bodies reports are given – about the work of the Association to Local Preachers Committees, and about Local Preachers affairs to LPMAA District meetings.

By 1988 the Standing Joint Committee had begun to look for ways of moving the process forward at national level. The feeling grew that it should be possible for the Association and the Local Preachers' Office to find a way for 'Becoming One'. This was the title of a discussion paper agreed by the Standing Joint Committee. It had its origins in an extended session of a working party of four representatives from LPMAA and four from the Division of Ministries, held at Luton Industrial College on 16th-17th September 1988. The initial statement, which was printed in the November magazine, concluded with the assertion that coming together as one body was an achievable objective. The full report of the Luton discussions was received and adopted by the General Committee on 21st January 1989, and resolutions were endorsed for the approval of the Aggregate Meeting at Wimborne in June that year. In principle these gave authority to the Officers of the Association to undertake further discussions through the working party and to bring specific recommendations in due course.

The result of these discussions was the adoption by the Standing Joint Committee, early in 1992, of the document 'Becoming One'. It was published in the May issue of *The Local Preachers Magazine* and the consultation process began. The document identified seven major guiding principles (some of them legal) and recognised the importance of safeguarding the position of Wesleyan Reform Union local preachers and several thousand Honorary Members within LPMAA. It then listed eleven 'Issues for Discussion' (see Appendix to this chapter) and invited responses before more specific plans for the union of LPMAA and the Local Preachers' Office were prepared. In September the Standing Joint Committee was informed that 28 written submissions had been made either to the Association's Head Office or the Connexional Office. More were received after the Autumn round of LPMAA Branch and District Meetings. The Senior

Honorary Secretary and the Connexional Local Preachers' Secretary were able to prepare, in the light of these, a fuller document for the consideration of the Joint Committee, setting out a possible model for the coming together of the two bodies.

This was due to be presented to the Joint Committee on 24th February 1994, but the General Committee meeting on 16th April 1994 heard what actually happened. The report of that General Committee in the August magazine summarised the position:

> A meeting of the Standing Joint Committee was held on 24th February 1994 and was adjourned until 11th May. A paper prepared jointly by Rev. J. S. Lampard and Mr G. J. H. Buss had been considered by the Connexional Local Preachers' Committee before it had been presented to the Standing Joint Committee for approval. Members of the Connexional Committee were not happy with the paper and it was agreed that the meeting should be adjourned to enable further discussion to take place. It is hoped there will then be agreement by all members of the Standing Joint Committee on a recommendation for the consideration of the LPMAA General Committee and the Board of the Division of Ministries.

By the time of Aggregate that year the adjourned meeting of the Standing Joint Committee had been held and a statement agreed. It listed the specific ways in which the Association and the Connexion were now co-operating:

> Cross-representation on committees
> LPMAA report to Conference
> Connexional Local Preachers newsletter sent to all preachers through *The Local Preachers Magazine*
> Grants from general church funds for the support of Local Preachers were authorised
> LPMAA to administer the Connexional Necessitous Local Preachers' Fund.

The statement then gave a summary of the difficulties that presently precluded the presentation of detailed proposals for full organisational unity. Disparity in size was a major factor. LPMAA has a staff about 30 times larger than the Local Preachers' Office, and a budget over 15 times larger. Differences in history and culture, raising issues of ownership, governance and people's perceptions of the two bodies, were also important. The Standing Joint Committee therefore unanimously supported LPMAA if it made application to the Secretary of Conference to become a discrete organisation within the Connexion. The 1994 Aggregate authorised the Association's Honorary Officers to proceed in doing so, and to bring necessary rule-changes for Aggregate approval in due course. To facilitate full discussion in Branches and Districts this information and the Agreed Statement were published in the August magazine.

THE LAST LAP

So it fell to the newly-elected Senior Honorary Secretary, David Mitchell, as one of his first tasks on taking office, to lead the negotiations with the Secretary of Conference to achieve this objective. The matter proceeded in a most cordial and helpful atmosphere so that by 1996 the fine details of the arrangement, and the necessary procedures and rule changes, had been agreed. The Aggregate Meeting, at Bromley that year, was able to approve the changes as part of the Association's celebration of the 200th anniversary of the formal establishment of Local Preachers Meetings (fuller details of the 1996 Aggregate are included in chapter 27). The changes became operative as soon as the Methodist Conference, later in June, had also approved the arrangements. The published Minutes of Conference record this in the report of the Methodist Council at item 3:

> *Local Preachers Mutual Aid Association*
> The Conference welcomed the satisfactory conclusion of the negotiations with the Local Preachers Mutual Aid Association for closer ties between the Association and the Conference. It rejoiced in the fact that in the year celebrating the two hundredth anniversary of local preaching this further step in the healing of earlier differences had been taken, and looked forward to the closer collaboration which the proposals made possible.

Later in the minutes, under 'Motions on other Matters', there appears the sub-heading 'LPMAA Appointments', and this resolution:

The Conference noted that prior to the amendment of its rules the Aggregate meeting of the Local Preachers Mutual Aid Association on 3rd June 1996 appointed Mr Brian Scorer as President-elect of the Association, Mr David L. Mitchell as Senior Honorary Secretary, Mr Noel Clarkson and Mr Alan Newcombe as Honorary Secretaries and Mr John E. T. Lawley as Honorary Treasurer for the year 1996-97. The Conference welcomed and endorsed these appointments.

Thus 147 years of sometimes uneasy co-existence came to an end, as LPMAA both accepted and was accepted into a place in the Connexional structures. The prolonged discussions that led to this outcome had been very valuable, not only in the result eventually achieved. They had also helped many people to understand more clearly the concerns and convictions that had caused and continued the separate existence of LPMAA throughout these years.

APPENDIX to Chapter 34
Becoming One

ISSUES FOR DISCUSSION

(a) If the Local Preachers' Office and LPMAA were to merge, what will be the position of the Division with regard to the existing work of the Association in terms of finance, accommodation and staffing?
(b) What will be the position of the Local Preachers' Office regarding its involvement in the support and running of the LPMAA Homes?
(c) Should discussions continue between Methodist Homes for the Aged and LPMAA in order to determine future levels of co-operation, without local preachers significantly losing the control and ownership of their benevolent work?
(d) As with any organisation the overall number of members actively involved in LPMAA is a minority. Are there ways in which more members of LPMAA, or all local preachers, could or should be involved in decision making?
(e) Should all LPs automatically be members of LPMAA? What

would be the position regarding subscriptions? Should there be two classes of LP members; those who pay voluntary subscriptions and those who do not?

(f) What should be the role of Honorary Members? Should they continue to be eligible to hold Branch Office and attend District and Aggregate meetings as delegates? Should they continue thus to have a role in decision making?

(g) What offices should be open to members of the Wesleyan Reform Union? Should they continue to be eligible for all offices?

(h) How can the different 'organisational cultures' of LPMAA and the Division be reconciled?

[The document summarised, in some detail, differences between the Board of the Division of Ministries and the LPMAA Aggregate Meeting, between the Connexional Local Preachers' Committee and LPMAA General Committee, and between the roles of the respective Secretariats.]

(i) Are there fears harboured within LPMAA about a possible 'take over'? How can these be explored in a non-threatening environment? How can a paper such as this assist?

(j) What will be the benefits resulting from LPMAA coming under Conference? What will be the disadvantages?

(k) All participants would wish to recognise the deep sense of commitment and devotion felt by some members of the LPMAA to its fellowship and good works. Nothing should deny or in any way negate this, as it is one of the great strengths of LPMAA. It is recognised that through Branch and District meetings a proportion of the members of LPMAA find a deep fellowship. How can this be maintained and the commitment of members harnessed to any new development?

35

Into the 21st Century

The Inevitability of Gradualness • Some Who Have Served
Looking Forward • . . . And New Doth Old Fulfil

THE INEVITABILITY OF GRADUALNESS

As its 150th Anniversary Year dawns, the Local Preachers Mutual Aid Association is emerging from a period of particularly intensive change. This has affected its formal relationship with Methodist Connexional structures, its own organisational arrangements, and the ways in which it has provided care and support for local preachers and their dependants. These changes are neither directly related to the approach of a new century (even millennium), nor to the 150th Anniversary celebrations. As this book has sought to show, LPMAA has always been changing, in order to continue the work for which it was brought into being. At certain periods of its history this has accelerated or intensified, as the social, political and ecclesiastical contexts have evolved. What is important is that the work goes on. As needs, and the ways of meeting them, continue to change, adaptability is essential.

This can be illustrated very simply by comparing the role of the General Committee in 1999, with the way it functioned a century ago. In 1900 it met each month to consider 20, 30 or 40 applications from members or dependants for a small weekly allowance or a funeral grant. Now it meets twice a year to determine policy, approve the actions of the Association's officers or the decisions of its small executive committee, and to prepare business for the Aggregate Meeting. In 1900, because of the cost in time and money of attending frequent meetings involving long journeys, the number present was usually between 15 and 20, out of a total exceeding 70. Now, from a committee similar in size, the attendance rarely falls below 50.

This kind of change has usually been evolutionary, which has been its strength. Significant changes have, of course, been made at particular points in time, but only after extended periods of discussion and consultation. They have then normally been phased in over several years. Other important changes have often been implemented gradually because time was needed to make plans and put them into operation. One example of this is the decision in the mid-1940s to embark on the provision of residential care for members and dependants requiring it.

Policies have sometimes taken many years to germinate and to mature. In 1954, what was then the Oxford and Gloucester District of LPMAA sent a resolution to the General Committee, expressing reservations about the residential homes policy. The resolution, which was referred to the General Purposes Committee for consideration and report, urged the purchase by the Association of:

> ... small houses in Districts, convenient for letting to aged Local Preachers at nominal rent, or free, thereby avoiding the movement of members to Homes long distances away, often to result in the breaking of many years' association with circuits, churches and friends.

No action was taken – LPMAA had already invested heavily in two residential homes, a third was about to be opened and a fourth was being contemplated. The initiative suggested by the resolution would not only have required the diversion of funds from the residential care policy, but would most probably have conflicted with it. Misgivings about that policy persisted, and surfaced from time to time. At one of its meetings in 1955, the Exeter District asked the General Committee to provide

> ... some new posters which do not over-stress the Homes and lead to confusion in the minds of our people.

In the debate on the Annual Report at the 1969 Aggregate Meeting, one member spoke forcefully about it. Saying that the Association should 'give up the idea of purchasing existing buildings for our work', he emphasised the need to look for ways of helping the elderly in their own homes.

The need for alternatives to residential Homes gradually became recognised and accepted. The investment in (by then) five establishments meant that considerable resources of money, time and energy still went into maintaining and operating them (see chapter 33). The joint enterprise with Methodist Homes in a sheltered housing development in Sheffield, which received its first LPMAA occupants in 1989, was a major step along a new road. This followed the acquisition of nomination rights in Hanover Housing (1975). As the Association reaches its 150th Anniversary consideration is being given to possible further participation in small-scale sheltered housing schemes, which would meet need without the upheaval of leaving the home area. With the backing of public policy, the practicability of local 'care at home' initiatives (as envisaged in the 1969 Aggregate debate, quoted above) is also being examined.

SOME WHO HAVE SERVED

Whilst this history of LPMAA has been in preparation, its work has, of course, continued, and changes have continued to take place. Some who have played a prominent part in its national leadership have died, others have stepped down from office after years of service, and new officers have been appointed in their place.

Amongst those who have died was one of the Association's great characters and for many years its Senior Trustee, **Charles Lemmon**. He attended over 60 Aggregate Meetings, and his collection of Aggregate Handbooks has been a valuable source of information for this book. Charles also left comprehensive memoirs of his personal experiences at many of those Aggregates. His service to LPMAA in Branches and Districts was in the Lincoln and East Anglia Districts. In the latter he played an important part as Chairman and Treasurer of the Local Arrangements Committee when Aggregate met at Norwich in 1977. Many delegates to Aggregate Meetings since 1974 remember particularly his lively presentation of the Trustees' Report. Always able to report that the deeds and investments were in order, he invariably took the opportunity to share some memory or gem of wisdom with the gathering. He continued to do this as Chairman of Mutual Aid Nominees and the Investments Sub-Committee, when the office of Trustee was discontinued. Charles Lemmon died in 1994, after a short period of residence in the LPMAA Home at Rickmansworth.

In the following year (1995) one of the Association's outstanding national officers died. **Alan Collen** became Honorary Treasurer in 1959, serving in that capacity until 1967, when he exchanged offices with the Honorary Secretary of the time, A. Wesley Blake. This made it logical for him to become Senior Honorary Secretary in 1968, when Albert Shaw retired from that office. Alan Collen gave eleven years of service in the senior position, a total of 20 years as an Honorary Officer. During his term as Treasurer he also served as President (1963-64). He brought his legal mind and experience to bear on the Association's affairs during a period when it was working out the implications of all that had happened during the 1960s (see chapter 32: 'The 1960s – A Decade of Transition'). The resolution of the Aggregate Meeting upon Alan Collen's retirement referred also to his compassion, loyalty and courtesy. It concluded by saying that 'his finest testimonial is the excellent condition of the Association today'.

The year 1996 saw the passing of two stalwarts of Mutual Aid. **Dr Donald Nuttall** died in June of that year. At the funeral service, Rev John Sadler paid tribute to his maturity in several dimensions – his grasp and understanding of the Gospel, his blending of faith and medical science, his perceptions of life, love and human relationships. All this gave a hint of 'the stature of the fullness of Christ'. Donald always remembered his early days in Scunthorpe; when the Aggregate met in Lincoln in 1995 he wrote to the preacher appointed at Centenary Chapel asking for his greetings to be given to friends there. Rev John Sadler described Donald as a man of integrity, resource, care and compassion, making reference to his committee work in the medical sphere, and to his long and varied service in LPMAA. This included the Senior Convenership in the Leeds District, and Honorary Medical Advisor to the Association. In this capacity, Donald Nuttall travelled many thousands of miles to meet prospective residents before recommending that they were offered a place in an LPMAA Home. He combined this role with the duties of Honorary Secretary for the LPMAA Homes from 1978 to 1986, and with the office of President in 1977-78.

Will Shapland died during the night at Willersley Castle, after the conference weekend in November 1996. He had taken an active part in the programme, contributing to the discussions and meal-table conversations in his own genial way. For many years he had been closely associated with the LPMAA Home at Minehead, not far from his home near Barnstaple. He served as President of the Association in 1981-82. His public life included long service as a Devon County Councillor. He was a Governor of Shebbear College and delighted to take his LPMAA visitors there, to see the school, the house where the Bible Christian movement began and the Bible Christian burial ground nearby. The Association benefited from Will Shapland's 13 years as Chairman of the Case Committee, which held its final meeting less than two months before his death. Its work was then absorbed by the recently-created LPMAA Executive Committee.

Shortly after it was wound up, Will wrote an article about the Case Committee. In it he reviewed the changes in the kinds of need that the Association was meeting, either with regular financial help or by single grants for special purposes. Instances of the latter included a contribution to the cost of installing gas heating in the home of a local preacher, and one for repairs to the car of a preacher so that he could continue taking appointments. Another example concerned a local preacher who was an electrician by trade. He was servicing an overhead electric crane motor when a colleague inadvertently operated a wrong switch. Receiving a high voltage electric shock, the electrician fell 30 feet, breaking an arm and losing consciousness. Full recovery took a year, but LPMAA met the cost of a seaside holiday for the member and his family, as soon as he had recovered sufficiently to benefit from it.

Another of the Association's senior figures and past-Presidents died in 1998. **G. Stanley Hollis** was neither the first nor the only LPMAA President to come from a railway background, working for many years as a coach and wagon examiner. Accredited as a local preacher in 1935, at the age of 23, he had been on 'full plan' for 63 years at the time of his death. His intellectual potential was not fully realised until he gained the London University Batchelor of Divinity degree in 1955, after five years of part-time study. He put his knowledge at the disposal of many people as a tutor for the Methodist Study Centre. In LPMAA he served as Secretary of the Banbury Branch for nearly 50 years, combining this with the office of Treasurer for a long period. A Convener of the Oxford and Leicester District, he became Senior Convener in 1981 until 1997, and was a member of the General Committee from 1966. He served as President in 1978-79.

LOOKING FORWARD

The changing function of the General Committee was mentioned in the opening section of this chapter. 'The inevitability of gradualness' can be seen at work again when the membership of the Committee is considered. In 1968 the North Lancs District sent a resolution recommending that the General Committee should be reduced from 70 elected members to 50, and that 10 should be elected annually instead of 14, to serve an initial term of five years. This was discussed in the Finance and General Purposes Committee, which recommended General Committee to appoint an ad hoc committee to examine the proposal in detail.

In May 1969 the General Committee received the ad hoc committee's recommendation that a strong executive body, smaller than the General Committee, was needed. A Council of 20 was suggested, plus the officers. (It was also recommended that the Aggregate Meeting should be reduced to 200 members.) By September these proposals had been referred back to the ad hoc committee, but they were returned, with a memorandum urging acceptance. This time they were rejected, though with agreement to discuss the matter again at a later date. The issue was 'waiting in the wings' throughout the whole period that Alan Collen was Senior Honorary Secretary. His last major achievement before he retired at the end of the 1978 Aggregate Meeting was to win conclusive support, in the face of strong opposition, for the proposals that had been embodied in the North Lancs resolution 10 years earlier.

Another 20 years elapsed before the General Committee was further reduced in size. The proposals were published in *The Local Preachers Magazine* in 1996, and the Aggregate Meeting of 1997, in Exeter, approved the necessary rule changes. A General Committee of 30 was established, to be phased in over five years. Six members are to be elected annually for an initial term of five years, with effect from 1998. Some of the arguments against change that had been advanced in 1978 were re-iterated, but the opposition focused chiefly on the proposal to discontinue the life membership of General Committee previously accorded to past-Presidents. The recommendation was approved and past-Presidents now continue as members of the Committee for five years only. In both stages of downsizing, the amendment that each District should appoint a General Committee member was proposed but not supported.

Following the adoption of the smaller Committee, a specification for the duties of its members was requested and referred to the LPMAA Executive. Its recommendations were adopted by General Committee in April 1998. This is obviously important now that the General Committee meets only twice per year; its members will be expected to work between meetings.

This latest phase of organisational change was led by the present Senior Honorary Secretary, David Mitchell, who, at the close of the 1997 Aggregate, signalled his intention to relinquish the position after the Aggregate Meeting of 1999. Having cemented the new relationship between LPMAA and the Methodist Connexion in 1996 (see chapter 34), and secured the restructuring of General Committee in 1997, he had one more important task to achieve for the Association before its 150th Anniversary. This was the preparation and adoption of a Business Plan to guide its work in the future. He had perceived the need for this at the time he succeeded to the Senior Office in 1994. Following the appointment of a new General Secretary in 1996 the preparatory work for a Business Plan was put in hand. As the Plan evolved it was presented in successive revisions to meetings of the LPMAA Executive during 1997. The final version was approved by General Committee in January 1998, as a definitive policy document to go to Aggregate. The Business Plan deals section by section with:

1. Introduction, explaining the legal status of LPMAA and associated bodies.
2. Mission, covering the purposes of LPMAA, and its relationship to the Methodist Conference and the Necessitous Local Preachers Fund.
3. Management and Organisation, including the Mutual Aid Homes Society.
4. Strategy – financial, marketing and publicity, sheltered housing.
5. The Market – in Methodism and ecumenically; other residential care providers.
6. Tactics, with emphasis on the need to revitalise Branch and District activity.
7. Finance and Investment Policy – income and capital growth.
8. Staff – recruitment, training, salaries, pensions, employee services.
9. Immediate Issues, including membership, Branches, sheltered housing, rules revision.

Its full importance will only be recognised over a period of time, depending upon how effectively the policies embodied in it are implemented. The key objective in the immediate future may well be the revitalisation of the Branches. This is where members should meet, where needs of every kind are first recognised, and where new members are enrolled. Branch meetings provide opportunities to encourage and support the work of leading worship and preaching. If Branches are not also alive to the physical, intellectual, emotional and social needs of all their members, the future for LPMAA will be in doubt.

This was a major topic, along with District and Branch celebrations for the 150th Anniversary Year, at a weekend conference for Senior District Conveners held in February 1998. As a first step the conference recommended the appointment of a small working party to examine Branch administration procedures. Two particular matters were identified: one, to simplify financial and membership records, the other to harmonise them with Head Office computerised systems. General Committee appointed the recommended working party in April, to report later in the year. A special Rules Revision Committee was appointed by the Aggregate Meeting, after the Business Plan had been formally adopted, to conduct a thorough review and overhaul of the Association's Rules for the needs of the future.

... AND NEW DOTH OLD FULFIL

This line, from Whittier's poem 'The Brewing of Soma' (the verse preceding 'Dear Lord and Father of mankind'), is a reminder of the inescapable continuity between past, present and future. Plans and people may change, but the present is no more than the future of yesterday, the past of tomorrow. Between 1994 and 1996, LPMAA saw a new team move into the Secretariat. David Mitchell became Senior Honorary Secretary, being followed by Noel Clarkson as Honorary Secretary and Editor. Dennis Corden completed his term as Honorary Secretary (Homes) and was followed by Alan Newcombe. Derek Bolton retired after 18 years as General Secretary and was succeeded by Godfrey Talford.

General Secretaries of LPMAA have invariably served for many years – Godfrey is only the seventh holder of the position in a century and a half. **Derek Bolton** had worked with three different Senior Honorary Secretaries and three Honorary Secretaries (Homes), maintaining the vital element of continuity when others changed. He was the second of his line to come into the Association's senior administrative post from Hartlepool. [William Noddings (1914-46) had also been employed there, before his appointment to LPMAA Head Office.]

The August 1996 edition of *The Local Preachers Magazine* contained several references to his retirement. His successor observed that both Derek Bolton and his predecessor (Squire Jones) were Lancastrians and that the red rose had now yielded to the white! In his own *Reflections*, Derek commented on the combined length of service of Squire Jones and William Noddings (65 years) saying that it was a daunting task to follow such men. He referred also to the plethora of legislation during the 1980s and 1990s affecting residential homes and care for old people. This had resulted in a greatly increased workload for himself and Head Office staff. The Aggregate Meeting report recorded the standing ovation given to Derek and his wife Pauline as he completed his term of office. Recalling that at his first Aggregate (1979) Rev. John Stacey had invited LPMAA to 'take Conference into its system', he noted that at this, his last Aggregate as General Secretary, the Rule-changes to bring that about had been approved. The Special Resolution of Aggregate 1996, on Derek Bolton's retirement, specifically mentioned his devotion to work beyond the call of duty, instancing the many occasions when urgent matters at one or other of the LPMAA Homes had required long journeys at short notice, and unexpected nights away from home.

Aggregate 1998 expressed its appreciation to a long-serving Honorary Officer who relinquished his responsibilities after 20 years – **John Lawley**, Honorary Treasurer. He was succeeded in that office by another member of the same District (Wolverhampton and Shrewsbury), Keith Rothery. The Special Resolution recognising John's service as Treasurer referred also to his other work for the Association. He chaired the Finance and General Purposes Committee for several years, was a Trustee of the staff pension fund, and travelled as President in 1989-90. The resolution also mentioned his enthusiasm for promoting legacies as an important way of supporting LPMAA, noting particularly that the level of legacies had doubled during his term of office. This had contributed to a fourfold growth in the value of the Association's investments during that time.

Note has already been taken of the announced retirement of David Mitchell as Senior Honorary Secretary, at the 150th Anniversary Year Aggregate Meeting. In 1998 the Aggregate took note of it, and nominated him for appointment by the Methodist Conference to serve as President, for a second time, in the Anniversary year.   The tradition that the Honorary Secretary usually succeeds to the senior office when that falls vacant suggests that Noel Clarkson will follow David in 1999. Beyond that, who can tell? One might envisage the appointment of a woman to a national honorary office, with the same trepidation that the writer of *A Goodly Fellowship* showed in 1949, when he said that few have dared to envisage the election of a feminine President. 'Plus ça change, plus ça meme chose.' (The more things change, the more they stay the same!)   The future will not wait, the 150th Anniversary will be celebrated, both nationally and in Districts and Branches. The celebrations are planned to reach their climax, on 2nd October 1999, in a service of Thanksgiving and Holy Communion at Wesley's Chapel, City Road. This will be exactly 150 years since hundreds of local preachers came to London for the Inaugural Aggregate Meeting of LPMAA on the following day. Thanksgiving to God for what has been accomplished, and renewed commitment for the future, are to be the keynotes of the celebrations.

This history is written, therefore, to inspire confidence, not only in what has been done in the past but also for what waits to be done in the future, through *Confidence in Mutual Aid*.

Chronology

1849

21 May   Francis Pearson talked with Joseph Marsden in the latter's home in Matlock.

6 June   The first of Pearson's four letters to *The Wesleyan Times* was published.

24 July   Twenty-four local preachers met in Birmingham to plan for a national gathering of Wesleyan local preachers later in the year.

3-4 October Over 600 met in the Freemasons' Hall, Great Queen Street, London, to establish a Friendly Society for Wesleyan Methodist Local Preachers.

1851

January   The first issue of *The Local Preachers Magazine and Mutual Aid Reporter* was published. It appeared monthly for many years. From 1853 to 1894 its title was *The Local Preachers Magazine and Christian Family Record.*

October   The Aggregate Meeting at Sheffield decided to retain in LPMAA membership any local preachers who were expelled from or left Wesleyan Methodism as a result of the Reform movement.

1857   The United Methodist Free Churches were formed by amalgamation of the Wesleyan Methodist Association and a substantial number of Reform movement members. United Methodist Free Church local preachers were eligible for membership of LPMAA, as before amalgamation.

1859   Most of the reformers who did not become part of the United Methodist Free Churches formally constituted the Wesleyan Reform Union. Wesleyan Reform Union local preachers continued to be eligible for LPMAA membership as before.

1862   The President's Bible was introduced. All former Presidents except Isaac English (1850) were still alive and able to sign its flyleaf. (English's signature, cut from a document, was pasted in.)

1870	Judge Samuel D. Waddy was elected as President of LPMAA, the first of a number of prominent Wesleyan laymen to serve in that office.
1878	Laymen were admitted to the Wesleyan Conference as members of a Representative Session.
1882	The Wesleyan Methodist Necessitous Local Preachers' Fund was established.
1896	Local Preachers of the Methodist New Connexion became eligible to join LPMAA.
1897	Women local preachers (relatively few in number then) were made eligible for LPMAA membership, on the same terms as men.
1899	The Jubilee Aggregate. Brigadier-General John Barnsley was elected President. The first retirement cottages for local preachers were opened at Fillongley, north of Coventry, as the result of a private initiative by David Barr, who later served as President (1906).
1907	Upon formation of the United Methodist Church, Bible Christian Local Preachers became eligible for membership of LPMAA.
1908	The introduction of state Old Age Pensions caused LPMAA to begin a long period of adjustment to a developing system of public benefits for people in need.
1911	The National Insurance Act, providing for sickness and unemployment benefit, led to major re-structuring of LPMAA membership and benefits.
1912	The 1911 Aggregate, having been adjourned, was reconvened to approve the rule changes which were necessary to achieve that restructuring. LPMAA did not become an 'approved society'.
1914-18	First World War (see chapter 16).
1918	Women over 30 were enfranchised for Parliamentary elections. The Wesleyan Conference put women local preachers on a basis more nearly equal to men.
1922	Royal patronage was first granted to LPMAA.

1923   For the first time Aggregate elected a woman to the General Committee.

1926   Dr T. E. Nuttall, President of the Association, made the first radio broadcast by a representative of LPMAA.

1929   Harry Dawson, President of the Association, spoke at the first Methodist Church Congress as a representative of local preachers, from the same platform as the three Presidents of the Conferences then preparing for Methodist Union.

1932   Methodist Union.   Primitive Methodist local preachers became eligible for membership of LPMAA, after a 'Lightning Effort' by the Primitive Methodist Connexion to raise the sum agreed to secure this right for them.

1939   Outbreak of the Second World War. The work of the Association was maintained, but *The Local Preachers Magazine* and the General Committee Meetings became less frequent. The Aggregate Meeting was reduced in size.

1942   The Report of the Beveridge Committee on Social Insurance was published. It was not immediately acted upon, but its principles influenced the postwar social legislation, which affected the work of Mutual Aid (chapter 15).

1944   Rev. Fred Farley, Connexional Local Preachers' Secretary, approached LPMAA regarding possible financial help for local preacher training.

1945   After careful consideration, the Aggregate Meeting voted in favour of a course of action to make that possible, but not by a sufficient majority for the necessary change of rules.   Lengthy and controversial correspondence followed in both the *Methodist Recorder* and *The Local Preachers Magazine*.

1949   The Centenary Year. *A Goodly Fellowship* (the centenary history of LPMAA) was published. F. Harold Buss was recalled for a second term as President. The first LPMAA residential home for retired preachers and dependants was opened at

Westcliff-on-Sea. Over 1300 members and dependants were receiving financial help.

1951/55/57 Further homes were opened at Grange-over-Sands, Woodhall Spa, Minehead.

1961 Non-member local preachers were made eligible for LPMAA benefits.

1963 Following a resolution of the Methodist Conference seeking better publicity for local preachers' affairs, Rev. David Francis (Connexional Local Preachers' Secretary) opened discussions with LPMAA about relations with the Connexional Local Preachers' Department.

1967 Agreement between LPMAA and the Local Preachers Department to sponsor Local Preachers Sunday jointly with combined leaflets.

1969 The first woman to serve as President, Alice Nuttall, was inducted to the office.

1979 Rev. John Stacey (Connexional Local Preachers' Secretary) addressed Aggregate, inviting LPMAA 'to take Conference into its system'.

1983 Reciprocal representation between the Association and the Division of Ministries and Connexional Local Preachers' Committee began. The first LPMAA report was presented 'for information only' to Conference.

1989 40th Anniversary of the opening of the first LPMAA residential care home. *More Precious Than Rubies*, by Alfred Gilliver, was published.

1996 Methodism celebrated 200 years since the first Conference minute on local preaching. *Workaday Preachers* was published. LPMAA became formally part of the Connexional structures.

1998 (November) The 150th Anniversary history of LPMAA, *Confidence in Mutual Aid*, was published as a prelude to the anniversary celebrations.

1999 The 150th Anniversary Year, springboard for Mutual Aid in the 21st century.

Glossary

Aggregate Meeting	The governing body of LPMAA; its annual meeting.
Benefit Members	Local preachers in membership of LPMAA before the 1911 National Insurance Act came into operation. They were entitled to benefit by right, not need.
Bible Christians	Became part of the United Methodist Church in 1907, their local preachers then being eligible for LPMAA membership and benefits.
Branch	The local operating unit of LPMAA, usually corresponding to a circuit, but sometimes covering two or more circuits.
Centenary	One hundred years of LPMAA were celebrated in 1949.
Charity	Prior to 1960, a body set up as a trust for defined charitable purposes and treated as a charity by the Inland Revenue for tax purposes. Since 1960, registration under the Charities Act of that year has been necessary.
Convener	A District Officer of LPMAA.
General Committee	Members (currently six annually) are elected by the Aggregate meeting, from nominations by Districts, Branches or Members, to serve for five years. The Committee is responsible for LPMAA affairs, in accordance with decisions of the Aggregate meeting.
General Secretary	The senior salaried officer of LPMAA, who manages the Association's business under the direction of the Senior Honorary Secretary.
Goodly Fellowship, A	The centenary history of the Association, written by F. Harold Buss and Richard G. Burnett (published 1949).
Honorary Members	Non-preachers who support the work of LPMAA by annual subscription. This used to

be approximately four times the subscription of a local preacher member, but is now about one half. Honorary members receive *The Local Preachers Magazine* each quarter.

Honorary Secretary

National Secretary of LPMAA. Originally one, but now three, one of whom is designated Senior Honorary Secretary.

Investments Sub-Committee

Responsible for the management of the Association's Investments.

Life Member

An ordinary member (local preacher) or honorary member (non-preacher) who pays twelve times the standard annual subscription in a lump sum.

Local Preacher

Anyone who has satisfied the requirements of the Methodist Conference, in respect of the study and training necessary for approval by the Circuit Meeting for admission as a Local Preacher, and has been commissioned for the work of a Local Preacher in a public service held for that purpose.

Local Preachers Magazine, The

The official organ of LPMAA. Now published quarterly and distributed to all members. At least one issue annually, containing the letter from the Connexional Local Preachers' Secretary, is sent to all local preachers and ministers.

LPMAA

The Methodist Local Preachers Mutual Aid Association, established in 1849, to provide care and financial help for local preachers and their dependants, and to encourage fellowship and mutual support amongst members.

Methodist Conference

The governing body of the Methodist Church. It is composed of both ministers and lay members, and meets annually in two sessions, one when ministers only are present.

Methodist Homes (for the Aged)

The body through which the Methodist Church makes its contribution to sheltered

Methodist New Connexion	Established as a body separate from the main Methodist movement in 1797, under the leadership of Alexander Kilham.
Methodist Recorder	The weekly independent newspaper which specialises in reports of Methodist news and affairs, and Christian comment upon current religious, political and social issues.
Methodist Union	Primitive, United and Wesleyan Methodism joined together as one Methodist Church. Wesleyan Reform Union (see below), Independent and Free Methodists continued as separate groups.
More Precious Than Rubies	The 40th Anniversary History of Mutual Aid Homes, written by Alfred Gilliver (published 1989).
Mutual Aid Homes Society	Composed of all members, at any time, of LPMAA General Committee. It appoints an executive committee annually to manage the Society's five residential homes, and can direct the Committee to take particular action. The financial needs of the Society are met from LPMAA General Funds.
Mutual Aid Nominees Ltd	The company whose members are appointed to hold the Association's investments.
Necessitous Local Preachers Fund	Established in 1882 by the Wesleyan Methodist Conference. Trustees, to hold the investment (initially £8,000), and a committee to supervise the distribution of interest, were appointed. Since 1993, the distribution has been administered by LPMAA in conjunction with its own benefit payments.
President	Is elected by the Annual Aggregate Meeting, since 1902 one year in advance.
Primitive Methodism	The Primitive Methodist Church maintained its own Local Preachers Aid Fund for many years. When the Primitive Methodist Church

housing, residential care, and live-at-home support for older people.

became part of the present Methodist Church (1932), its local preachers were made eligible for LPMAA membership by payment of £20,000 from Primitive Methodism to LPMAA.

Royal Patronage — This was granted in 1922, by George V and Queen Mary, and has been continued by subsequent sovereigns.

Trustees — Were the legal holders of the Association's investments. This function is now fulfilled by Mutual Aid Nominees Ltd (see above). No new Trustees have been appointed since 1984.

United Methodist Free Churches — Formed in 1857 by amalgamation of the Wesleyan Methodist Association and a substantial number of Reform movement members.

United Methodist Church — Formed in 1907 by amalgamation of Methodist New Connexion, United Methodist Free Churches and the Bible Christians.

Watchman, The — The Wesleyan newspaper of the mid-19th century (pro-establishment).

Wesleyan Methodist Association — Formed in 1836, by amalgamation of the Wesleyan Association and other separated groups, following controversy over theological training for ministers.

Wesleyan Reform Union — Formed in 1859 by reformers who did not enter the United Methodist Free Churches (see above) in 1857.

Wesleyan Times, The — A newspaper that was more liberal in its reporting of mid-19th century Methodist affairs.

Workaday Preachers — A connexional history of Local Preaching (edited by Geoffrey Milburn and Margaret Batty). Published by Methodist Publishing House to mark the bi-centenary in 1996 of the first Conference minutes on local preaching.

Notes on Sources

As the text of the chapters shows, information about the history of LPMAA has been drawn from a wide range of sources. Specialist readers require detailed references to these, whilst general readers usually prefer something that can be read without consulting footnotes or an appendix. A compromise has been evolved. At some of the seven evaluation conferences, which reviewed sections of the text, members were invited to express opinions. Several historians and a number of other LPMAA members were also consulted. As a result, fairly generous use has been made of brief extracts from original material, and of relevant indications in the text. Nevertheless, for the benefit of readers who wish to have fuller information, the principal sources for each chapter are listed here.

AMH   Aggregate Meeting Handbooks
AMJ   Aggregate Meeting Journal
AR   Annual Reports of LPMAA
BDG   *Birmingham Daily Gazette*
BLO   Bodleian Library, Oxford
BRL   Birmingham Reference Library
CRO   Coventry Record Office
GCM   General Committee Minutes
HO   Head Office of LPMAA
JRL   John Rylands University of Manchester Library (Connexional Archives)
LPM   *The Local Preachers Magazine*
MM   *The Methodist Magazine*
MMC   Minutes of Methodist Conference
MR   *Methodist Recorder*
MRO   Matlock Record Office
QCB   Queen's College Birmingham (library)
RLP   Rules of LPMAA
WCB   Wesley College, Bristol (library)
WHS   Wesley Historical Society Library
WMC   Wesleyan Methodist Conference Minutes
WT   *The Wesleyan Times*

Section 1   Before LPMAA

1   **Who Were the Local Preachers?**
Workaday Preachers (ed. Geoffrey Milburn and Margaret Batty)
WMC (JRL)   Trades Union Library, Tolpuddle

2   **Public Policy for Relief of the Poor**
Report of Poor Law Commission, 1834
Report of the Inaugural Aggregate Meeting, 1849

3   **The Friendly Society Movement in the 19th Century**
Self-Help: Voluntary Associations in the 19th Century –
J. Gosden (BRL)
Town Porters Friendly Society Rules, 1833 (BRL)

4   **Wesleyan Methodism in the 1830s and 1840s**
Historic Sketches of Free Methodism – J. Kirsop (WHS)
United Methodist Free Churches – O. Beckerlegge (WHS)
Stages in the Development and Control of Wesleyan Lay Leadership – M. Batty (WHS)
The Significance of 1849 – E. C. Urwin (WHS)
Workaday Preachers (ed. Geoffrey Milburn and Margaret Batty)

5   **Mutual Aid amongst Local Preachers before 1849**
Stephens' MM (QCB) LPM (JRL)   WT (WCB)
Rochdale LP Friendly Society Minute Book (in private possession)

6   **Mid-19th Century Society**
Contemporary works, as quoted or referred to.

Section 2   The Origin and Early Years of LPMAA

7   **Francis Pearson, the Initiator of Wesleyan Methodist LPMAA**
LPM (JRL)   Marriage Registers (MRO)
Cromford Circuit Plans and LP Meeting Minutes (MRO)
Census Returns 1851 (MRO)

8   **The *Wesleyan Times* Correspondence**
WT (WCB)

9   **The Inaugural Aggregate (Day 1)**
Report of the Aggregate Meeting of October 1849 (HO)

10   The Inaugural Aggregate (Day 2)
As for chapter 9
A Tribute to Francis Pearson (see source notes appended)

11   Struggles in the 19th Century
LPM (JRL)   WT (WCB)   AR (HO)

12   Relations With Methodism to 1907
LPM (JRL)   MR (JRL)   AR (HO)   MM (WCB)
British Trade Journal, December 1894 (copy in private possession)
WMC minutes (JRL) (WCB)
The Waddy Family – J. Leonard Waddy (WHS)

13   Homes for Retired Preachers (19th Century)
Climbing the Ladder – David Barr (autobiography) (BLO)
MR (JRL)   LPM (JRL)   BDG (BRL)
Fillongley Cottage Homes Trust documents (CRO)

Section 3   Change in the 20th Century

14   The Fillongley Retirement Homes (continued)
As for chapter 13   Correspondence files (HO)

15   The Effects of Public Policy
LPM (JRL)   AMJ (JRL)   AR (HO)   GCM (JRL)
Hall's Social Services of England and Wales (ed. Forder)
Introduction to Social Services – W. E. Baugh
Appendix 2 draws on the article about Beveridge in the *Dictionary of National Biography*

16   War and Peace
LPM (JRL)   GCM (JRL)   AR (HO)   AMJ (JRL)
A Goodly Fellowship – Buss and Burnett (1949)
More Precious Than Rubies – Gilliver (1989)

17   Methodist Union and Afterwards
AMJ (JRL)   File notes (HO)   AR (HO)
Report of Methodist Church Congress (QCB)
Primitive Methodist Year Book, 1932
The Methodist Local Preachers' Who's Who, 1934
MR (JRL)   GCM (JRL)   LPM (JRL)

18   Social Change and LPMAA
LPM (JRL)   AMJ (JRL)   RLP (HO)   MR (JRL)
A Goodly Fellowship – Buss and Burnett (1949)

Section 4   Our Roots are our Branches

19-26   District and Branch Minute Books
Other local records, and personal memories
Miscellaneous local newspapers
Various issues of LPM & MR (JRL)
Research by officers and members in their own Districts

Section 5   Continuity and Change

27   **The Aggregate Meeting (Some Places, People, Programmes)**
AMH (JRL; HO; personal copies)
AMJ (JRL)   LPM (JRL)   MR (JRL)
Nottingham and Derby District minutes

28   *The Local Preachers Magazine*
LPM (JRL)   GCM (JRL)   AMJ (JRL)   RLP (HO)
A Goodly Fellowship – Buss and Burnett (1949)

29   **Intellectual and Spiritual Aid**
Report of Inaugural Aggregate Meeting, 1849
LPM (JRL)   Various Districts' records

30   **The Wider View**
LPM (JRL)   AMJ (JRL)   GCM (JRL)
Text of lecture on Sierra Leone LPMAA (private possession)

31   **The Impact of Technology**
GCM (JRL)   LPM (JRL)   AMJ (JRL)
Personal input (past and present officers and staff)
Mutual Aid Homes Executive Committee minutes (HO)

Section 6   Living Memory and Present Hope

32   **The 1960s – a Decade of Transition**
LPM (JRL)   AMJ (JRL)   GCM (JRL)
AR (HO)   RLP (HO)   MMC (JRL)
Charity Commission file (HO)
More Precious Than Rubies – Gilliver (1989)

33   **Residential Homes in the 1990s**
AR (HO)   AMJ (JRL)   LPM (JRL)
Mutual Aid Homes General Meeting minutes (HO)

34   The Association and Methodism in the late 20th Century
LPM (JRL)   GCM (JRL)   MMC (JRL)   AMJ (JRL)
Standing Joint Committee minutes (HO)

35   Into the 21st Century
LPM (JRL)   GCM (JRL)   RLP (HO)
AMJ (JRL)   Business Plan (HO)

INDEX

This index does not include every name of person or place mentioned in the text, nor every event recorded. It itemises those which are considered to have had a bearing on the formation of the Association, both at its inauguration and subsequently as changes took place in structure or rules to meet the changing needs of those it sought to serve.

Thus a name may be entered of someone recorded as speaking on only one occasion, but whose ideas contributed to our constitution; conversely not where a person is simply identified as an office holder, or a branch or district as existing. Lists of these may be found elsewhere. Likewise Aggregate and, particularly, General Committee meetings are noted only when there was an event or decision of significance. Note: when an 'f' is attached to a page number, a reference will also be found on the one or more following pages.

Geoffrey Buss

*Geoffrey Buss died as he was on the point of completing this Index.
We are deeply grateful to him for carrying out this demanding task,
and rejoice in the memory of his life and work.*

Honorary Secretaries 82, 95f, 105,
113, 124, 149, 154, 156, 159f,
179, 181, 230f, 251, 254f, 279,
283, 287, 358, 370
Honorary Secretary (Homes) 248,
263, 331, 362
Hornsea Branch 224f
Hughes, Rev Hugh Price 135

Ibberson, Herbert 191, 195f, 225
Industrial and Provident Societies
Acts 331
Izzett, P. 198

Jameson, William 302
Jebson 102, 105
Jephson (Huddersfield) 78
Johnson, John 240, 243
Johnson, Matthew 25
Johnson, Russell 124, 283
Johnson, Samuel 68
Jones, Squire 243, 322, 363

Kalamazoo System 316f
Kay, Lady Alice May Newbald 204
Keet, Rev Henry 128f
Key Hill Cemetery 56f, 72f, 147f,
239
Keed(Lynn) 69, 82, 292
Kievill, John W. N. 241f, 263
Kilner, William 123f, 132, 303
Kirkham, Walter 196, 245, 247
Kirsop, Joseph 23, 25
Knaggs (York) 106
Kneen, W. H. 197, 206, 257
Knight, Sir George 192f

Lampard, Rev John S. 351
Lawley, John E. T. 342,353,363
Lean, Garth 6
Leeds Branches 223
Leeds District 358
Lemmon, Charles 357

Lewis, Rev Greville 198
Leybourne, John P. 220
Lidgett, Rev J. Scott 188
Lightning Fund 186f, 367
Lincoln & Grimsby District 245,
296
Lindley, Richard 272, 306
Liverpool District 170
Local Preachers Magazine 60, 95 97f,
109, 197, 216, 237, 275, 283f,
288, 292f, 297, 302, 306, 308,
310, 312f, 315f, 322, 328, 331f,
348, 365, 367, 370
Local Preachers' Committee 183,
187f, 194f, 218, 351, 368
Local Preachers' Department 191f,
197f, 332f, 335, 368
Local Preachers' Relief Fund 34
Local Preachers' Sunday 189, 332f,
334, 368
Local Preachers' Who's Who 187f
Lockett, Malcolm 236, 244
London Districts 257, 296f
Lord, Rev John H. 115
Loveless, George 6
Lovely (London) 77f, 82
Luckham (Bath) 78
Lump-Sum Grants 161
Lunn, George 175
Lyndon, Rev E. I. 148

Mabbott, Howell 259, 261
Madder, Charles S. 255f
Mallinson, George 99, 106
Manchester and Stockport District
233
Mann (Hinde Street) 68
Marsden, William 53f
Maxfield, Thomas 71
McLean, Rev John 40f
Meikle (Holmfirth) 100
Melson, John B. 57, 72f, 82
Membership 79, 102, 108f, 125,
162, 169f, 175, 187, 245, 275
Methodist Church Congress 184
Methodist Homes 340, 357, 370